THE EURO

General Editors:

The European Uni... ...ranging from
general introduct... ...sues, policies
and policy proces...

Books in the serie... ...up-to-date
research and deba... ...on for a wide
audience of stude...

The series editors ...of European
Integration, Manc... ...; Director of
the Institute of G... ...nan British
Forum. Their co-e... ...Nuffield
College, Oxford U...

Feedback on the s... ...o
Steven Kennedy, ...S, UK
or by e-mail to s.k...

General textbc... ...b **The European
and Practice of**

Published ...[Rights: Europe only]

Desmond Dinan **En...** **Enlargement
Union** [Rights: Eur... ...**Politics of the**
Desmond Dinan **Eu...**
European Union ...dencies and Canada]
Desmond Dinan **Ev...** ...**erg Decision**
Introduction to
(3rd edn) [Rights: ...an Integration
Mette Eilstrup Sang...
European Integration. A Reader

Simon Hix **The Political System of the European Union (2nd edn)**

Paul Magnette **What is the European Union? Its Nature and Prospects**

John McCormick **Understanding the European Union: A Concise Introduction (4th edn)**

Laurie Buonanno and Neill Nugent **Policies and Policy Processes of the European Union**

David Howarth **The Political Economy of European Integration**

Philippa Sherrington **Understanding European Union Governance**

Series Standing Order (outside North America only)
ISBN 0–333–71695–7 hardback
ISBN 0–333–69352–3 paperback
Full details from www.palgrave.com

**Visit Palgrave Macmillan's
EU Resource area at**
www.palgrave.com/politics/eu/

The major institutions and actors

The main areas of policy

The member states and the Union

Issues

Understanding the European Union

A Concise Introduction

Fourth Edition

John McCormick

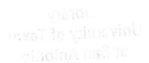

First published 2008 by
PALGRAVE MACMILLAN
Houndmills, Basingstoke, Hampshire RG21 6XS and
175 Fifth Avenue, New York, N.Y. 10010
Companies and representatives throughout the world

PALGRAVE MACMILLAN is the global academic imprint of the Palgrave
Macmillan division of St. Martin's Press, LLC and of Palgrave Macmillan Ltd.
Macmillan® is a registered trademark in the United States, United Kingdom
and other countries. Palgrave is a registered trademark in the European
Union and other countries.

ISBN-13: 978 0 2302 0101 9   hardback
ISBN-10: 0 2302 0101 6   hardback
ISBN-13: 978 0 2302 0102 6   paperback
ISBN-10: 0 2302 0102 4   paperback

This book is printed on paper suitable for recycling and made from fully
managed and sustained forest sources. Logging, pulping and manufacturing
processes are expected to conform to the environmental regulations of the
country of origin.

A catalogue record for this book is available from the British Library.

A catalog record for this book is available from the Library of Congress.

10 9 8 7 6 5 4 3 2 1
17 16 15 14 13 12 11 10 09 08

Printed and bound in China

Contents

List of Boxes, Tables, Figures and Maps

Boxes

Tables

Figures

Maps

List of Abbreviations and Acronyms

ACP   African, Caribbean, Pacific
CAP   Common Agricultural Policy
CFSP   Common Foreign and Security Policy
Coreper   Committee of Permanent Representatives
DG   directorate-general
EADS   European Aeronautic Defence and Space company
EAGGF   European Agricultural Guidance and Guarantee Fund
EC   European Community
ECB   European Central Bank
ECSC   European Coal and Steel Community
Ecofin   Economic and Financial Affairs Council
ecu   European currency unit
EDC   European Defence Community
EEA   European Economic Area/European Environment Agency
EEC   European Economic Community
EFTA   European Free Trade Association
EMS   European Monetary System
EMU   economic and monetary union
EP   European Parliament
EPC   European Political Cooperation
ERDF   European Regional Development Fund
ERM   Exchange Rate Mechanism
ESDP   European Security and Defence Policy
ESF   European Social Fund
EU   European Union
EU-15   The 15 member states of the EU prior to the 2004 enlargement
EU-27   The 27 member states of the EU following the 2004–07 enlargement
Euratom   European Atomic Energy Community
Europol   European police intelligence agency
GAERC   General Affairs and External Relations Council
GATT   General Agreement on Tariffs and Trade
GDP   gross domestic product
GNP   gross national product
IGC   intergovernmental conference

IGO   intergovernmental organization
IO   international organization
IR   international relations
MEP   Member of the European Parliament
MLG   multi-level governance
NAFTA   North American Free Trade Agreement
NATO   North Atlantic Treaty Organization
NGO   non-governmental organization
OECD   Organization for Economic Cooperation and Development
OEEC   Organization for European Economic Cooperation
PR   proportional representation
QMV   qualified majority voting
SAP   Social Action Programme
SEA   Single European Act
TEN   trans-European network
UN   United Nations
USSR   Union of Soviet Socialist Republics
VAT   value-added tax
WEU   Western European Union
WTO   World Trade Organization

The member states:

AT	Austria	IT	Italy
BE	Belgium	LT	Lithuania
BG	Bulgaria	LU	Luxembourg
CY	Cyprus	LV	Latvia
CZ	Czech Republic	MT	Malta
DE	Germany	NL	Netherlands
DK	Denmark	PL	Poland
EE	Estonia	PT	Portugal
EL	Greece	RO	Romania
ES	Spain	SE	Sweden
FI	Finland	SI	Slovenia
FR	France	SK	Slovakia
HU	Hungary	UK	United Kingdom
IE	Ireland		

Introduction

This is a book about the politics and policies of the European Union (EU). The impact of the EU on the lives of Europeans and non-Europeans has deepened dramatically in recent years, but it still has a remarkable capacity to confuse, bemuse and confound. The problem starts with trying to decide how we can best understand its character and personality. In other words, just what is 'it'? It is much more than a standard international organization, because its powers, roles and responsibilities go far beyond those of any other international organization that has ever existed. But it has not yet become a European superstate, or a United States of Europe, and indeed there are many in Europe who are keen to make sure that it is never allowed to go that far. Just where it sits on the continuum between an international organization and a superstate remains unclear.

In addition to the basic challenge of defining the EU, we are faced with a host of additional problems and questions. How significant a role does it play in the daily life of politics, economics and society in its 27 member states? Can we yet think of it as a bona fide political system, and if so, how do we explain and characterize its relationship with the 27 national governments? Is it still reasonable to think of the member states as independent actors, or should we think of them as part of a club, whose rules, norms and expectations they must follow? What are the implications of the EU for democracy and for policy making in Europe? And what has been the impact of the EU on the identity and meaning of Europe, particularly now that it is much more than a group of wealthy western industrialized democracies? Is it any longer realistic or useful to make a distinction between Europe and the European Union?

And what of Europe's place in the world? What difference has the EU made to how Europe deals with the rest of the world, and to how the rest of the world deals with Europe? Are the statistics as impressive as they seem: the biggest capitalist marketplace in the world, one of the world's two leading international currencies, the biggest trading power in the world, the biggest market for mergers and acquisitions in the world, and the biggest source of foreign direct investment and overseas development assistance in the world? Or are there still too many divisions among Europeans to allow Europe to flex its international political and economic muscle, and is there still only one true superpower (the United States)?

The number of competing answers to these questions has grown with time, but agreement on the best answer is as remote as it has ever been. We cannot even agree on whether the EU is a good idea, and a project worth pursuing, or whether it has involved the surrender of too much national sovereignty and identity, and has aspirations above its station. Opinion polls find that only about half of Europeans approve of the European Union, while the other half either disapproves or is not yet sure what to think. Critics point accusing fingers at interfering Eurocrats, and disapprove of the authority given to European institutions that are portrayed as secretive, elitist, and unaccountable. They also question the extent to which integration can be credited with the peace, economic growth and prosperity that has come to Europe since 1945. But supporters take the opposite view, see many political and economic advantages in integration, and are ready to credit much of Europe's renewal and revival to the opportunities provided by integration, and to think of themselves more as Europeans than as citizens of particular states.

Whether we like it or not, the European Union is here to stay. Its member states have spun a web of links that would be all but impossible to unravel. Most of the laws that limited free movement and trade among European states have gone forever. The physical and psychological barriers that for so long reminded Europeans of their differences have come down, and while national and regional identities are still alive and well, Europeans are no longer willing to fight each other to assert those identities. Twenty years ago, the EU was only a marginal factor in the lives of most Europeans, but today – with the completion of the single market, policy cooperation on a wide range of issues, the development of a system of European law, the adoption of the euro, eastern enlargement, moves towards a common foreign policy, and important global challenges that demand response from its leaders – Europe has become impossible to ignore.

This is an introductory book about the European Union, written for anyone who wants to understand how it works and what it means for the nearly half a billion people who live under its jurisdiction. It sets out to introduce the EU from first principles: to look at the debates over what it is and how it has evolved, to describe and assess the way it works and reaches decisions, to examine its impact on the individual states of Europe and their citizens, to review the effects of European integration on a range of critical policy issues, and to discuss its changing global role. The analysis has been coloured by three core influences.

First, I approach the EU from the vantage point of a British citizen living in the United States. I last lived in Western Europe in the 1980s, when it was still the European Community, when there were still many barriers to the single market, when the European corporate world was dominated by national champions, and when most Europeans were barely aware of the changes that Europe had made to their lives. My annual trips back to Europe have since allowed me over the years to compare public and media responses to the EU on both sides of the Atlantic, and to gain the kind of perspective that distance often allows. My snapshot visits have also made it easier to see the changes that Europe has wrought.

Second, my academic specialities are comparative politics and public policy, which makes me a member of a minority in the field of EU studies, dominated as it has been for many years by the sub-discipline of international relations. Like a growing number of political scientists, I believe that the EU is best approached and understood as a political system in its own right, and that the discipline needs to make better use of the analytical tools made available by comparative politics and public policy.

Finally, I believe that much of the academic writing on the EU – particularly at the introductory level – has done us a disservice by shrouding the EU in a fog of theoretical debates, treaty articles, arcane jargon, and convoluted philosophical theses that have helped make one of the most fascinating developments in European history sound dull and bureaucratic, and that too often divorces European integration from the real, daily life of Europeans. Politics at the European level is just as full of drama, of success and failure, of bold initiatives and weakness, and of visionary leadership and mercenary intrigue as politics at the national level, and it is important in books such as this to show clearly why the EU changes all of our lives in real and substantial ways.

It was my concern with the tone of most of the texts then available that prompted me in 1994–95 to write a book titled *The European Union: Politics and Policies*, which was published in 1996 by Westview Press and aimed mainly at college and university classes on the EU in the United States and Canada. In 1997, Steven Kennedy at Palgrave Macmillan asked me to write a shorter book that was more introductory and broad-ranging, and aimed at a wider readership. The first edition of *Understanding the European Union* was published in 1999, its main goal being to demystify the European Union, to help readers come to grips with this unique economic and political entity, and to do this as clearly as possible.

Apparently it struck a note, new editions were published in 2002 and 2005, and this fourth edition follows in short order. There is something of a myth in the academic world that new editions of books rarely involve many changes. But given how quickly the EU evolves, how often its rules are amended, how much its personality changes in response to new problems and opportunities, and how often new layers of analysis and interpretation are added to the debate on the EU, light tinkering with new editions is not an option. Although this fourth edition preserves the overall goals and structure of its predecessors, it has been substantially reworked in response to recent developments, and looks quite different in several places.

Chapter 1 on theory has been thoroughly reorganized and revised in order to distinguish explanations of how the EU evolved (which come mainly out of international relations theory) from explanations of what the EU has become (which come mainly out of comparative politics and public policy). A section in earlier editions on regional integration around the world has been removed to make room.

Chapter 2 on the meaning of Europe has also been overhauled, and a section in earlier editions on the political, economic and administrative features of European states has been replaced with an expanded section on the meaning of Europe, discussing its political, economic and social norms and values.

Chapter 3 on the history of the EU has been updated to include developments since the last edition, taking the story up to the Lisbon treaty, and more attention has been paid to external influences on the EU, particularly the role of the United States.

Chapter 4 on institutions has been revised and updated, with more information on constitutional developments, and more on the informal practices of EU institutions.

Chapter 5 has undergone a fundamental change of personality. Where before it was primarily a study of the relationship between the EU and the member states that included a study of the EU policy process, it has been converted into a full-blown study of the policy process.

Chapter 6 on the EU and its citizens has had new material injected on public opinion, Euroscepticism, and the democratic deficit, and has seen the sections on representation and participation fine-tuned.

Chapter 7 on economic policy has seen much of the historical background taken out, more details added on the effects of the single market (and particularly on competition policy), and more details and discussion incorporated on developments with the euro.

Chapter 8 has also seen a reduction in historical background, a thorough update of developments on agricultural and environmental policy, and a reassessment of cohesion policy.

Chapter 9 includes more on trade policy and on EU relations with its neighbourhood, and offers more in the way of discussion about the changing global role of the European Union.

Meanwhile, several boxes have been replaced, some tables and figures have been removed and new ones added, the arguments and analysis have been developed, and the core findings of recent scholarship on the EU have been briefly summarized. Through all this, one key element of the book remains unchanged: *Understanding the European Union* remains an introduction. Brevity has always been my watchword, and while other texts on the EU seem to grow in both length and density, and several of them now top a remarkable 600 pages, this one has always deliberately been short, never breaking the 270-page mark. It was never intended to offer a thorough and detailed analysis of the EU, but nor was it designed to be a whistle-stop description of the EU, reciting a series of key facts, names and dates. Instead, it sets out to paint a broad portrait of the EU in such a way as to both engage and challenge its readers, tying up the basic facts with original analysis.

Writing it has, as usual, been made that much easier by the excellent judgement, advice and patient nudging of my publisher Steven Kennedy, to whom I owe my continuing gratitude. My thanks also to Neill Nugent for his work as series editor, to three anonymous reviewers for their suggestions (many of which I took on board), and to all the production staff at Palgrave Macmillan. Finally my thanks and love to my support team: Leanne, Ian and Stuart.

JOHN McCORMICK

Map 0.1   *The European Union*

EU member states	1. Slovenia	5. Montenegro
	2. Croatia	6. Republic of Macedonia
	3. Bosnia and Herzegovina	7. Albania
	4. Serbia	

Table 0.1   *The European Union in figures*

	Area (000 sq. km)	Population (million)	Gross domestic product (billion $)	Per capita gross national income ($)
Germany	357	82.5	2,782	25,250
UK	245	60.2	2,193	28,350
France	552	60.7	2,110	24,770
Italy	301	57.5	1,723	21,560
Spain	506	43.4	1,127	16,990
Netherlands	41	16.3	595	26,310
Belgium	33	10.5	365	25,820
Sweden	450	9.0	354	28,840
Austria	84	8.2	305	26,720
Poland	323	38.2	299	5,270
Denmark	43	5.4	254	33,750
Greece	132	11.1	214	13,720
Ireland	70	4.1	196	26,960
Finland	338	5.2	193	27,020
Portugal	92	10.6	173	12,130
Czech Republic	79	10.2	122	6,740
Hungary	93	10.1	109	6,330
Romania	238	21.6	99	2,310
Slovakia	49	5.4	46	4,920
Slovenia	20	2.0	34	11,830
Luxembourg	2	0.5	34	43,940
Bulgaria	111	7.7	27	2,130
Lithuania	65	3.4	25	4,490
Latvia	65	2.3	16	4,070
Cyprus	9	0.8	15	12,320
Estonia	45	1.3	13	4,960
Malta	0.3	0.4	6	9,260
Total	4,343	488.6	13,429	
United States	9,364	303.0	12,455	43,740

Source: Population and economic figures from World Development Indicators database, World Bank website, http://www.worldbank.com (2007). All figures are for 2005, and countries are ranked by GDP.

Chapter 1

What is the European Union?

When we study world politics, and try to understand our place in the international system, most of us think in terms of states, and of ourselves as citizens of one or other of those states. World maps show continents divided by state frontiers, marking out territories under the administration of sovereign governments and subject to independent systems of law. When we travel from one state to another, we must usually show passports or other documents, and are reminded that we are in transit until we return to the state to which we 'belong', and with which we feel an identity and which we consider home.

States dominate our thinking because they have been the primary actors in the global system for 300 years or more, and because the study of world politics has long involved the study of alliances, changing patterns of cooperation and conflict, and fluctuations in the balance of power between and among states. But there are many who argue that the state system is in decline, its credibility undermined by its long-time association with nationalism and war, and the differences among states reduced by the effects of globalization. Borders no longer matter as much as they once did, runs the logic, and in order to truly understand the modern world we need to expand our analytical horizons.

In few places has the prestige and grip of the state been more aggressively challenged than in Europe, where centuries of conflict and tension reached a climax with the horrors of two world wars, driving home the dangers of nationalism and emphasizing the urgency of interstate cooperation. Political divisions were further emphasized by the cold war, which made many people realize that states seemed unable to guarantee their safety except through a balance of violence with other states, and also found Europe caught in the middle of political and ideological competition between the superpowers, the west obliged to follow the lead of the United States, and the east trapped in the Soviet bloc.

Alarm at the internal and external threats to European security led to a new debate about how best to build a permanent state of peace in the region, the most important result of which was what we now know as the European Union. But although it is now a fixed part of the international political landscape, there is little agreement on how it evolved, or on what it has become. Did it grow out of the deliberate actions of governments, or was there a more complex set of internal and external pressures at work? Were states the core elements in the story, or was cross-state functional cooperation

1

the key element in the equation? And what has been the end result? The EU is clearly more than a typical international organization, but it is not a European superstate. So what exactly is it?

Most explanations of European integration have come out of the study of international relations, because the EU (and the European Community before it) has been regarded by most scholars of integration – and by European political leaders – as an international organization. But recent years have seen new support for understanding the EU as a political system in its own right, and for looking at explanations coming out of the fields of comparative politics and public policy. There is still no grand theory of European integration, and no agreement about what the EU has become, or how best to understand it, but the parameters of the debate are changing, as this chapter will show.

The EU in the international system

Look at a map of the world and you will find it divided into nearly 200 states. As a unit of administration, the state has dominated the way we think about political relations among humans for generations – some say since the Renaissance, some since the 1648 Peace of Westphalia (see Chapter 2), and others since the beginning of the nineteenth century. A state is a legal entity which has four key qualities:

- It operates within a fixed *territory* marked by borders, and controls the movement of people, money, goods, and services across those borders.
- It has *sovereignty* over that territory and over the people and resources within its borders, and has the sole right to impose laws and taxes within its borders.
- It is legally and politically *independent*, and both creates and operates the system of government under which its residents live.
- It has *legitimacy*, meaning that it is normally recognized both by its people and by other states as having jurisdiction and authority within its territory.

None of these qualities is absolute: there may be political disputes that create uncertainties about the borders of a territory; there may be legal, economic or political difficulties that limit the sovereignty of a state; the independence of states is qualified by external economic and political pressures; and levels of legitimacy vary according to the extent to which the citizens of a state (and the governments of other states) respect the powers and authority of that state (see Vincent, 1987; Gill, 2003). Furthermore, the viability of the state system has come under increased scrutiny of late, and there are many who argue that the state is in retreat (see Strange, 1996), the result mainly of three critical developments.

First, public loyalty to the state – and the strength of state identity – has long been undermined by the division of most states into different nations, or groups of people linked by history, language and culture. Occasionally, a nation will coincide with a state (for example, Japan is predominantly Japanese, Swaziland is predominantly Swazi, and Portugal is predominantly Portuguese), but most states are home to multiple different nationalities. Thus Spain is a state, but its population is divided among Andalusians, Aragonese, Basques, Cantabrians, Castilians, Catalans, Galicians, Navarese, Valencians and others. The focus of people's allegiance has changed as national minorities within states have become more assertive and demanded greater self-determination, and even independence in some cases, as with the Scots in Britain, the Kurds in Turkey/Iraq, and the Québécois in Canada.

Second, international borders have been weakened by the building of political and economic ties among states, driven mainly by the need to trade, to expand markets, to develop security alliances, and to borrow money. To these pressures have been added in recent decades the effects of globalization: increased economic interdependence, changes in technology and communications, the rising power of multinational corporations, the growth of international markets, the spread of a global culture, and the harmonization of public policies, the latter driven by the need to respond to shared or common problems such as terrorism, transboundary pollution, illegal immigration, and the spread of disease. At the same time, people have become more mobile: complex new patterns of emigration have emerged, based on a combination of economic need and personal choice, and mass tourism has broken down many of the psychological borders among states.

Third, states have not always been able to meet the demands of their residents for security, justice, prosperity, and human rights. States have gone to war with each other with depressing frequency, their democratic records have been mixed, many have failed to manage their economies and national resources to the benefit of all their residents, and both poverty and social division persist, even in the wealthiest and most progressive of states. States have also often failed to meet the needs of their consumers for goods and services, a problem that has combined with the rise of multinational corporations in search of new markets and profits to change the nature of production, and to make state boundaries more porous.

The decline of the state has run in tandem with growing cooperation among states on matters of mutual interest. This cooperation has taken many forms, from the narrowly focused to the broadly idealistic, and has achieved its most tangible form in the creation of international organizations (IOs). These promote voluntary cooperation and coordination between or among their members, but have neither autonomous powers nor the authority to impose their rulings on members. Some IOs have national governments as members; they include the United Nations (UN), the World Trade Organization (WTO), and the North Atlantic Treaty Organization (NATO). Others consist of national non-governmental organizations, whether multinational corporations (such as Royal Dutch/Shell, Sony, or Wal-Mart), or interest groups that cooperate in order to pursue the collective goals of their members (such as the International Red Cross, Amnesty International, and Friends of the Earth).

Where governments take part in the work of IOs, decision making is described as *intergovernmental*: the IOs are used as forums within which government representatives can meet, share views, negotiate, and work to reach agreement. Membership is voluntary, and the IOs lack the power to raise taxes, depending instead for revenue on contributions from their members. They do not have independent powers, their decisions being the result of the joint will of their members. They do not have the power to enforce their decisions, and normally cannot impose fines on recalcitrant members, or impose sanctions other than those agreed by the membership as a whole. In most cases, the only pressure IOs can impose on members is either moral (playing by the rules), or the threat of having their membership suspended or terminated.

In some ways, the European Union looks and functions much like a standard IO. It is a voluntary association of states in which many decisions are taken as a result of negotiations among the leaders of the states. Its taxing abilities are limited and its revenues small. It has few compelling powers of enforcement, and – contrary to one of the most common myths perpetuated by Eurosceptics (critics of the EU) – its institutions have little independence, their task being mainly to carry out the wishes of the member states. None of its senior officials are directly elected to their positions, most being either appointed (as in the case of European commissioners or judges on the European Court of Justice) or holding *ex officio* positions (as in the case of members of the Council of Ministers, who hold their positions by virtue of being ministers in their home governments).

However, on closer examination, it is clear that the EU is much more than a standard IO. Its institutions have the power to make laws and policies that are binding on the member states. In policy areas where the member states have ceded or transferred authority to the EU (that is, where the EU has 'competence'), European law overrides national law. Its members are not equal, because many of its decisions are reached using a qualified majority voting system that is weighted according to the population size of its member states. In some areas, such as trade, the EU has been given the authority to negotiate on behalf of the member states collectively, and other countries work with the EU institutions rather than with the governments of the member states. In several areas, such as agriculture, the environment, and competition, policies are driven more by decision making at the level of the EU than of the member states, leading to the phenomenon of Europeanization: the process by which laws and policies in the member states are brought into alignment with EU law and policy.

Where cooperation leads to the transfer of this kind of authority, we move away from an intergovernmental arrangement and into the realms of *supranationalism*. This is a form of cooperation which results in the creation of a new level of authority that is autonomous, above the state, and has powers of coercion that are independent of those of its member states. Rather than being a meeting place for governments, and making decisions on the basis of the competing interests of those governments, a supranational organization rises above individual state interests, and makes decisions on the basis of the shared or cumulative interests of the whole.

Debates have long raged about whether the EU is intergovernmental, supranational, or a combination of the two. Some of its institutions – notably the European Council and the Council of Ministers – are more clearly intergovernmental, because they are meeting places for the representatives of the governments of the EU member states, and decisions are reached as a result of compromises based on competing national positions. Some of the other institutions – notably the European Commission and the European Court of Justice – are more clearly supranational, because they focus on the general interests of the European Union, and their decision makers are not national representatives. But the debate about the logic and personality of the EU has provided few hard answers, in large part because of competing opinions about how the EU has evolved.

Understanding the process of integration

In spite of the apparent permanence of states, the boundaries between them have often changed, become more porous, or been removed altogether, for a variety of reasons:

- States may be brought together by force, as they were in Europe by Napoleon and Hitler.
- They may come together out of the need for security in the face of a common external threat, as did the members of NATO during the cold war.
- They may share common values and goals, and agree to cooperate or share resources in selected areas, as have the Nordic states on transport, education, and passports.
- They may decide that they can promote peace and improve their quality of life more successfully by working together rather than separately, as have the members of the United Nations.

Interstate relations in Europe were long influenced and driven by the first two motives, but since 1945 there has been a shift to the third and the fourth. In other words, compulsion has been replaced by encouragement. But just why and how the process has unfolded and evolved the way it has remains a matter of debate. At first, there was an idealistic notion that out of the ruins of postwar Europe, and before state governments could reassert themselves, there was an opportunity to break with the past and create a new European federation. *Federalism* was based on the argument that states had lost their political rights because they could not guarantee the safety of their citizens (Spinelli, 1972), and that if the prewar system was rebuilt there would be a return to nationalism and further conflict. Federalists argued instead for a federal Europe, hoping that political integration would be followed by economic, social and cultural integration. With this optimistic idea in mind, the European Union of Federalists was created in 1946, but by the time it met at its first Congress in 1948, national political systems were on the mend and federalist ideas fell by the wayside. The Congress was able to agree the creation of the Council of Europe, but it had to compromise with the more modest goal of intra-European cooperation.

Postwar thinking about international relations instead came to be dominated by the more pessimistic notion of *realism*, which argues that states are the most important actors on the world stage (because there is no higher sovereign power), and that states strive to protect their interests relative to each other. Realists speak of the importance of survival in a hostile global environment, and argue that states use both conflict and cooperation to ensure their security through a balance of power with other states. Under this analysis, the EU today would be a gathering of sovereign states, which retain authority over their own affairs, transfer authority to new cooperative bodies only when it suits them, and reserve the right to take back that authority at any time. In short, realists argue that the EU exists only because the governments of the member states have decided that it is in their best interests. Realism was a response to the tensions that arose out of the nuclear age, but it did not explain the rising tide of cooperation that followed the Second World War, and left many unanswered questions about the motives behind international relations.

An alternative view was offered by *functionalism*, which was based on the idea of incrementally bridging the gaps between states by building functionally specific organizations. So instead of trying to coordinate big issues such as economic or defence policy, for example, functionalists believed they could 'sneak up on peace' (Lindberg and Scheingold, 1971, p. 6) by promoting integration in relatively non-controversial areas such as the postal service, or a particular sector of industry, or by harmonizing technical issues such as weights and measures. While realists spoke of competition, conflict, and self-interest, functionalists focused more on cooperation. While realists were

Box 1.1 The pros and cons of regional integration

Few Europeans would seriously question the merits of peace, cooperation and trade, but opinions about the benefits of regional integration as a means to achieving these ends are mixed. Some feel that they can be achieved without the compromises that are demanded by integration, while others argue that the record of centuries of conflict and war proves that only integration can keep Europeans peaceful and prosperous. In the resulting debate, it has so far been easier to assess the costs than to outline the benefits. Those costs include the following:

1. Loss of sovereignty and national independence.
2. Loss of national identity as laws, regulations and standards are harmonized.
3. Reduced powers for national governments.
4. The creation of a new level of distant and impersonal 'big government' in Brussels.
5. Too little reference to public opinion regarding key decisions on integration.
6. Increased competition and job losses brought by the removal of market protection.
7. Progressive states are handicapped as standards are reduced to help integrate states with lower standards.
8. Increased drug trafficking, crime and illegal immigration arising from the removal of border controls.
9. Problems related to controversial initiatives such as the Common Agricultural Policy.

For pro-Europeans, the benefits of integration include the following:

1. Cooperation makes war and conflict less likely.
2. The single market offers European businesses a larger pool of consumers.
3. Mergers and takeovers create world-class European corporations, helping the EU better compete in the global marketplace.
4. There is greater freedom of cross-border movement within the EU.
5. It pools the economic and social resources of multiple member states.
6. Member states working together enjoy new global power and influence.
7. Less advanced member states 'rise' to standards maintained by more progressive states.
8. Funds and investments create new opportunities in the poorer parts of the EU.
9. Democracy and capitalism are promoted in less advanced member states.

Public opinion on integration has moved in cycles (see Chapter 6), with polls finding that only about half of all Europeans generally support the idea, and that there has been a recent decline in the number of people who think that their country has benefited from membership. But – at the same time – few Europeans know much about the EU or about how it works, which raises questions about how much faith can be placed in the results of polls (see Box 6.1).

concerned with relations among governments, functionalists argued that cooperation was better promoted by technical experts than by government representatives. They concentrated on the internal dynamic of cooperation, arguing that if states worked together in certain limited areas and created new bodies to oversee that cooperation, they would come to work together in additional areas through an 'invisible hand' of integration. In short, functionalists argued that European integration had its own logic that participating states would find hard to resist.

The thinker most often associated with these ideas was the Romanian-born British social scientist David Mitrany (1888–1975), who defined the functional approach as an attempt to link 'authority to a specific activity, [and] to break away from the traditional link between authority and a definite territory' (Mitrany, 1966, p. 27). He argued that transnational bodies would not only be more efficient providers of welfare than national governments, but that they would help transfer popular loyalty away from the state, and so reduce the chances of international conflict (Rosamond, 2000, p. 33). He argued for the creation of separate bodies with authority over functionally specific fields, such as security, transport, and communication. They should be executive bodies with autonomous tasks and powers, he argued, and do some of the same jobs as national governments, only at a different level. This focus on particular functions would encourage international cooperation more quickly and effectively than grand gestures, and the dimensions and structures of these international organizations would not have to be predetermined, but would instead be self-determined (Mitrany, 1966, pp. 27–31, 72).

Once these functional organizations were created, Mitrany argued, they would have to work with each other. For example, rail, road, and air agencies would need to collaborate on technical matters, such as the coordination of timetables, and agreement on how to deal with different volumes of passenger and freight traffic. As different groups of functional agencies worked together, there would be coordinated international planning. This would result not so much in the creation of a new system as in the rationalization of existing systems through a process of natural selection and evolution. States could join or leave, drop out of some functions and stay in others, or try their own political and social experiments. This would eventually lead to 'a rounded political system ... the functional arrangements might indeed be regarded as organic elements of federalism by instalments' (Mitrany, 1966, pp. 73–84).

Ironically, Mitrany felt that peace could not be achieved by regional unification, because this would simply expand the problems of the state system, and replace interstate tensions with inter-regional tensions. Neither did he support the idea of world government, which he felt would threaten human freedom. Nonetheless, his ideas were at the heart of the thinking of the two men most often described as the founders of the European Union, French businessman Jean Monnet and French foreign minister Robert Schuman (see

Chapter 3). They believed that the integration of a specific area (the coal and steel industry) would encourage integration in other areas. As Schuman put it, 'Europe will not be made all at once or according to a single plan. It will be built through concrete achievements which first create a *de facto* solidarity' (Schuman Declaration, reproduced in Weigall and Stirk, 1992, pp. 58–9).

Studies of the early years of European integration led to the expansion of Mitrany's theories as *neofunctionalism*. This argues that preconditions are needed before integration can occur, including a switch in public attitudes away from nationalism and towards cooperation, a desire by elites to promote integration for pragmatic rather than altruistic reasons, and the delegation of real power to a new supranational authority (see Rosamond, 2000, Chapter 3). Once these changes take place there will be an expansion of integration caused by spillover, described by Lindberg as a process by which 'a given action, related to a specific goal, creates a situation in which the original goal can be assured only by taking further actions, which in turn create a further condition and a need for more action' (Lindberg, 1963, p. 10). For example, the integration of agriculture will only really work if related sectors – say transport and agricultural support services – are integrated as well. Equally, the integration of an international rail system will inevitably increase the pressure to integrate road systems and air routes as well.

Spillover is a valuable analytical concept, but it is broad and ambiguous, and is better understood when it is broken down into more specific varieties, of which there are at least three:

- *Functional spillover* implies that economies are so interconnected that if states integrate one sector of their economies (for example), it will lead to the integration of other sectors (Bache and George, 2006, p. 10). So many functional IGOs would have to be created to oversee this process, and so many bridges built among states, that the power of national government institutions would decline, leading eventually to economic and political union.

- *Technical spillover* implies that disparities in standards will cause states to rise (or sink) to the level of the state with the tightest (or loosest) regulations. For example, Greece and Portugal – which had few if any environmental controls before they joined the EU – were encouraged to adopt such controls because of the requirements of EU law, which had in turn been driven by economic pressures from states with tight environmental controls, such as Germany and the Netherlands.

- *Political spillover* assumes that once different functional sectors are integrated, interest groups (such as corporate lobbies and labour unions) will switch from trying to influence national governments to trying to influence regional institutions (which will encourage them in an attempt to win new powers for themselves). The groups would appreciate the benefits of integration and would act as a barrier to a retreat from integration, and politics would increasingly be played out at the regional rather than the national level (Bache and George, 2006, p. 10).

The forerunner of today's European Union was the European Coal and Steel Community (ECSC) (see Chapter 3). Founded in 1951, it was created partly for short-term goals such as the encouragement of Franco-German cooperation, but Monnet and Schuman also saw it as the first step in a process that would eventually lead to political integration. Few people supported the ECSC at the start, but once it had been working for a few years, trade unions and political parties became more enthusiastic because they began to see its benefits, and the logic of integration in other sectors became clearer. But there was only so far it could go, argues Urwin, because it 'was still trying to integrate only one part of complex industrial economies, and could not possibly pursue its aims in isolation from other economic segments' (Urwin, 1995, p. 76). This was part of the reason why – six years after the creation of the ECSC – agreement was reached among its members to achieve broader economic integration within the European Economic Community.

Neofunctionalist ideas dominated studies of European integration in the 1950s and 1960s, but briefly fell out of favour in the 1970s, in part because the process of integrating Europe seemed to have ground to a halt, and in part because the theory of spillover needed further elaboration. The most common criticism of neofunctionalism was that it was too linear, and needed to be expanded or modified to take account of different pressures for integration, such as changes in public and political attitudes, the impact of nationalism on integration, the influence of external events such as changes in economic and military threats from outside, and social and political changes taking place separately from the process of integration (Haas, 1968, pp. xiv–xv).

Variations on the theme of spillover were described by Philippe Schmitter (1971), including the following:

- *Spillaround*: an increase in the scope of the functions carried out by an IO (breadth) without a corresponding increase in authority or power (depth). For example, governments of the EU member states have allowed the European Commission to become involved in new policy areas, but have worked to prevent it winning too many new powers over the policy process.
- *Buildup*: an increase in the authority or power of an IO (depth) without a corresponding increase in the number of areas in which it is involved (breadth). Nye has written about 'rising transactions' (or a growing workload) which 'need not lead to a significant widening of the scope (range of tasks) of integration, but to intensifying of the central institutional capacity to handle a particular task' (Nye, 1971a, p. 67). This, for example, would explain why the workload of the European Court of Justice led to the creation in 1989 of a subsidiary Court of First Instance to deal with less important cases (see Chapter 4).

- *Retrenchment*: an increase in the level of joint arbitration between or among member states at the expense of the power and authority of the IO. This has happened at times of crisis in the EU, such as when member states pulled out of attempts to build exchange rate stability in the 1980s and early 1990s as a prelude to establishing the single currency.
- *Spillback*: a reduction in both the breadth and depth of the authority of an IO. This has yet to happen in the case of the EU, although the powers of the Commission over policy initiation have declined in relative terms as those of the European Parliament and the European Council have grown.

Neofunctionalism was given a boost by Nye (1971b, pp. 208–14) when he wrote about taking it out of the European context and looking at non-western experiences. He concluded that experiments in regional integration involve an *integrative potential* that depends on several different conditions, including the economic equality or compatibility of the states involved, the extent to which the elite groups that control economic policy in the member states think alike and hold the same values, the breadth of interest group activity, and the capacity of the member states to adapt and respond to public demands, which in turn depends on the level of domestic stability and the capacity – or desire – of decision makers to respond.

On all these counts the EU has always had a relatively high integrative potential: the member states are economically compatible (in the sense that their goals and values are generally the same, even if Eastern European members still have much to do in order to complete their transition away from central planning), elite groups may disagree on the details but they tend to have broadly similar goals and values, interest groups have taken advantage of the rise of a new level of European decision making (see Chapter 6), and the democratic processes and structures of EU member states are responsive to public demands, even if there is sometimes a mismatch between what majority public opinion says and what political leaders do. By contrast, similar exercises in integration in other parts of the world generally have more handicaps to overcome (see Box 1.2).

A response to criticisms of neofunctionalism came in the form of *intergovernmentalism*, a theory which draws on realism and takes neofunctionalism to task for concentrating too much on the internal dynamics of integration without paying enough attention to the global context, and for overplaying the role of interest groups. Intergovernmentalism argues that while organized interests play an important role in integration, as do government officials and political parties, the pace and nature of integration are ultimately determined by national governments pursuing national interests; they alone have legal sovereignty, and they alone have the political legitimacy that comes from being democratically elected. Put another way, governments have more autonomy than the neofunctional view allows (Hoffman, 1964). A variation on this theme is *liberal intergovernmentalism*, a theory which emerged in the

Box 1.2 Regional integration around the world

The European Union is the example of regional integration that has drawn the most international attention and that has had the most clearly evident effects both on its member states and on states doing business with the EU. But regional integration is very much a global affair, and there are similar experiments underway on every continent. Levels of progress have been mixed, regional groupings do not always have the same levels of ambition, and their integrative potential varies. Extrapolating from the arguments made by Nye, the chances of success are greatest where the countries involved have the most in common and where there are obvious advantages to integration. So, for example, while the three-member East African Community and the 16-member Economic Community of West African States (ECOWAS) bring together countries with often common historical experiences and comparable political and economic conditions, the 53-member African Union faces enormous challenges in bringing its members together.

One of the best-known attempts to build a regional market has been in North America, where the North American Free Trade Agreement (NAFTA) has tried to open up trade among the United States, Canada, and Mexico. But it has been handicapped by economic differences, minimal political support, public indifference, and concerns about international terrorism and the enormous challenge of controlling illegal immigration into the United States. The US may be a strong driving force in NAFTA, but it is much wealthier than Mexico, elite groups in Mexico are more in favour of state intervention in the marketplace than those in the United States and Canada, trade unions in the United States have been critical of NAFTA, public opinion in Mexico is more tightly controlled and manipulated than in the United States and Canada, and both Mexico and Canada are wary of the political, economic and cultural force of their giant neighbour.

Elsewhere, the ten-member Association of Southeast Asian Nations (ASEAN), the four-member Mercosur grouping in Latin America, the five-member Central American Common Market, the 14-member Caribbean Community (CARICOM), and the 21-member Asia-Pacific Economic Cooperation (APEC) have all had teething troubles, but have made progress toward encouraging their member states to work together on issues of mutual interest, most notably internal trade. With its common history, language, religion and culture, the Arab world would seem to offer strong prospects for integration, but the Arab League, the Council of Arab Economic Unity, the Arab Cooperation Council, and the Arab Maghreb Union have all been undermined by the political and religious squabbles dividing the region.

1980s and 1990s, and combined the neofunctionalist view of the importance of domestic politics with the role of the governments of the EU member states in making major political choices. Proponents argue that European integration has moved forward as a result of a combination of factors such as the commercial interests of economic producers, and the relative bargaining power of important governments (see Moravcsik, 1998).

Whatever the debates about how and why the EU evolved, there is no question that its institutions as a group constitute an additional level of political authority in Europe, making decisions that impact both the governments and the residents of the member states. So while the debates over how the EU reached its present state are interesting, even if frustrated by the lack of general agreement, they are now mainly of only historical interest; more relevant to an understanding of what the EU has become is the debate over its contemporary personality and character. Here again, unfortunately, there are many competing explanations, and no grand theory.

Explaining the EU today

The EU today sits somewhere along the continuum between an international organization and a state, and has been moving away from the former and closer to the latter. But just where it sits on that continuum has been a matter for intense debate:

- As noted earlier, it has many of the typical features of an international organization, in that membership of the EU is voluntary, the balance of sovereignty lies with the member states, decision making is consultative, and the procedures used to direct the work of the EU are based on consent rather than compulsion.
- It also has many of the typical features of a state, in that it has internationally recognized borders, there is a European system of law to which all member states are subject, it has authority that impacts the lives of Europeans, the balance of responsibility and power in many policy areas has shifted to the European level, and in some areas – such as trade – the EU functions as a unit, has become all but sovereign, and is recognized by other states as a legitimate player.

That so much emphasis has been placed on analyzing the EU as an international organization can be explained in part by the dominance in the academic debate of principles coming out of international relations (IR) theory. Certainly IR has made important contributions to the debate, but it is primarily concerned with interactions between or among states, and pays little attention to the internal characteristics and qualities of the states themselves. As long as the EU was primarily an association of states, this presented few problems, but once the EU began to develop a life and personality of its own, and its institutions accumulated greater powers, so IR analyses became less useful. As a result, there has been growing support since the early 1990s for approaching the EU as a political system in its own right (Hix, 2005), and for making greater use of the analytical methods of comparative politics and public policy.

With its focus on institutions and processes, comparative politics can help us better understand how political power is exercised at the European level, how Europeans relate to EU institutions, and how EU-wide government is influenced by political parties, elections, and interest groups (Sbragia, 1992; Hix, 1994). In other words, instead of studying the mechanics of the process of integration, we can use the comparative method to better understand how the EU actually works today. We can focus less on assessing the EU as an international organization, and more on comparing its institutions and procedures with those found in states, and in other regional groupings of states. Meanwhile, the methods and theories of public policy can help us better understand the European decision making process: the forces and limitations that come to bear on decision making, the relative balance of influence of the EU and the member states, and the steps involved in setting the European agenda, developing plans of action, implementing decisions, and evaluating the results. There are many different models and theories of the policy process that are applicable to the EU case, including the process model, rational choice, incrementalism, group theory, elite theory, and game theory – see Chapter 5 for more details.

The greatest problem with trying to encourage the use of comparative and public policy analyses is that few European leaders or students of the EU are willing to agree that there is such a thing as a European government. The term *government* is typically used in reference to the institutions and officials that make up the formal administrative structure of a state, and the context in which it is mainly used implies that they have independent powers to make laws and set the political agenda. But while the EU clearly has a network of 'governing' institutions and full-time officials, that network is rarely described in the language used to describe national systems of government. Instead, it is more usual to see the system of authority within the EU described as *governance*, a term which plays down the role of institutions and focuses instead on processes: governance is the exercise of authority through interactions involving a complex variety of actors, which in the case of the EU includes member state governments, EU institutions, interest groups, and other sources of influence.

At the heart of any discussion is the controversial question of *sovereignty* – what it is, who has it, and what impact integration has on the powers enjoyed by the member states. Sovereignty is usually defined as the right to hold and exercise authority. So a state is sovereign over its territory, for example, in that it has the power to decide what happens within that territory, and to make laws that govern the lives of the people who live there. More specifically, sovereignty is usually said to lie in the hands of the people or institutions that exercise control over the territory. In democratic systems, this usually means the national executive, legislature and judiciary. Theoretically, there are no legal constraints on a sovereign power, only moral and practical ones

– sovereign institutions are not answerable to any higher authority, but can only exert their powers to the extent that those under their authority will allow, and to the extent that they can practically implement their decisions.

In a democracy, sovereign institutions may not answer to any higher (supranational) authority, but they do answer to the people, because it is the will of the people that decides who exercises power. So sovereignty lies with the people, even though power is usually exercised by the institutions that the people elect to represent their interests. This means that the common complaint made by Eurosceptics that integration means a loss of sovereignty is not entirely accurate. Sovereignty has not been lost in the European Union, but rather has been redistributed. Where sovereign power was once monopolized by national governments in the member states, it is now shared by those governments and by the institutions of the European Union. But just how is it shared, and how do national governments interact with EU institutions?

One analytical concept that has gained popularity in recent years has been *multi-level governance* (MLG), which describes a system in which power is shared among the supranational, national, sub-national, and local levels, with considerable interaction among them all (see Marks, 1993; Hooghe and Marks, 2001; Bache and Flinders, 2004). The debate within academic circles about the value of MLG has been vigorous, but once again inconclusive. And what almost everyone has failed to acknowledge is that MLG is a conceptual cousin of two other, older concepts which also play a role in the debate. The most important of these is federalism, which has been given surprisingly little attention by scholars of the EU, despite the often heated debates it has generated among European political leaders and publics. Less important, but only because it has rarely been discussed in the context of the EU, is confederalism, a looser form of administration which historically has been a stepping stone to federalism.

Federalism

A federal system is one in which at least two levels of government – national and local – coexist with separate or shared powers, each having independent functions, but neither having supreme authority over the other. A federation usually consists of an elected national government with sole power over foreign and security policy, and separately elected local governments with powers over such issues as education and policing. There is a single national currency and a common defence force, a written constitution that spells out the relative powers of the different levels of government, a court that can arbitrate disputes between them, and at least two major sets of law, government, bureaucracy, and taxation. The cumulative interests of the local units help define the interests of the national government, which deals mainly with those matters better addressed at the national rather than the local level.

There are several federations in the world, including Australia, Canada, Germany, India, Mexico, and Nigeria, but the best known and most thoroughly studied is the United States. It has been a federal republic since 1788, when nine of the original 13 states agreed to replace their confederal structure with a federal union, voluntarily giving up power over such areas as security, but retaining their own sets of laws and a large measure of control over local government. American states today can raise their own taxes, and they have independent powers over such policy areas as education, land use, the police, and roads. However, they are not allowed to make treaties with other states or foreign nations, or to have their own currencies, to levy taxes on imports and exports, or to maintain their own armies. Meanwhile, the federal government in Washington DC cannot unilaterally redraw the borders of a state, impose different levels of tax by state, give states different levels of representation in the US Senate (where each state has two representatives), or amend the US constitution without the support of two-thirds of the states. Meanwhile – an important point – the US constitution (in the Tenth Amendment) reserves to the states or the people all the powers not delegated to the national government by the constitution or prohibited by it to the states.

EU member states can still do almost everything that the states in the US model *cannot* do: they can make treaties, still have a near monopoly over tax policy, maintain independent militaries, and – in a dozen member states – use their own national currencies. The EU institutions, meanwhile, have few of the powers of the federal government in the US model: they cannot levy taxes, they can make few independent decisions on law and policy, they do not yet enjoy the undivided loyalty of most Europeans, and they do not have sole power to negotiate all agreements on behalf of the member states with the rest of the world. Despite this, the EU does have some of the features of a federal system:

- It has a complex system of treaties and laws that are uniformly applicable throughout the EU, to which all the member states and their citizens are subject, and that are interpreted and protected by the European Court of Justice.
- In those policy areas where the member states have agreed to transfer authority to the EU – including intra-European trade, the environment, agriculture, and social policy – EU law supersedes national law.
- It has a directly elected representative legislature in the form of the European Parliament, which has growing powers over the process by which European laws are made. As those powers grow, so the powers of national legislatures are declining.
- Although still small by comparison to most national budgets (just €129 billion in 2008), the EU budget gives the EU institutions an element of financial independence.

- The European Commission has the authority to oversee negotiations with third parties on behalf of all the member states, in those areas where it has been given authority by the member states.
- Fifteen of the EU member states have their own currency, the euro, meaning that they have transferred monetary policy from their own national central banks to the European Central Bank in Frankfurt.

One way of looking at the practice of European federalism is to picture the EU as a network in which individual member states are increasingly defined not by themselves but in relation to their EU partners, and in which they prefer to interact with one another rather than third parties because those interactions create incentives for self-interested cooperation (Keohane and Hoffmann, 1991, pp. 13–14). It has been argued that the EU has become 'cooptive', meaning that its participants have more to gain by working within the system than by going it alone (Heisler and Kvavik, 1973). Once they are involved, governments of the member states must take some of the responsibility for actions taken by the EU as a whole, and find it increasingly difficult to blame the European institutions.

Federalism is not an absolute or a static concept, and it has taken on different forms in different situations and at different times according to the relative strength and nature of local political, economic, social, historical, and cultural pressures. For example, the US model of federalism was in place long before that country began its westward expansion, explicitly includes a system in which the powers of the major national government institutions are separated, checked, and balanced, and was adopted more to avoid the dangers of chaos and tyranny than to account for social divisions. Furthermore, it has changed over time as a result of an ongoing debate over the relative powers of national and local government. In India, by contrast, federalism was seen as a solution to the difficulty of governing a state that was already in place, and that had deep ethnic and cultural divisions; the national government has a fused executive and legislature on the British model, and while India is a federal republic like the United States, political reality has ensured that powers have often been much more centralized in the hands of the national government.

The most committed European integrationists would like to see a federal United States of Europe in which today's national governments would become local governments, with the same kinds of powers as the *Länder* governments have in Germany or state governments in the United States. Before this could happen, there would need to be – at the very least – a directly elected European government, a constitution, a common tax system, a single currency, and a common military, and EU institutions would have to be able to act on behalf of all the member states in foreign relations. But just how far the process of integration would have to go before there was a federal Europe is a debatable point. There is no reason why European federalism would have to look exactly like the US, Indian or even German models.

Confederalism

A confederation is a loose system of administration in which two or more organizational units keep their separate identities but give specified powers to a central authority for reasons of convenience, mutual security, or efficiency. A discussion of the features of confederalism can be found in Lister (1996, especially pp. 22–3). He argues that if a federation is a union of peoples living within a single state, then a confederation is a union of states. The balance of power in a confederation is tilted towards the member states, central authorities are kept subordinate, the shifting of authority to those authorities must be approved by the states, ultimate authority remains firmly fixed with the national governments of the member states (which exercise it jointly in the various confederal decision making bodies), and the loyalty of individuals remains focused on their home states. 'In a confederal setting,' Lister argues, 'the central institutions are both the agents of the member states and the instruments that enable those states to attain the degree of political union that is provided for in their treaty-constitutions' (Lister, 1996, p. 83).

Put another way, the member states in a confederation are sovereign and independent, and the central authority is relatively weak, existing at the discretion of the members, and doing only what they allow it to do. If states were to form a confederation, then the citizens of those states would continue to relate directly to their own governments, and only indirectly to the higher authority (see Figure 1.1). Unlike a federal system, where government exercises power over both its constituent units and its citizens, and there is a direct relationship between citizens and each level of government, the higher authority in a confederation does not exercise power directly over individuals.

One example of confederalism in practice was the United States in 1781–88. Following the end of the War of Independence, the original 13 states cooperated under a loose agreement known as the Articles of Confederation, or a 'league of friendship'. Central government could declare war, coin money, and conclude treaties, but could not levy taxes or regulate commerce, and founded its system of 'national' defence on a network of state militias. The Articles could not be amended without the approval of all 13 states, and treaties needed the consent of at least nine states. There was no national executive or judiciary, and the powers of the confederation lay in the hands of an elected Congress in which each state had one vote. Congress rarely met though, and had no permanent home, so its powers were exercised by committees with variable membership. The assumption was that the states might cooperate enough eventually to form a common system of government, but they did not. It was

Figure 1.1   *Federalism and confederalism compared*

```
                    FEDERALISM
Central government

        ↑
    States          Power is divided between central government and the states.
                    Both levels derive authority from the people, and exercise
        ↓           authority over them.

    People


                    CONFEDERALISM
Central government

        ↑
    States          Power is held by independent states. Central government
                    derives authority from the states, and has no direct authority
        ↑           over the people.

    People
```

only in 1787 that work began on developing the federal system of government that we find in the United States today.

Confederalism was also used in Germany in 1815–71, when a 39-member confederation was created under the domination of Austria and Prussia following the Congress of Vienna in 1815. Based on the old Holy Roman Empire, it was more an empire than a new state. Few restrictions were placed on the powers of the member kingdoms, duchies, and cities, whose representatives met sporadically (just 16 times in the history of the confederation) in a diet in Frankfurt. Amendments to the constitution needed near-unanimity, and most other measures required a two-thirds majority. Regular business was conducted by an inner committee in which the 11 largest states had one vote each, and the smallest had six between them. There were no common trade or communications policies, and the development of a common army was frustrated by the refusal of smaller states to cooperate (Carr, 1987, pp. 4–5).

Switzerland, too, was confederal until 1798, and although it now calls itself a federation, it has given up fewer powers to the national government than has been the case with other federations, such as Germany, the United States, or Russia. Its 1874 constitution allocates specific powers to the federal government, the rest being reserved to the 20 cantons and six half-cantons. The Swiss encourage direct democracy by holding national referendums, have a Federal Assembly elected by proportional representation, and are governed by a seven-member Federal Council elected by the Assembly. Comparable arrangements can be found today in Bosnia and Hercegovina. Even though it is formally described as a federation, and the federal government has accumulated more powers with time, the two partner states – the Bosnian Muslim-Croat Federation of Bosnia and Hercegovina and the Bosnian Republika Srpska – still have considerable independence. Each has its own system of government, with a president, a legislature, a court, a police force and other institutions, but they come together under a joint Bosnian government with a presidency that rotates every eight months between a Serb, a Bosnian Muslim and a Croat.

The European Union has several of the features of a confederal system:

- The citizens of the member states do not relate directly to any of the EU institutions except Parliament (which they elect), instead relating to them mainly through their national governments. Despite their powers of making and implementing policy, the key institutions of the EU – the European Commission, the Council of Ministers, the European Council, and the European Court of Justice – derive their authority not from the citizens of the member states, but from the leaders and governments of the member states. They are run either directly by national government leaders (the Council of Ministers and the European Council), or are appointed by those leaders (the Commission and the Court of Justice).
- The member states still have their own separate identities, have their own systems of law, can sign bilateral treaties with other states, can act unilaterally in most areas of foreign policy, and can argue that the EU institutions exist at their discretion. There is no European government in the sense that the EU has obvious leaders – such as a president, a foreign minister, or a cabinet – with substantial power to make policy for the EU member states. The most important political leaders in the EU are still the heads of government of the individual member states.
- There is no generalized European tax system. The EU raises funds in part through levies and customs duties, which are a form of tax, but the vast majority of taxes – income, corporate, property, sales, estate, capital gains, and so on – are raised by national or local units of government, which also make tax policy.
- There is no European military or defence system. The armies, navies, and air forces of the member states still answer to the governments of the member states, although contingents have come together as the seeds of a European security force (see Chapter 9). In this sense they are the functional equivalent of the militias that existed in the American confederal system.
- The EU may have its own flag and anthem, but most of the citizens of the member states still have a greater sense of allegiance to their own national flags, anthems, and other symbols, and there has been only limited progress towards building a sense of a European identity (see Chapter 6).

Interestingly, the concept of confederalism is rarely mentioned in conjunction with the EU, in spite of how much it clearly offers the debate. There are several possible reasons for this: federalism is more often found in practice and has been more thoroughly studied, federalism has been at heart of the criticisms directed by Eurosceptics at the EU, confederalism falls short of what the most enthusiastic European federalists would like for Europe, and in those few cases where confederalism has been tried in practice it has always evolved ultimately into a federal system. In his 1981 study of confederation and the European Economic Community (EEC), Forsyth argued that studies of federalism seemed to have little connection with the realities of European integration, and that if we were to look more closely at historical examples of confederations, we would find that the EEC was clearly an economic confederation in both content and form (Forsyth, 1981, pp. x, 183). Lister agrees, describing the EU as a 'jumbo confederation' whose member states and governments continue to dominate the EU's institutions (Lister, 1996, Chapter 2).

Conclusions

What, then, is the European Union? The answer depends upon who you ask, and what preferences they bring to their analysis. It is clearly far more than a conventional international organization, and although it is still sometimes spoken of in the same breath as the United Nations, or the World Trade Organization, or the World Bank, it is also generally understood that it is in a class apart. At the same time, it has not yet been comfortably slotted in to discussions about the state. It often appears in the company of states, as in peacekeeping operations in world trouble spots, where EU soldiers might be operating alongside those from individual nations, or as in so many of those statistical tables produced by the UN that list all the countries of the world and will often have a separate listing for the EU. But, once again, it is generally understood that it is in a class apart.

In spite of all the energy that has been devoted since the 1950s to first understanding the process of European integration, and then to understanding the personality of the EU, about all that anyone can agree is that there is nothing in the political lexicon that captures the essence of the EU, and that it is *sui generis* (unique). To describe it as such is really to avoid the question, and to avoid taking a position. And yet to take a position, and to describe the EU as federal, confederal, quasi-federal, an exercise in multi-level governance, or any of the other labels that have appeared in the debate, is to invite additional debate which rarely results in a conclusion. To take the plunge and to argue that it is an arrangement on the road to a United States of Europe is to risk either the ire or the confusion of others in the debate. This is one of the great frustrations of studying the EU. No-one can quite agree on what it is, it constantly changes form, it is on the path to an end-state whose features are unknown, everyone has different opinions about when the end-state will be reached, and it is unlikely that we will even know we have reached it until many years after the event.

Whatever it is, the EU is an entity with which we are all becoming more familiar. This is especially true in Europe, because the laws and decisions that govern the lives of Europeans are being made less at the local or national level, and increasingly as a result of negotiations and compromises among the EU member states. Developments at the EU level are becoming as important for Europeans to understand as those in their national capitals. Not long ago an 'informed citizen' was someone who knew how their national system of government worked, how their national economy functioned and how their national society was structured. To be 'informed' now demands a broader horizon, and familiarity with a new set of institutions, processes, and political, economic, and social forces.

Opinions on the value of regional integration – and its long-term prospects – will remain divided as long as they are confused and obscured by questions and doubts about the conditions that encourage integration, the logic of the steps taken towards integration, and the end product. Comparing the European Union with a conventional state can give us more insight, but we are still some way from agreement on what drives the process, and from understanding what we have created. Most confusingly, the goals of regional integration are only vaguely defined. The next three chapters will attempt to address some of the confusion by looking at the personality, evolution, and structure of the European Union.

Chapter 2

The Idea of Europe

We live in a European world. It is a multicultural world, to be sure, but most of it has been colonized at some point by one European power or another, and the majority of people today live in societies that are either based on the European political and cultural tradition or influenced on a daily basis by the norms and values of that tradition. The 'world culture' described by the American political scientist Lucien Pye (1966) is ultimately European in origin, even if it is most actively promoted and exported by the United States (which is itself primarily a product of European culture). For 'western', we could as easily think 'European'.

It is all the more ironic, then, that the idea of Europe is so hard to pin down. Its political and cultural identity is hard to define (beyond being an accumulation of national identities), its geographical boundaries remain uncertain, and there is little agreement on what 'Europe' represents. Europeans have had much to unite them over the centuries, but they have had much more to divide them. Their common historical experiences have been rare, they speak many different languages, they have struggled with religious and social divisions, their views of their place in the world have changed, they have gone to war with each other with alarming frequency, and they have often redrawn their common frontiers in response to changes in political affiliations.

But all is changing. In the immediate postwar years, Europeans were diverted by the need to rebuild their economies, their political systems, and their faith in one another, and were conscious of their perilous situation astride the divisions of the cold war. But with the rise of the European Community and then of the European Union, and the end of the cold war, Europeans have discovered their common interests, goals and values, and have had to accept the new responsibilities that have come with renewed global power and influence. Outsiders have also had to review their perception of Europe, which is now less a collection of sovereign states and more a global superpower. North American and Asian business and government leaders see the EU as a new source of competition for economic power and political influence, while most Eastern Europeans and Russians see it as an assertive new force for democratic and free market change.

The idea of European unity that has taken root and expanded since 1945 is nothing new. In fact it is an old idea that has simply been revived and, more importantly, adopted voluntarily by a large number of Europeans for the first time. Monarchs, Popes, generals, and philosophers have dreamed about European unity since the Early Middle Ages, and have written and spoken about unity as a means of defending Europe against itself and outsiders since at least the fourteenth century. But for them it was no more than an ideal; for modern Europeans it has much greater immediacy, the effects of integration are impossible to ignore, and the implications for the idea of Europe have been profound. As a result, it has become more important to understand the meaning of Europe. What are its political, economic, social, and cultural dimensions, and how can these help us better understand the significance and impact of European integration? Has integration simply been an intergovernmental project pursued by elites and bureaucrats, or does it build upon – and help strengthen – a distinctively European political, economic and social model, and a distinctively European way of interpreting domestic and international problems, and of addressing those problems?

The changing identity of Europe

Defining 'Europe' and 'European' has never been simple, thanks to disagreements about the outer limits of the region and the inner character of its inhabitants. The rise of the EU has added a new dimension to the challenge, obliging us to think of inhabitants of the region not just as Spaniards or Belgians or Poles or Latvians, but also as 'Europeans'. And to add yet more spice to the debate, macro-integration has been accompanied by a micro-level loosening of ties as national minorities in several countries – such as the Scots in Britain, the Catalans in Spain, the Flemings and Walloons in Belgium, and multiple nationalities in the Balkans – express themselves more vocally, and remind us that European identity is being reformed not only from above but also from below.

   Europe has never been united, and its long history has been one of repeated fragmentation, conflict, and the reordering of political boundaries. Parts of Europe have been brought together at different times for different reasons – beginning with the Romans and moving through the Franks to the Habsburgs, Napoleon, and Hitler – but while many have dreamed of unification, it has only been since the Second World War that the idea of setting aside insular nationalism in the interests of regional cooperation has won wide public and political support. For the first time in its history, almost the entire region has been engaged in a joint integrative exercise that has encouraged its inhabitants to think and behave as Europeans rather than as members of smaller cultural or national groups that just happen to inhabit the same landmass. But there is one key quality that crops up repeatedly throughout European history: Europeans have often been better at defining themselves in relation to outsiders than in relation to each other. External threats and opportunities have helped give tighter definition to the European Union, just as they helped give tighter definition to earlier understandings of the meaning of Europe.

The word 'Europe' is thought to come from Greek mythology: Europa was a Phoenician princess who was seduced by Zeus disguised as a white bull, and was taken from her homeland in what is now Lebanon to Crete, where she later married the King of Crete. It is unclear when the term 'European' was first applied to a specific territory or its inhabitants, but it may have been when Greeks began to settle on the Ionian Islands and came across the Persians. The expansion of the Persian Empire led to war in the fifth century BC, when Greek authors such as Aristotle began to make a distinction between the languages, customs and values of Greeks, the inhabitants of Asia (as represented by the Persians) and the 'barbarians' of Europe, an area vaguely defined as being to the north. Maps drawn up by classical scholars subsequently showed the world divided into Asia, Europe and Africa, with the boundary between Europe and Asia marked by the River Don and the Sea of Azov (Delanty, 1995, pp. 18–19; den Boer, 1995).

The Roman Empire – whose power peaked from approximately 200 BC to 400 AD – brought much of Europe under what has been described as a 'single cultural complex' (Cornell and Matthews, 1982) for the first time. The Roman hegemony also came with a common language (Latin), a common legal and administrative system, and – following the adoption of Christianity in AD 391 – a common religion. However, the Roman Empire was centred on the Mediterranean and included North Africa and parts of the Middle East as well, and so was not exclusively European. Because the Romans presided over an empire, there was no prevailing sense that everyone living under Roman rule was part of a region with a common identity. Furthermore, the inhabitants of Europe were known as Franks or Romans by inhabitants of the Middle East and North Africa. The situation was further confused with the end of Roman hegemony in the last part of the fourth century AD, when Rome was invaded by the northern 'barbarians' and Europe broke up into feuding kingdoms. The invasions separated Europe culturally from its classical past, and the Dark Ages that followed witnessed redefining movements of people as different tribes – notably the Huns, the Vikings, and the Magyars – invaded other parts of Europe.

The birth of Europe is often dated to the Early Middle Ages (500–1050), which saw the emergence of a common civilization with Christianity as its religion, Rome as its spiritual capital, and Latin as the language of education. The new sense of a European identity was strengthened by the development of a rift between the western and eastern branches of Christianity, the expansion of Frankish power from the area of what are now Belgium and the Netherlands, and the development of a stronger territorial identity in the face of external threats, notably from the Middle East. The retreat of Europeans in the face of Asian expansionism reached its peak in the seventh and eighth centuries with the advance of Arab forces across North Africa and into Spain and southern France. They were turned back only in 732 with their epic defeat by Charles Martel at Poitiers, in west central France.

The term 'European' was used by contemporary chroniclers to describe the forces under the command of Martel (Hay, 1957, p. 25), but it would not become more widely used until after 800, when his grandson Charlemagne was crowned Holy Roman Emperor by the Pope and hailed in poems as the king and father of Europe. His Frankish Empire covered most of what are now France, Switzerland, Austria, southern Germany and the Benelux countries. (As champions of European unity in the 1950s liked to point out, this area coincided closely with the territory of the six founding member states of the European Economic Community.) Although the Frankish Empire helped promote the spread of Christianity, it was quickly divided among Charlemagne's sons after his death in 814, and while the Holy Roman Empire persisted until the middle of the fourteenth century, it was to be famously dismissed by the French writer Voltaire as 'neither Holy, nor Roman, nor an Empire'.

Medieval Europe was technologically backward in comparison with China, and peripheral to the development of civilization. Central authority declined and intra-European trade ended in the wake of further invasions from Scandinavia and central Europe, and feudalism strengthened as large landowners exercised new authority over their subjects. By the beginning of the High Middle Ages in the mid-eleventh century, however, commerce had revived, agricultural production and population were growing, towns were becoming centres of intellectual and commercial life, a new class of merchants was emerging, monarchs and the aristocracy were imposing greater control over their territories, and the threat of invasion from outside Europe had largely disappeared. Indeed Europe now became the aggressor. As Christian armies gathered from all over the region to take part in the Crusades (1095–1291), aimed at recapturing Jerusalem and the Holy Land from the Muslims, the concept of Europe developed a tighter identity.

Safe from invasion, European culture took root and by the fifteenth century it had become more usual for scholars to use the term 'Europe', which to outsiders was synonymous with 'Christendom'. This was ironic given the turbulence that followed in the wake of famines, the Black Death and the Hundred Years' War (1337–1453), which saw the emerging power of monarchs, and challenges to the authority of the papacy that led to the Reformation and the growth of the modern state system. Religious divisions strengthened as a multitude of Protestant churches expressed their independence from the Roman Catholic Church, and for much of the sixteenth and early seventeenth century Europe was destabilized by religious warfare. But this did not stop Europeans from embarking on voyages of discovery to Africa, the Americas, and Asia, there was an expansion of education based on the classical works of Greek and Latin authors, and a revolution in science was sparked by the findings of Copernicus, Sir Isaac Newton, and others. These developments combined to give Europeans a new confidence and a new sense of their place in the world.

Delanty (1995, p. 42) argues that cultural diversity within Europe ensured that the idea of European unity was restricted to matters relating to foreign conquest. The earliest proponents of unity were moved in part by their belief that a united Christian Europe was essential for the revival of the Holy Roman Empire and by concern about Europe's insecurity in the face of gains by the Turks in Asia Minor; most of the proposals for unity were based on the argument that the supremacy of the papacy should be revived (Heater, 1992, p. 6). One example was the suggestion made in 1306 by the French advocate Pierre Dubois (1255–1312). Noting that war was endemic in Europe despite the teachings of Christianity, Dubois suggested that the princes and cities of Europe should form a confederal 'Christian Republic', overseen by a permanent assembly of princes working to ensure peace through the application of Christian principles. In the event of a dispute, a panel of nine judges could be brought together to arbitrate, with the Pope acting as a final court of appeal (Heater, 1992, p. 10; Urwin, 1995, p. 2).

The Renaissance (roughly 1350–1550) saw loyalty shift away from the Church, with growing support for individualism and republicanism, and the early development of the state system, beginning in England and France. Under the circumstances, the idea of regional unity was far from the minds of all but a small minority of idealists. Among these were King George of Bohemia and his diplomatist Antoine Marini, who proposed a European confederation to respond to the threat posed by the Turks in the mid-fifteenth century. Their plan – which was remarkably similar to the structure eventually set up for the European Union – involved an assembly meeting regularly and moving its seat every five years, a college of permanent members using a system of majoritarian decision making, a council of kings and princes, and a court to adjudicate disputes (de Rougemont, 1966, p. 71).

The Church had become so divided by the end of the sixteenth century that the idea of a united Christian Europe was abandoned, and those who still championed the idea of European unity saw it as based less on a common religion than on addressing the religious causes of conflict and the growing threat of Habsburg power. These were the motives behind the Grand Design outlined by the Duc de Sully (1560–1641) in France in the early seventeenth century. He proposed a redrawing of administrative lines throughout Europe so as to achieve equilibrium of power, and the creation of a European Senate with 66 members serving three-year terms (Heater, 1992, pp. 30–5). But by now the borders of European states were achieving new clarity and permanence, weakening the notion of a wider European identity. When the Peace of Westphalia came in 1648, with two treaties bringing an end to the Thirty

Years' War and the Eight Years' War and leaving many territorial adjustments in its wake, a new permanence was given to the idea of state sovereignty.

But dreamers dreamt on, and one of those influenced by de Sully's ideas was William Penn (1644–1718), who in the middle of yet another war between England and France (the War of the Grand Alliance) published *An Essay Towards the Present Peace of Europe* (1693). In it he proposed the creation of a European diet or parliament that could be used for dispute resolution, and suggested that quarrels might be settled by a three-quarters majority vote, something like the qualified majority voting system used today in the EU Council of Ministers (see Chapter 4). This would be weighted according to the economic power of the participating states: Germany would have 12 votes, France ten, England six, and so on (Heater, 1992, pp. 53–6; Salmon and Nicoll, 1997, pp. 3–6). In 1717 the Abbé de Saint-Pierre (1658–1743) published his three-volume *Project for Settling an Everlasting Peace in Europe*, in which he argued for free trade and a European Senate. His ideas were to inspire the German poet Friedrich von Schiller to write his 'Ode to Joy' in 1785. Sung to Beethoven's Ninth Symphony, it has become the European anthem: 'Thy magic reunites those whom stem custom has parted, All men will become brothers under thy gentle wing'.

Several prominent thinkers and philosophers subsequently explored the theme of peace through unity. Jean-Jacques Rousseau wrote in favour of a European federation; Jeremy Bentham, in *A Plan for an Universal and Perpetual Peace* (1789), wrote of his ideas for a European assembly and a common army; Immanual Kant's *Thoughts on Perpetual Peace* (1795) included suggestions for the achievement of world peace; and the Comte de Saint-Simon, in response to the Napoleonic Wars, published a pamphlet in 1814 titled *The Reorganization of the European Community*, in which he argued in support of a federal Europe with common institutions, but within which national independence would be maintained and respected.

The desire to overcome Europe's divisions led some political leaders to the conclusion that conquest was the best response, but they found themselves foiled by the sheer size of the task and by the resistance from key actors to changes in the balance of power. The attempts by Charlemagne, Philip II of Spain and the Habsburgs to establish a European hegemony all failed, argues Urwin (1995, p. 2), because of the 'complex fragmented mosaic of the continent ... [and] the inadequate technical resources of the would-be conquerors to establish and maintain effective control by force over large areas of territory against the wishes of the local populations'. The first attempt to achieve unity by force in modern times was made by Napoleon, who brought what are now France, Belgium, the Netherlands, Luxembourg, and parts of Germany and Italy under his direct rule. He saw himself as the 'intermediary' between the old order and the new, and hoped for a European association with a common body of law, a common court of appeal, a single currency, and a uniform system of weights and measures.

Despite rapid economic, social and technological change, nineteenth-century Europe was driven by nationalism, founded in the effects of the 1815 Congress of Vienna on the encouragement of great-power rivalry, and tracing its development through to the unification of Italy in the 1860s and of Germany in 1871, and beyond. It also prompted rivalry among European states, both within Europe and further afield in the competition to build colonial empires. Dreams of a United States of Europe nonetheless continued to inspire nineteenth-century intellectuals such as the French poet and novelist Victor Hugo, who in 1848 declared that the nations of Europe, 'without losing [their] distinctive qualities or ... glorious individuality, will merge closely into a higher unity and will form the fraternity of Europe ... Two huge groups will be seen, the United States of America and the United States of Europe, holding out their hands to one another across the ocean.' But nationalism won out, feeding into militarization and the outbreak in 1914 of the Great War, when all the competing tensions within Europe finally boiled over in what was, to all intents and purposes, a European civil war. One of the effects was chaos in much of central Europe, and the peace arranged under the 1919 Treaty of Versailles did little more than fan the fires of nationalism, particularly in Germany.

Before, during and after the war, philosophers and political leaders continued to ponder the challenge of encouraging Europeans to rise above national identity and consider themselves part of a broader sub-continental culture, thereby helping remove the causes of conflict, and allowing Europe to better defend itself against external threats. Where Dubois, Penn, Saint-Simon, and others had been writing in a vacuum of public interest, the horrors of the Great War now created an audience that was more receptive to the idea of European cooperation, and the new debates involved not just intellectuals but politicians as well. The strongest support came from the leaders of smaller states that were tired of being caught up in big-power rivalry, and several made practical moves towards economic cooperation. Thus Belgium and Luxembourg created a limited economic union in 1922, including fixing the exchange rates of their currencies relative to each other, and in 1930 joined several Scandinavian states in an agreement to limit tariffs.

One of the most convinced champions of European unity was Count Richard Coudenhove-Kalergi, who in the early 1920s proposed a Pan-European Union that might reverse the internal decline of Europe (Box 2.1). He failed to generate a mass following, but his ideas caught the attention of leading figures in the arts, such as the German composer Richard Strauss and the Spanish philosopher Ortega y Gasset, as well as several contemporary or future political leaders, including Georges Pompidou, Thomas Masaryk, Konrad Adenauer, Winston Churchill, and two French prime ministers, Edouard Herriot and Aristide Briand.

Box 2.1 Paneuropa

The years of peace after the First World War saw the publication of a flood of books and articles exploring variations on the theme of European unity. The most influential of these were written by Count Richard Coudenhove-Kalergi (1894–1972), the son of an Austrian diplomat and his Japanese wife, and co-founder in 1922 with the Archduke Otto von Habsburg of the Pan-European Union.

The problems facing Europe after the war convinced Coudenhove-Kalergi that the only workable guarantee of peace was political union, and he outlined his ideas in a manifesto titled *Paneuropa*, published in 1923. He argued that while Europe's global supremacy was over, the internal decline of Europe could be avoided if its political system was modernized, with a new emphasis on large-scale cooperation. Changes in Europe could not happen in isolation from those in the rest of the world, however, and Coudenhove-Kalergi felt that the best hope for world peace lay in the creation of five 'global power fields':

- the Americas (excluding Canada)
- the Soviet Union (USSR)
- Eastern Asia (China and Japan)
- Paneuropa (including continental Europe's colonies in Africa and southeast Asia)
- Britain and its empire (including Canada, Australia, southern Africa, the Middle East and India).

He excluded the USSR from Europe because it was too diverse and did not have the democratic traditions necessary for the development of Paneuropa. He was uncomfortable about excluding Britain, but did so because he felt it was so powerful as to be a political continent in its own right. It could serve as a mediator with the United States, however, and could become part of Paneuropa if it lost its empire.

Coudenhove-Kalergi argued that an arms race among European states would be destructive and keep Europe in a permanent state of crisis. Instead, he proposed a four-stage process for the achievement of European union: a conference of representatives from the 26 European states, the agreement of treaties for the settlement of European disputes, the development of a customs union, and the drafting of a federal European constitution. He also presciently suggested that English should become the common second language for Europe, since it was becoming the dominant global language.

The prevailing view in France was that European cooperation was an impossible dream, and that the best hope for peace lay in French strength and German weakness (Bugge, 1995, p. 102). Herriot disagreed, and in 1924 he called for the creation of a United States of Europe, to grow out of the postwar cooperation promoted by the League of Nations. For his part, Briand called for a European confederation working within the League of Nations, and in May 1930 distributed a memorandum to governments outlining his ideas (Salmon and Nicoll, 1997, pp. 9–14). In it he wrote of the need for 'a permanent regime of solidarity based on international agreements for the rational organization of Europe'. He used such terms as 'common market' and 'European Union', and even listed specific policy needs, such as the development of trans-European transport networks, and anticipated what would later become the regional and social policies of the EU. He is often described in France as one of the founding fathers of European integration, but the impact of his memorandum was undermined by the gathering tensions sparked by the rise of Nazism.

Adolf Hitler was obsessed with correcting the 'wrongs' of Versailles and creating a German 'living space'. He spoke of a 'European house', but only in terms of the importance of German rule over the continent in the face of the perceived threat from communists and 'inferior elements' within and outside Europe. The nationalist tensions that had not been resolved by the Great War now boiled over once again into pan-European conflict. Hitler was able to expand his Reich to include Austria, Bohemia, Alsace-Lorraine, and most of Poland, and to occupy much of the rest of continental Europe.

With the end of the Second World War in 1945, the pre-existing economic and social divisions of Europe were joined by the ideological rift between a capitalist west and a socialist east. The circumstances would have seemed unfavourable to supporters of unity and regional integration, and yet it was to be the very depth of the threats posed to Europe by the cold war that was to allow the dreamers to begin taking the substantive actions needed to move beyond theory and philosophy into the realms of practical political, economic and social change. Europe was threatened less by itself (as it had been during the centuries of great-power rivalry) than by external tensions growing out of superpower rivalry. At no time in its history had it been so divided, or had its future been so patently out of its control. The dismay at the depths to which it had been reduced by centuries of conflict now combined with discomfort at the opposing directions in which Europe was being pulled by the United States and the Soviet Union to lead to a new focus on European cooperation and independence. By the time the cold war came to an end in 1990–91, the ideological and social divisions that had been represented by the Berlin Wall and the Iron Curtain were well on their way to extinction. Encouraged by the removal of the economic and political barriers that had for so long kept them apart, Europeans were setting aside their differences and focusing new attention on their common political, social and cultural values.

Europeans still make many distinctions among themselves. Eastern Europe still struggles to rid itself of the heritage of state socialism and central planning, Germans still distinguish between those from the east and those from the west, Italy is culturally and economically divided into north and south, and Britain is an amalgam of English, Scottish, Welsh, and Northern Irish influences. Cultural and economic differences also continue to complicate European identity: the Mediterranean states to the south are distinctive from the maritime states to the west or the Scandinavian states to the north. And the rivalries, suspicions and stereotypes that have their roots in centuries of conflict still surface periodically. But compared with just a generation ago, what separates Europeans has become less distinct and important than what unites them. A host of critical changes – including the increased mobility of Europeans, a communications revolution that has made Europe a smaller place, the growth in intra-European trade, the rise of pan-European corporations, and a new sensitivity to the differences that exist between Europe, the United States and Russia, and of course the rise of the European Union – have combined to strengthen the sense that there is less to distinguish Europeans from one another today than they once thought.

Where is Europe?

In spite of all the political, economic, and social changes that have taken place in Europe since 1945, many doubts remain about the wisdom and the future of European integration. Most of those doubts have their roots in four main problems. First, few of the EU's member states are culturally homogeneous, and there is no such thing as a European race. The constant reordering of territorial lines over the centuries has bequeathed to almost every European state a multinational society, and has left several national groups – such as the Germans, the Poles, the Basques and the Irish – divided by national frontiers. Many states have also seen large influxes of immigrants since the 1950s, including Algerians to France, Turks to Germany and Indians to Britain. Not only is there no dominant culture, but most Europeans rightly shudder at the thought of their separate identities being subordinated to some kind of homogenized Euroculture. At least part of the resistance to integration is generated by concerns about threats to national cultural identity. Europeans might be striving to create unity out of diversity, but the cry of '*Vive la différence*!' is not forgotten.

Second, the linguistic divisions of Europe are substantial: its natives speak more than 40 languages, which are often vigorously defended as symbols of national identity; by contrast, one of the factors that helped the development of the United States was the existence of a common language. Multilingualism in Europe also means that all official EU documents are translated into the 23 official languages of the member states,[1] although the work of EU institutions is increasingly carried out in English and French. Supported by its rapid spread as the language of global commerce and diplomacy, the dominance of English

---

1. Bulgarian, Czech, Danish, Dutch, English, Estonian, Finnish, French, German, Greek, Hungarian, Irish Gaelic, Italian, Latvian, Lithuanian, Maltese, Polish, Portuguese, Romanian, Slovak, Slovenian, Spanish, Swedish.

grows, and it is slowly becoming the language of Europe. This worries the French in particular and other Europeans to some extent, but it is probably irresistible and will at least give Europeans a way of talking to each other, and help reduce the cultural differences that divide them.

Third, the histories of European states overlapped for centuries as they colonized, went to war, or formed alliances with each other. But those overlaps often emphasized their differences rather than giving them the sense of a shared past, and European integration grew in part out of the reactive idea of ending the conflicts that arose from those differences. Historical divisions were further emphasized by the external colonial interests of European powers, which encouraged them to develop competing sets of external priorities at the expense of cultivating closer ties with their immediate neighbours. Even now, Britain, France, Spain, and Portugal have close ties with their former colonies, while Germany – for different reasons – has interests in Eastern Europe. Many Europeans still need to be convinced that internal links are as important as external links.

Finally, and perhaps most fundamentally, the political and geographical boundaries of Europe have never been settled. It is often described as a 'continent', but continents are defined by geographers as large, unbroken, and discrete landmasses that are almost entirely surrounded by water. Strictly speaking, Europe is no more than part of the Asian continent, but no-one would seriously describe Europeans as Asians, even if there is no agreement on where Europe ends and Asia begins. The western, northern, and southern boundaries of Europe offer no difficulties, because they are conveniently demarcated by the Atlantic, the Arctic, and the Mediterranean. Unfortunately, there is no handy geographical feature to mark Europe's eastern boundary. It is usually defined as running down the Ural Mountains, across the Caspian Sea, along the southern edge of the Caucasus Mountains, across the Black Sea and through the Bosporus Strait. But these are no more than convenient physical features that have been adopted despite political realities.

Consider the problem of the Urals, which were nominated as a boundary by an eighteenth-century Russian cartographer, Vasily Tatishchev, so that Russia could claim to be an Asian as well as a European power. If we accept them as a boundary, then six former Soviet republics – Belarus, Moldova, Ukraine, and the three Baltic states (Estonia, Latvia, and Lithuania) – are part of Europe. The Baltic states offer few problems, because they have historically been bound to Europe, and are now members of the European Union and NATO. But questions remain about the orientation of Belarus, Moldova, and Ukraine, all three of which are still caught in a residual struggle for influence between Russia and Europe. Belarus is a political outlier, since it has resisted the wave of democracy that has swept over most of its neighbours. Ukraine underwent its famous Orange Revolution in 2004 that confirmed President Viktor Yushchenko in office, and he made clear his aspirations for Ukrainian membership of the EU, but there are many political and economic hurdles to cross before that becomes a reality. In Moldova, meanwhile, political leaders have hinted at an interest in EU membership, but the country is poor and has strong historical and cultural links with Russia.

The major problem with the Urals is that they do not mark the political border between two states, but are deep in the heart of Russia. Russians have sometimes been defined – and have seen themselves – as European, and Russia west of the Urals was long known as Eurasia because of the distinctions imposed on the region by Europeans, but opinion on Russia's identity remains mixed: some Russians see it as part of Europe and the West, others distrust the West and see Russia as distinctive from both Europe and Asia, and yet others see it as a bridge between the two (Smith, 1999, p. 50). The most obvious problem with defining Russia as European is that three-quarters of its land area is east of the Urals, and many of the more than 40 ethnic minorities that live in Russia – such as the Siberian minorities of Buryatia, Evenki, Khakassia, and Selkup – are unquestionably non-European. Further south, meanwhile, the Caucasus Mountains present similar problems; should the republics of Armenia, Azerbaijan and Georgia be considered European (they are all members of the Council of Europe, after all, and there have been hints here, too, as in Ukraine, of EU and NATO membership down the line) or are they too politically and economically tied to Russia?

In central Europe, changes in the balance of power long meant that the Poles, the Czechs, and the Slovaks were caught in the crossfire of great-power competition, which is why this region was known as the 'lands between'. The west looked on the area as a buffer against Russia, a perception that was helped by the failure of its people to form lasting states identified with dominant national groups. During the cold war the distinctiveness of Eastern Europe was further emphasized by the ideological divisions between east and west, despite the historical ties that meant Poland was actually closer to Western Europe than to Russia. But the end of the cold war meant a rapid reorientation of central Europe towards the west, and all states in the region are now members of the EU and NATO.

For their part, the Balkans occupy an ambiguous position between Europe and Asia, being a geographical part of the former but historically drawn towards the latter. They were long regarded as an extension of Asia Minor, and until relatively recently were still described by Europeans as the Near East (Hobsbawm, 1991, p. 17). Most Europeans have traditionally regarded them as a zone of transition between two 'civilizations', whether the term is applied to religions (the boundary between Islam, Catholicism, and Eastern Orthodoxy) or to political communities (the boundary between the eastern and western Roman Empires, between the Habsburg and Ottoman Empires, and more recently between Slavic-Russian, western, and eastern influences).

The Balkans have come under the authority of the Macedonians, the Romans, the eastern Roman empire, Slavic tribes, Christianity, the Kingdom of Hungary, the Venetians, and – from the sixteenth century until 1918 – the Ottoman Turks. Except during the Tito regime (1945–80), the region has never been united, and the allegiance of its inhabitants has always been divided. These changes created what Delanty (1995, pp. 51–2) describes as 'frontier societies in the intermediary lands' between great powers. The Slavs in particular were split between those who accepted Catholicism, Greek Orthodoxy, or Islam, which resulted in cultural heterogeneity in spite of the greater linguistic homogeneity that existed among Slavs than among the peoples of Western Europe (Delanty, 1995, p. 54). Slavs continue to have affiliations with Russia, which is part of the reason why NATO was wary about becoming too deeply involved in the conflicts in Bosnia and Kosovo in the 1990s. Since the breakup of Yugoslavia there has been a trend for Balkan national groups to look to the EU; the Slovenians were the first to become members in 2004, Croatia and Macedonia have been accepted as candidate countries, and other Balkan republics have broached the prospect of eventual EU membership. (The Balkans also include part of Turkey, discussion about whose European identity creates its own set of problems – see Box 2.2.)

So where, then, is Europe? If its borders with Turkey, the Caucasus and Russia are taken as its eastern limits, then it consists today of 39 countries: the 27 members of the EU, three other Western European states (Iceland, Norway and Switzerland), and nine Eastern European states.[2] If a broader definition of Europe's boundaries is accepted, then it includes four more countries: Armenia, Azerbaijan, Georgia, and Turkey. Stretching the limits of credibility, some (such as former Italian prime minister Silvio Berlusconi) have even suggested that Israel should be considered European, and might qualify for EU membership, but this view has little support.

Whatever Europe's external boundaries, its inner personality has been driven by two critical developments. First, the cold war division of Europe has faded into the mists of history as Western and Eastern Europeans have buried their political, economic and ideological differences, and as the bonds among them have tightened and strengthened. Political and economic investments have flowed from west to east, and workers in search of new opportunities have moved from east to west. Second, enlargement has helped reduce the differences between 'Europe' and the 'European Union'. As recently as 2004, less than half the states of Europe were members of the EU, which was home to only two-thirds of Europeans. Today, the EU covers three-quarters of the land area of Europe, includes two-thirds of the states of Europe, accounts for 93 per cent of the economic wealth of Europe, and is home to four out of every five Europeans. We may still quibble about the eastern borders of Europe,

2. Albania, Belarus, Bosnia and Herzegovina, Croatia, Macedonia, Moldova, Montenegro, Serbia, and Ukraine. The number will increase to ten if and when the independence of Kosovo is agreed.

Box 2.2   The Turkish question

When it comes to defining the borders of Europe, and deciding the limits of EU enlargement, no question is as troubling as that of Turkey. The European Community agreed as long ago as 1963 that Turkish membership was possible, and it became an associate member of the Community that same year. It applied for full membership in 1987, a customs union between the EU and Turkey came into force in December 1995, Turkey was formally recognized as an applicant country in 2002, and negotiations on EU membership opened in 2005. But a string of troubling questions has muddied the waters. Perhaps most fundamental has been the matter of whether or not Turkey is a European country. Most Europeans see it as part of Asia Minor and part of the Islamic sphere of influence, but the Bosporus is usually regarded as the border between Europe and Asia, which means that about 4 per cent of the land area of Turkey lies inside Europe. And the geographical argument has been undermined since Cyprus became an EU member in 2004; Nicosia is further from Brussels than Ankara.

But the real barriers to Turkish membership of the EU are less geographical than they are political, economic and religious. The EU has agreed three criteria for aspiring members, known as the Copenhagen conditions: an applicant must be democratic, capitalist, and willing to adopt the existing body of EU laws. Turkey is clearly capitalist, and has made great efforts to meet the third of these requirements, most notably abolishing the death penalty in 2004. But while it is clearly capitalist it is also poor, with a per capita GDP one-tenth that of the EU, and current EU members fear not only that billions of euros in subsidies and investments will be diverted to Turkey if it joins the EU, but that numerous Turks will move to richer parts of the EU in search of jobs. As to Turkish democracy, its record on human rights has been poor, with concerns – for example – about the role of the military in politics, about the treatment of the Kurdish minority, and about women's rights.

But the most telling – if usually unspoken – concern about prospective Turkish membership of the EU is religious. Turkey is a Muslim state, and even though its brand of Islam is secular and western-oriented, the potential difficulties of integrating 72 million Turkish Muslims into a club that often emphasizes its Christian credentials, and that has been struggling with accommodating its own existing Muslim minorities, are substantial. If Turkey was small, poor and Muslim it might be less of a problem, but its size means that it would become the second largest member state of the EU by population after Germany. The resulting doubts have divided European public and political opinion, which tends to focus on the challenges rather than the opportunities offered by Turkish membership. Among the latter: a large new market and labour pool, and the importance of Turkey in helping Europe strengthen its geopolitical relationship with the Middle East and the Muslim world. (For further discussion, see Morris, 2005.)

but the differences between the EU and Europe are rapidly disappearing, with the result that the location and the mission of Europe have never been clearer than they are today.

The Meaning of Europe

There is an old and well-worn joke that heaven is where the police are British, the cooks are French, the mechanics are German, the lovers are Italian and everything is organized by the Swiss. Meanwhile, hell is where the police are German, the cooks are British, the mechanics are French, the lovers are Swiss, and everything is organized by the Italians. National stereotypes such as these abound in Europe (as they do everywhere), some based on a modicum of truth, some with no redeeming qualities, and most nonetheless perpetuated by the media and popular culture. But even if such stereotypes are typically wrong (or wrong-headed), what they tell us is that Europe is a region of enormous diversity. Nationalism and national identity are alive and well, and every country claims to have a distinctive personality arising out of a combination of history, culture, norms, and values. A country may share many of its norms and values with other countries, and its population may be divided internally by multiple different social and political values, but each is branded with a personality that is usually assumed to be unique to each country.

Out of this melange of competing identities, how is it possible to pin down a distinctive European personality? Surely the histories, cultures and social structures of European states are too deeply ingrained to make such an exercise credible? And those who doubt the wisdom and effects of European integration are more than ready to point to the many instances where EU member states still squabble and disagree. The open disagreement over the US-led invasion of Iraq in 2003 is a prime example, often touted as evidence of the underlying weaknesses of the European experiment, notably in the area of foreign policy. But what almost all the analysts and observers failed to mention was that the disagreement was primarily between European governments, and not between Europeans themselves. Indeed, opinion polls found a near uniformity of opinion across Europe, with 70–90 per cent of those polled expressing opposition to the war, even in countries whose governments supported the war, including Britain, Spain, Italy, Denmark, and the Netherlands.

At the same time, a growing body of research indicates that there are many increasingly common values and opinions across the EU on a broad array of issues, ranging from welfarism to capital punishment, immigration, international relations, environmental protection, and the relationship between Church and state. Much remains to be done to better understand and clarify the commonalities, and to move the analysis beyond the increasingly tired obsession with what divides rather than unites Europe, but the outlines of Europeanism have achieved a new clarity in recent years, particularly since the end of the cold war finally allowed Europeans from east and west to begin expressing and exerting themselves without being limited by the constraints of rivalry between the Americans and the Soviets.

'Europeanism' is usually understood to mean support for the process of European integration. Hence Scruton (1996, p. 180) defines it as the 'attitude which sees the well-being, destiny and institutions of the major European states as so closely linked by geographical and historical circumstances that no cogent political action can be successfully pursued in one state without some reference to, and attempt to achieve integration with, the others'. But perhaps it is time to move beyond the narrow focus on integration, and to think instead of Europeanism as signifying the collective values and principles associated with Europe and Europeans. An initial attempt was made to pin them down in 2003, when – inspired by the massive demonstrations against the impending invasion of Iraq that were held in every major European city on 15 February – the German and French philosophers Jürgen Habermas and Jacques Derrida hailed what they optimistically saw as the birth of a 'European public sphere', noted that there had been a reaction to nationalism that had helped give contemporary Europe 'its own face', and argued that a 'core Europe' (excluding Britain and Eastern Europe) should be built as a counterweight to US influence in the world. They listed several features of what they described as a common European 'political mentality', including secularization, support for the welfare state, a low threshold of tolerance for the use of force, and support for multilateralism (Habermas and Derrida, 2003 [2005]).

During the cold war, the outlines of a distinctive European identity were hard to find, divided as the sub-continent was by the lines of the conflict, and subject as most European states were to the political lead of the United States (in the west) or of the Soviet Union (in the east). European priorities were subsumed under the broader goals of cold war conflict, and neither group of states was in the position to offer much resistance to the lead of the superpowers. This did not stop the governments of western states from privately resisting US policy (for example, in Vietnam and the Middle East), or those of eastern states from occasionally resisting Soviet control. But it was only with the end of the cold war that Europe was once again in the position to be able to pursue more freely the policies and goals that best suited European needs and best reflected European values. The result has been a new awareness of what makes Europe different, the key elements of which can be found in four major areas: political values, economic values, social values, and attitudes towards international relations.

On the political front, the Europeans are clearly champions of democracy, but they also have a particularly European view of the nature and purposes of democracy. The structure and distribution of power is driven by the parliamentary system, which – while not peculiar to Europe – was born in Europe and today forms the basis of all national European political systems, albeit with local variations. One effect of the system is that political parties play a more central role in European politics than they do in much of the rest of the world (in spite of the many suggestions that European party systems are on the decline), the distribution of seats in national legislatures determining the make-up of governments, and the variety and ideological spread of parties reflecting and driving the diversity of voter opinion. Although the rigidity of social class has declined with the growth of social mobility, and neither voting nor party identification are as class driven as they once were, in comparison to the United States there is a greater sense of class consciousness in Europe. If class identification is on the decline, national and ethnic political divisions have been on the rise thanks to a combination of resurgent local nationalism and of immigration first from former European colonies and more recently from neighbouring states. Finally, national politics in Europe is heavily influenced by the impact of integration, which has had an homogenizing effect on political culture and on the content of national laws and policies.

On the economic front, Europeans are committed capitalists and supporters of the free market, but they place a premium on the redistribution of wealth and opportunity, and on the responsibility of government to maintain a level playing field. As Prestowitz puts it, one of the most fundamental differences between the American and European economic models is that 'Americans emphasize equality of opportunity, [while] Europeans focus more on equality of results' (Prestowitz, 2003, pp. 236–7). Europeans have a higher level of tolerance than Americans for government intervention in the marketplace, and generally support the idea that key services should be managed and offered by the government, and paid for out of taxes. One American observer – Jeremy Rifkin – has gone so far as to talk of a new European dream that is threatening to eclipse the much-vaunted American dream. He contrasts the American emphasis on economic growth, personal wealth, and individual self-interest with the European emphasis on sustainable development, quality of life, and community, and concludes that the EU is developing a new social and political model better suited to the needs of the globalizing world of the new century (Rifkin, 2004). Europeans have not yet been able to address the problems of persistent poverty and widespread unemployment (just as no-one has), but their approaches stand in contrast to those of the United States, which places an emphasis on self-reliance and on the private delivery of key services.

There has been recent debate about just how much European governments agree on the economic responsibilities of the state, and an interest in the distinctions between the 'Anglo-Saxon' and 'continental' or Rhenish European economic models. The former – so called (see Albert, 1993) because it is associated with English-speaking countries such as Britain, Ireland, the US and Canada – features lower levels of tax and regulation, a greater reliance on the private sector to provide key services, and a greater level of market freedom. The latter takes the opposite view, arguing that the state must intervene more actively to redistribute wealth and address poverty. Those who support the Anglo-Saxon model like to point to its successes in achieving higher levels of productivity and lower levels of unemployment and inflation. But they also fail to note that the Anglo-Saxon economies differ substantially in several respects, most obviously in contrasting attitudes towards the welfare state. Meanwhile, supporters of the continental model argue that it offers corporations and workers more protection, particularly from the pressures of globalization, and that it generates less economic inequality and creates less poverty. But they fail to note that poverty is still a widespread problem throughout Europe, and that the wealth of the European single market has grown on the back of globalization. The existence of two models also rather overlooks the homogenization of the structure of European economies that has taken place as a result of the single market, increased intra-European trade and investment, corporate mergers and acquisitions, and common policies on competition.

On the social front, there is not yet a distinctive European society, in spite of the long tradition of cultural superiority that Europeans felt over much of the rest of the world, particularly over those regions that were colonized at least in part out of a sense of a mission to civilize. Considerable barriers are created today by language differences, by the absence of pan-European media, and by cultural differences (see Box 2.3), and yet there are many trends which suggest substantial agreement among Europeans on a variety of issues. Thus there is strong support for the idea that government should provide basic services such as education and health care (existing alongside private alternatives), a view which sees its most essential occurrence in the welfare state. Hutton (2003, pp. 54–8) argues that while the American liberal definition of rights does not extend beyond the political to the economic and social, the European conception of rights is broader, encapsulating free health care, free education, the right to employment insurance, and so on.

At the same time, Europeans are resistant to suggestions that government should be active in making moral decisions or defining the social choices of individuals. This can be seen in the predominantly liberal positions on issues such as abortion, capital punishment, gun control, censorship, doctor-assisted suicide, and same-sex civil unions and marriage. Many of these views are related to European support for the gap between Church and state.

Despite the central role that the Church has played in European public and political life over the centuries, it has never been a uniting force (Dunkerley et al., 2002, p. 115). First there was the division between the Latin and Orthodox Churches, then the division between the Catholic and Protestant Churches, and more recently there has been the rise of religious diversity as new immigrants have brought Islam, Hinduism, Buddhism, Sikhism and other religions into the equation. During the discussions over the European constitutional treaty, it was suggested that the preamble should include reference to the Christian heritage of Europe, but this was turned down on the grounds that it would not reflect the religious diversity of the new Europe, and would

Box 2.3   Promoting European culture

The stability of a state is usually predicated upon a high degree of legitimacy (public acceptance), which is in turn predicated upon a strong sense of national identity, in which a sense of a common culture is a critical element. Conversely, the instability of states often arises out of social and cultural divisions, which weaken the sense of a common national identity. France is an example of a state with a high level of cultural unity, while British national identity is weakened by divisions among the English, the Scots, the Welsh, and the Northern Irish, and Belgium is weakened by divisions between its Flemish and Wallonian communities.

Historically and culturally speaking, Europeans are insular and inward-looking, often knowing little about the history or culture of even their closest neighbours. The EU has tried to address this problem by promoting the idea of a common European culture (even though such promotion may be anathema to some – how can culture be legislated or 'promoted' as a policy goal?). Despite the results of Eurobarometer polls showing a majority in favour of cultural policy being left to the member states, Maastricht introduced a commitment that the EU would 'contribute to the flowering of the culture of the Member States' with a view to improving knowledge about the culture and history of Europe, conserving European cultural heritage, and supporting and supplementing non-commercial cultural exchanges and 'artistic and literary creation'.

What this has so far meant in practice has been spending money on restoring historic buildings, supporting training schemes in conservation and restoration, preserving regional and minority languages, subsidising the translation of works by European authors (particularly into less widely spoken languages), and supporting cultural events. For example, the EU has funded a Youth Orchestra and a Baroque Orchestra to bring young musicians together, declared since 1985 European 'Capitals of Culture' (including Graz in Austria, Genoa in Italy, and Cork in Ireland) and established a European Cultural Month in cities in non-member states (such as Basel, Cracow, and St Petersburg).

While the sentiments behind these projects are laudable, it is difficult to see how cultural exchanges and the development of a European cultural identity can work unless they are driven by Europeans themselves. It is easy to argue that Shakespeare, Michelangelo, Voltaire, Goethe, Picasso and Mozart are all part of the heritage of Europe, but the notion of promoting a modern pan-European popular culture is a beast of an entirely different stripe. Even the most mobile of art forms – film and rock music – come up against the barrier of national preferences, and little that is not produced in English has had commercial success outside its home market.

send a particularly worrying message to Muslims and Jews (see discussion in Schlesinger and Foret, 2006).

European society has also been distinguished by important demographic changes that are routinely quoted as sources of concern and as indicating weaknesses in the future success of Europe. Prime among these has been the aging of European societies and declining birth rates, the combination of which has meant that the costs of health care and social security are falling on the shoulders of a shrinking workforce. A related factor has been the impact of immigration, which can be interpreted as an opportunity to make up for the problems posed by aging and population decline, but can also be interpreted as a problem in respect of the social and political conflict created by ethnic and religious cleavages.

In international relations, Europeans have a preference for multilateralism, the use of soft power (encouragement and opportunity) rather than hard power (coercion and force) (see Chapter 9), and for using civilian means for dealing with conflict. They take a liberal view of the international system, arguing that states can and must cooperate and work together on matters of shared interest, and placing an emphasis on the importance of international organizations and international law. The European view stands in particular contrast to that of the United States, which has a reputation (not always entirely deserved) for unilateralism, the promotion of national interests, an emphasis on military solutions to problems, and a distrust of international organizations. While Europeans have become used to working together, the United States has long been wary of alliances and jealously guards its independence. This can be seen in the contrasting positions of Europeans and Americans towards international peacekeeping efforts; while Europeans are willing to work through the United Nations and to commit their troops to joint commands, the United States refuses to allow its troops to wear the blue helmets of the United Nations or to allow them to be controlled by foreign officers or political leaders. Where many Europeans long ago acknowledged that they were citizens of an international system, and are prepared to act multilaterally, there are still many Americans for whom there are only two realistic options: American leadership, or isolationism.

The best-known recent analysis of the contrasting worldviews of the EU and the US was offered in 2003 by Robert Kagan, an American political commentator (Kagan, 2003). He argued that the two sides no longer share a common view of the world, and that 'Americans are from Mars and Europeans are from Venus'. What he meant was that while Europe has moved into a world of laws, rules, and international cooperation, the United States believes that security and defence depend on the possession and use of military power. While the United States sees the world as divided between good and evil, and between friends and enemies, Europeans see a more complex global system, and prefer to negotiate and persuade rather than to coerce. Kagan argues that the differences are a reflection of the relative positions of the two actors in the world; when Europe was powerful it was willing to use violence to achieve its goals, while Americans had no choice but to use soft power. But now that they have traded places, they have also traded perspectives. Critics have taken issue with this analysis, arguing that Europeans do not use soft power because they have no choice, but precisely because they have a choice.

Europe is not a continent of pacifists, but one where the 'just' causes of war are actively debated and where there are different opinions about the role of military force (Menon *et al.*, 2004).

These four sets of features can help us pin down the nature of Europeanism, but – just as with its eastern borders – it is not easy to draw firm lines around the features, many of which are shared with other parts of the world. In geographical, political, economic, and social terms it has never been easy to pin down Europe, particularly given its enormous internal diversity. But one of the effects of integration has been to encourage more efforts to understand what Europeans have in common. There is still much resistance among political leaders, academics and Europeans themselves to the idea that generalizations can be drawn across national borders, but the common themes in both the meaning of Europe and in the values and norms that are represented by Europe are easier to identify today than ever before.

Conclusions

The idea of European unity is nothing new. The conflicts that brought instability, death, and changes to the balance of power in Europe over the centuries prompted many to propose unification – or at least the development of a common system of government – as a means to the achievement of peace. The rise of the state system undermined these proposals, but interstate conflict ultimately reached a level at which it became clear that only cooperation could offer a path to peace. The two world wars of the twentieth century – which in many ways began as European civil wars – emphatically underlined the dangers of nationalism and of the continued promotion of state interests at the expense of regional interests.

The new thinking has dramatically altered the idea of Europe over the past two generations, and the nature of the internal relationship among the states that make up Europe has changed out of all recognition. For the first time, the concept of European unity has found a widespread audience. The audience may not always have been enthusiastic, but there has been a generational shift since 1945 as those who witnessed the horrors of the Second World War are superseded by those who have known nothing but a general peace in the region. Where intellectuals and philosophers once argued in isolation that the surest path to peace in Europe was cooperation, or even integration, the costs of nationalism are now more broadly appreciated, ensuring a wider and deeper consideration of the idea of regional unity.

Europeans still have much that divides them, and those differences are obvious to anyone who travels across the region. There are different languages, cultural traditions, legal, education and health care systems, social priorities, cuisines, modes of entertainment, patterns of etiquette, styles of dress, ways of planning and building cities, ways of spending leisure time, attitudes towards the countryside, and even sides of the road on which to drive (the British, Irish, Cypriots, and Maltese drive on the left, everyone else on the right). Europeans also have differences in the way they govern themselves, and in what they have been able to achieve with their economies and social welfare systems.

Increasingly, however, Europeans have more in common. The economic and social integration that has taken place under the auspices of the European Union and its precursors since the early 1950s has brought the needs and priorities of Europeans closer into alignment. It has also encouraged the rest of the world to see Europeans less as citizens of separate states and more as citizens of the same economic bloc, if not yet the same political bloc. Not only has there been integration from the Mediterranean to the Arctic Circle, but the 'lands between' – which spent the cold war as part of the Soviet bloc and part of the buffer created by the Soviet Union to protect its western frontier – are now becoming part of greater Europe for the first time in their history. The result has been a fundamental redefinition of the idea of Europe. In the next chapter we will look at the steps taken by European governments to build the European Union, the underlying motives of integration, and the debates involved in the process.

Chapter 3

The Evolution of the EU

The idea of 'Europe' may have been with us for centuries, but serious efforts to promote voluntary European unity date back less than 60 years. It was only after the Second World War that the theories about the possible benefits of European integration were finally tested in practice. The critical first step was taken on 9 May 1950, at a press conference held at the French Foreign Ministry in Paris. To the attendant journalists, French foreign minister Robert Schuman announced a plan under which Europe's national coal and steel industries would be brought together under the administration of a single joint authority.

The European Coal and Steel Community was founded in 1952 with just six member states (France, West Germany, Italy and the three Benelux countries), but from this modest first step a complex process of experimentation, political action, opportunism, intrigue, crisis and serendipity would eventually lead to the European Union as we know it today. The original priorities were threefold: postwar economic construction, the desire to prevent European nationalism leading once again to conflict, and the need for security in the face of the threats posed by the cold war. At the core of this thinking was concern about the traditional hostility between France and Germany, and the argument that if these two could cooperate it might provide the foundations for broader European integration.

The next step was the creation in 1958 of the European Economic Community, with the same six members but a more ambitious set of goals. These included agreement on a common external tariff for all goods coming into the Community, the development of a single market, within which there would be free movement of people, goods, money, and services, and a common agricultural policy. As it became clear that the Community was working, other countries applied for full or associate membership. The first enlargement came in 1973 with the accession of Britain, Denmark, and Ireland, followed in the 1980s by Greece, Portugal, and Spain, and in 1995 by Austria, Finland and Sweden.

The single market was given a much-needed boost in 1986 with agreement of the Single European Act, setting a five-year deadline for removal of the remaining barriers. There was progress, too, on monetary union, with the launch in 1999 of the euro. Enlargement remained high on the agenda, the focus shifting to Eastern Europe. After lengthy preparations, 12 new mainly

Eastern European countries joined the EU in 2004–07, bringing membership to 27 and the population of the EU to nearly 490 million.

Along the way, progress was made on developing common policies on a wide range of issues, although those who hoped that Europe would play a more assertive and united role in foreign and security policy were to be disappointed. There was also disappointment for supporters of a new European constitution, which was drafted in 2005 but collapsed after negative public votes in France and the Netherlands. As this book went to press, agreement had been reached on a slimmed down Lisbon treaty that preserved most of the content of the constitutional treaty, aimed at making the larger EU more efficient. Meanwhile, many Europeans remain ambivalent about the European Union, and others are patently hostile. While some see strong signs of progress, others remain doubtful about the unfinished business on the European agenda, and about the direction of the road ahead.

Postwar Europe

The European Union was born out of the ruins of the Second World War. Before the war, Europe had dominated global trade, banking and finance, its empires had stretched across the world and its military superiority had been unquestioned. But Europeans had often fallen out with each other, and their conflicts undermined the prosperity that cooperation might have brought. Pacifists hoped that the Great War of 1914–18 might conclusively prove the futility and brutality of armed conflict, but it was to take yet another conflagration finally to convince Europeans that they needed to change how they related to each other if a lasting peace was to be achieved.

The Second World War left more than 40 million dead and widespread devastation in its wake. European cities lay in ruins, agricultural production was halved, food was rationed, and communications were disrupted by the destruction of bridges, railways and harbours. While the physical damage caused by the First World War had been relatively restricted, every country involved in this latest conflict sustained heavy casualties and physical damage. The war also dealt a near-fatal blow to Europe's global power and influence, clearing the way for the emergence of the United States and the Soviet Union as superpowers, and creating a nervous new bipolar balance in the distribution of international political influence.

Against this troubled background a number of European leaders began to champion the idea of European states setting aside their differences and building bridges of cooperation aimed at removing the causes of war, and perhaps even promoting European economic and political union. Their priorities were quite different: France and the Benelux countries sought security from Germany, Germany and Italy sought new respectability, Britain saw its primary interests lying outside Europe, the Nordic states were pursuing their own cooperative plans, Portugal and Spain were marginalized and uninterested in regional cooperation, and Eastern Europe was under the political control of the Soviet Union. But while their domestic priorities were sometimes different, Western European governments quickly realized that changes taking place at the global level demanded new thinking. In July 1944, representatives from 44 countries – including the United States and all the allied European states – had met at Bretton Woods in New Hampshire to make plans for the postwar global economy. All agreed to an Anglo-American proposal to promote free trade, non-discrimination and stable exchange rates, and supported the view that Europe's economies should be rebuilt and placed on a more stable footing.

Because Europe's wartime resistance had been allied with left-wing political ideas, there was a political shift to the left after the war, with socialist and social democratic parties winning power in several European countries. Many of the new governments launched programmes of social welfare and nationalization, emphasizing central economic planning. Fundamental to this approach were the theories of the British economist John Maynard Keynes, who argued for government control over some aspects of the economy in order to manage the cycle of booms and busts. Keynesianism became the basis of postwar economic reconstruction and Western European governments increasingly intervened in their economies to control inflation and rebuild industry and agriculture. However, it soon became clear that substantial capital investment was needed to bolster reconstruction. The readiest source of such capital was the United States, which saw Europe's welfare as essential to its own economic and security interests, and made a large investment in the future of Europe through the Marshall Plan (see Box 3.1).

As one of the two new postwar superpowers, the United States also found itself playing the role of global policeman, its primary goal being to defend Western Europe (and ultimately itself) from the Soviet threat. Its assumptions that Europe had enough people, money and resources to recover from the war, and that the allies would continue to work together, both proved wrong (Urwin, 1995, pp. 13–14). Furthermore, its European allies were divided over how far they felt they could rely on the United States to defend them, and the doubters began to think in terms of greater European cooperation.

Most immediately, the western allies were undecided about what to do with Germany. In June 1948 they united their three zones of occupation into a new West German state with a new currency. The Soviets responded with a blockade around West Berlin, prompting a massive western airlift to supply the beleaguered city. The US Congress was resistant to direct American commitments or entanglements in Europe, but saw the need to counterbalance the Soviets and to ensure the peaceful cooperation of West Germany. In 1949 the North Atlantic Treaty Organization (NATO) was created, by which the United States agreed to help its European allies 'restore and maintain

Box 3.1   The Marshall Plan, 1948–51

US policy after 1945 was to withdraw its military forces as quickly as possible from Europe. However, it soon became clear that Stalin had plans to expand the Soviet sphere of influence, and the US State Department began to realize that it had underestimated the extent of Europe's economic destruction; despite a boom in the late 1940s, sustained growth was not forthcoming. When an economically exhausted Britain ended its financial aid to Greece and Turkey in 1947, President Truman argued the need for the United States to fill the vacuum in order to curb communist influence in the region.

US policy makers also felt that European markets needed to be rebuilt and integrated into a multilateral system of world trade, and that economic and political reconstruction would help forestall Soviet aggression and the rise of domestic communist parties (Hogan, 1987, pp. 26–7). Thus Secretary of State George Marshall argued that the United States should provide Europe with assistance to fight 'hunger, poverty, desperation and chaos'. The original April 1947 State Department proposal for the plan made clear that one of its ultimate goals was the creation of a Western European federation (quoted in Gillingham, 1991, pp. 118–19).

The European Recovery Programme (otherwise known as the Marshall Plan) provided just over $12.5 billion in aid to Europe between 1948 and 1951 (Milward, 1984, p. 94), the disbursement of which was coordinated by the Organization for European Economic Cooperation (OEEC), a new body set up in April 1948 with headquarters in Paris. Governed by a Council of Ministers made up of one representative from each member state, the OEEC's goals included the reduction of tariffs and other barriers to trade, and consideration of the possibility of a free trade area or customs union among its members. Opposition from several European governments (notably Britain, France, and Norway) ensured that the OEEC remained a forum for intergovernmental consultation rather than becoming a supranational body with powers of its own (Wexler, 1983, p. 209; Milward, 1984, pp. 209–10).

Although the effects of the Marshall Plan are still debated, there is little question that it helped underpin economic and political recovery in Europe, and helped bind more closely the economic and political interests of the United States and Western Europe. It was a profitable investment for the United States, in both political and economic terms, but it also had critical influence on the idea of European integration – as Western Europe's first venture in economic cooperation, it encouraged Europeans to work together and highlighted the mutual dependence among their economies (Urwin, 1995, pp. 20–2). It also helped liberalize intra-European trade, and helped ensure that economic integration would be focused on Western Europe.

the security of the North Atlantic area'. Canada, too, joined, along with the Benelux countries, Britain, Denmark, France, Iceland, Italy, Norway, and Portugal.

NATO members agreed that an attack on one of them would be considered an attack on all of them, but each agreed only to respond with 'such actions as it deems necessary'. The Europeans attempted to take their own defence a step further in 1952 by proposing the creation of a European Defence Community, but this failed after political opposition in Britain and France (see below). Nonetheless, Britain was anxious to encourage some kind of military cooperation, and invited France, West Germany, Italy, and the Benelux states to become founding members of the Western European Union (WEU), whose members agreed to give all possible military and other aid to any member that was attacked. The WEU went beyond purely defensive concerns, and the agreement signed by the seven founding members in Paris in October 1954 included the aim 'to promote the unity and to encourage the progressive integration of Europe'. Within days of the launch of the WEU in May 1955 and the coincidental admission of West Germany into NATO, the Soviet bloc created the Warsaw Pact. The lines of the cold war were now defined, and its implications were clearly illustrated by events in Egypt and Hungary in 1956.

In July, seeking funds to help him build a dam on the Nile, Egyptian president Gamal Abdel Nasser nationalized the Suez Canal, still owned and operated by Britain and France, and seen as vital to the international interests of both countries. Their governments immediately conspired with that of Israel to launch an invasion of the canal, in the face of hostile international public and political opinion, and – most tellingly – the ire of the Americans. Then, in October, the government of Imre Nagy in Hungary announced the end of one-party rule, the evacuation of Russian troops, and withdrawal from the Warsaw Pact. Just as Britain and France were invading Egypt to retake the Suez Canal, the Soviets were sending tanks into Hungary. The United States wanted to criticize the Soviet use of force and boast to the emerging Third World about the moral superiority of the west, but obviously could not while British and French paratroopers were storming the Suez Canal. In the face of US hostility, Britain and France were ostracized in the UN Security Council and the attempt to regain the Suez was abandoned.

The combined effects of the French defeat in Indochina in 1954, the Suez crisis and the Hungarian uprising were profound: Britain and France began to reduce the size of their armed forces, finally recognizing that they were no longer world powers capable of significant independent action in the Middle East, or perhaps anywhere; both embarked on a concerted programme of decolonization; Britain began to look to Europe for its economic and security interests; and it became obvious to Europeans that the United States was the dominant partner in the North Atlantic alliance, a fact that particularly concerned the French.

First steps towards integration (1945–58)

The priority for European leaders after the Second World War was to create the conditions that would prevent Europeans from ever going to war with each other again. For many, the major threats to peace and security were nationalism and the nation state, both of which had been discredited by the war. For most, Germany was the core problem – peace was impossible, it was argued, unless Germany could be contained and its power diverted to constructive rather than destructive ends. It had to be allowed to rebuild its economic base and its political system, but in ways that would not threaten European security.

Meanwhile, tensions between the United States and the Soviet Union led Europeans to worry that they were becoming pawns in the cold war. There was clearly a need to protect Western Europe from the Soviet threat, but there were also doubts about the extent to which Europeans and Americans could find common ground, and to which Western Europe could rely on US protection. Europe might be better advised to take care of its own security, but this would require a greater sense of unity and common purpose than it had ever been able to achieve.

The spotlight fell particularly on Britain, which had taken the lead in fighting Nazism and was still the dominant European power. In 1942–43, Winston Churchill had suggested the development of 'a United States of Europe' operating under 'a Council of Europe' with reduced trade barriers, free movement of people, a common military and a High Court to adjudicate disputes (quoted in Palmer, 1968, p. 111). He made the same suggestion in a speech at the University of Zurich in 1946, but it was clear that Churchill felt this new entity should be based around France and Germany and would not necessarily include Britain – before the war he had argued that Britain was 'with Europe but not of it. We are interested and associated, but not absorbed' (Zurcher, 1958, p. 6).

National pro-European groups decided to organize a conference aimed at publicizing the cause of regional unity. The key result of the Congress of Europe, held in The Hague in May 1948, was the Council of Europe, founded with the signing in London in May 1949 of a statute by ten Western European states. The statute noted the need for 'closer unity between all the like-minded countries of Europe' and included among the Council's aims 'common action in economic, social, cultural, scientific, legal and administrative matters'. Although membership of the Council expanded, however, it never became more than a loose intergovernmental organization, and was not the kind of body that European federalists wanted. Those looking for something more substantial included the French entrepreneur and postwar planner Jean Monnet (1888–1979) and French foreign minister Robert Schuman (1886–1963). Both were committed Europeanists, felt that practical steps needed to be taken that went beyond the broad statements of organizations such as the Council of Europe, and agreed that the logical starting point should be the resolution of the perennial problem of Franco-German relations.

By 1950 it was clear to many that West Germany had to be allowed to rebuild its industrial base if it was to play a useful role in the western alliance. This would best be done under the auspices of a supranational organization that would tie West Germany into the wider process of European reconstruction. Looking for a starting point that would be meaningful but not too ambitious, Monnet opted for the coal and steel industries, because they were the building blocks of industry, because the heavy industries of the Ruhr had been the foundation of Germany's power, and because integrating coal and steel would make sure that West Germany became reliant on trade with the rest of Europe, underpinning its economic reconstruction while helping the French overcome their fear of German industrial domination (Monnet, 1978, p. 292). He knew from personal experience that intergovernmental organizations had a tendency to be hamstrung by the governments of their member states, and to become bogged down in ministerial meetings. To avoid these problems he proposed a new institution independent of national governments, which would be supranational rather than intergovernmental in nature.

The plan was announced by Robert Schuman at his May 1950 press conference. In what later became known as the Schuman Declaration, he argued that Europe would not be united at once or according to a single plan, but step by step through concrete achievements. This would require the elimination of Franco-German hostility, and Schuman proposed that French and German coal and steel production be placed 'under a common High Authority, within the framework of an organization open to the participation of the other countries of Europe'. This would be 'a first step in the federation of Europe', and would make war between France and Germany 'not merely unthinkable, but materially impossible' (Schuman, quoted in Stirk and Weigall, 1999, p. 76).

Although membership of the new body was open to all Western European states, only four accepted: Italy, which wanted respectability and economic and political stability, and the three Benelux countries, which were small and vulnerable, had twice in recent memory been invaded by Germany, were heavily reliant on exports, and felt that the only way they could have a voice in world affairs and ensure their security was to become part of a bigger regional unit. The other Western European governments had different reasons for not taking part: Britain still had extensive interests outside Europe, exported little of its steel to the continent, and the new Labour government had recently nationalized Britain's coal and steel industries and did not like the supranational character of Schuman's proposal; Ireland was predominantly agricultural and tied economically to Britain; for Denmark and Norway the memories of German occupation were too fresh; Austria, Finland, and Sweden were keen on remaining neutral; and Portugal and Spain were dictatorships with little interest in international cooperation.

The lines of thinking now established, the governments of 'the Six' opened negotiations and on 18 April 1951 signed the Treaty of Paris, creating the European Coal and Steel Community (ECSC). The new organization began work in July 1952 after ratification of the terms of the treaty by each of the member states. It was governed by a nominated nine-member High Authority (with Jean Monnet as its first president), and decisions were taken by a six-member Special Council of Ministers. A nominated 78-member Common Assembly helped Monnet allay the fears of national governments regarding the surrender of powers, and disputes between states were to be settled by a seven-member Court of Justice.

The founding of the ECSC was a small step in itself, but notable in that it was the first time that European governments had transferred significant powers to a supranational organization. It was allowed to reduce tariff barriers, abolish subsidies, fix prices, and raise money by imposing levies on steel and coal production, its job made easier by the fact that some of the groundwork had been laid by the Benelux customs union (founded in 1948). Although the ECSC failed to achieve many of its goals (notably the creation of a single market for coal and steel), it had ultimately been created to prove a point about the feasibility of integration, which it did. But if the ECSC was at least a limited success, two much larger, more ambitious and arguably premature experiments in integration did not fare so well:

- The European Defence Community (EDC) was intended to promote cooperation on defence and bind West Germany into a European defence system. A draft treaty was signed by the six ECSC members in May 1952 but it failed to be ratified, mainly because the French were nervous about the idea of German rearmament so soon after the war and did not want to give up control over their armed forces. Also, Britain – still the strongest European military power – was not included, and there could be no workable European defence force without a common foreign policy (Urwin, 1995, p. 63).
- The European Political Community was intended as the first step towards a European federation. A draft plan was completed in 1953 but with the collapse of the EDC all hope of a political community died, at least temporarily.

The failure of these two initiatives was a sobering blow to the integrationists and sent shock waves coursing through the ECSC. Monnet resigned the presidency of the High Authority in 1955, disillusioned by the political resistance to its work and impatient to further the process of integration (Monnet, 1978, pp. 398–404).

The European Economic Community (1958–86)

Europeanists now took a different approach to their attempts to give momentum to the cause of integration. A meeting of the ECSC foreign ministers at Messina in Italy in June 1955 resulted in agreement to adopt a Benelux proposal 'to work for the establishment of a united Europe by the development of common institutions, the progressive fusion of national economies, the creation of a common market, and the progressive harmonization of their social policies' (Messina Resolution, in Weigall and Stirk, 1992, p. 94). A new round of negotiations led to the signing in March 1957 of the two Treaties of Rome, one creating the European Economic Community (EEC) and the other the European Atomic Energy Community (Euratom), both of which came into existence in January 1958. The EEC had a similar administrative structure to the ECSC, with a nine-member quasi-executive Commission, a Council of Ministers with powers over decision making, and a seven-member Court of Justice. A new 142-member Parliamentary Assembly was also created to cover the EEC, ECSC and Euratom; in 1962 it was renamed the European Parliament.

The EEC Treaty committed the Six to the creation of a common market within 12 years by gradually removing all restrictions on internal trade, setting a common external tariff for goods coming into the EEC, reducing barriers to the free movement of people, money, goods and services among the member states, developing common agricultural and transport policies, and creating a European Social Fund and a European Investment Bank. Action would be taken in areas where there was agreement, and disagreements could be set aside for future discussion. The Euratom Treaty, meanwhile, was aimed at creating a common market for atomic energy, but Euratom was to remain a junior actor in the process of integration and focused primarily on research.

By January 1958, then, the founding members of the European Communities had signed three treaties, created a network of joint institutions, and agreed a number of ambitious goals aimed at integrating many of their economic activities. But it was still an exclusive club of six, and the logic of enlargement became increasingly clear. Most obvious by its absence was Britain, which continued to think of itself as a world power. That notion was sent reeling by the 1956 Suez crisis, which made clear that most of the key decisions on global political and economic issues were being driven by the United States and the USSR. Britain was not opposed to European cooperation, but had doubts about what the EEC was trying to achieve, and instead championed a looser exercise in cooperation known as the European Free Trade Association (EFTA). With a goal of free trade rather than economic and political integration, EFTA was founded in January 1960 with the signing of the Stockholm Convention by Austria, Britain, Denmark, Norway, Portugal, Sweden, and Switzerland. EFTA helped cut tariffs, but achieved relatively little in the long term, mainly because several of its members did more trade with the EEC than with their EFTA partners.

It soon became clear to Britain that true political influence in Europe lay with the EEC, that it risked political isolation if it stayed out of the EEC, and that the EEC was actually working: the member states had made impressive economic and political progress and British industry wanted access to the rich EEC market. In August 1961, barely 15 months after the creation of EFTA, Britain applied for EEC membership, along with Denmark and Ireland, and they were joined in 1962 by Norway. Denmark's motive was mainly agricultural: it was producing three times as much food as it needed, and the EEC represented a big market for those agricultural surpluses, as well as a boost for Danish industrial development; Norway also realized the importance of the EEC market. Ireland saw EEC membership as a way of furthering its industrial plans, reducing its reliance on agriculture, and loosening its ties with Britain. With four of its members now trying to defect, EFTA ceased to have much purpose, so Austria, Sweden, and Switzerland all applied for associate membership of the EEC; they were followed in 1962 by Malta, Portugal, and Spain.

Negotiations between Britain and the EEC opened in early 1962, and appeared to be on the verge of a successful conclusion when they fell foul of Charles de Gaulle's Franco-German policy. De Gaulle had plans for an EEC built around a Franco-German axis, saw Britain as a rival to French influence in the Community, was upset that he had not been given equal status at the wartime summits of the allied powers, resented Britain's lack of enthusiasm for the early integrationist moves of the 1950s, and felt that British membership would give the United States too much influence in Europe. Monnet, however, was keen on British membership, and even tried to bring West German chancellor Konrad Adenauer around to his point of view, but the latter shared de Gaulle's anglophobia, and agreed that development of the Franco-German axis was the key. In the space of just ten days in January 1963 de Gaulle signed a new Franco-German treaty and vetoed the British application. Since it was part of a package with Denmark, Ireland and Norway, they too were rejected. Britain reapplied in 1967, but de Gaulle again vetoed its application. Following his resignation in 1969 Britain applied for a third time, and this time its application was accepted, along with those of Denmark, Ireland, and Norway. Following membership negotiations in 1970–71, Britain, Denmark, and Ireland finally joined the EEC in January 1973. Norway would have joined as well but a public referendum in September 1972 narrowly went against membership.

An additional round of enlargements in the 1980s pushed the borders of the EEC further south and west. Greece had made its first overtures to the EEC in the late 1950s, but had been turned down on the grounds that its economy was too underdeveloped. It was given associate membership in

Box 3.2   Early progress on the road of integration

Numerous problems were encountered in the early years of European integration, but there were also many achievements along the way:

- Although the 12-year deadline for the creation of a common market was not met, internal tariffs fell quickly enough to allow the Six to agree a common external tariff in July 1968, and to declare an industrial customs union.
- Decision making was streamlined in April 1965 with the Merger treaty, which combined into one the separate councils of ministers and commissions of the three communities. The decision making process was given both authority and direction by the formalization in 1975 of regular summits of EEC leaders coming together as the European Council. The EEC was also made more democratic with the introduction in 1979 of direct elections to the European Parliament.
- Integration meant the removal of the quota restrictions that member states had used to protect their domestic industries from competition from imported products. Intra-EEC trade between 1958 and 1965 grew three times faster than that with third countries (Urwin, 1995, p. 130), the GNP of the Six grew at an average annual rate of 5.7 per cent, per capita income and consumption grew at 4.5 per cent, and the contribution of agriculture to GNP was halved (Ionescu, 1975, pp. 150–4).
- In the interests of removing non-tariff barriers to the free movement of goods across borders – including different standards and regulations on health, safety and consumer protection – standards were harmonized during the 1960s and 1970s. It was not until the passage of the 1986 Single European Act, however, that a concerted effort was made to bring all EEC members into line.
- Another priority was to lift restrictions on the free movement of workers. While some limits remain even today, progress was made towards easing them during the 1960s and 1970s.
- Agreement on a Common Agricultural Policy (CAP) was achieved in 1968, creating a single market for agricultural products, and assuring EEC farmers of guaranteed prices for their produce. CAP initially encouraged both production and productivity, but it became increasingly controversial, not least because of its cost (see Chapter 8).
- The Six worked more closely together on international trade negotiations, achieving a joint influence that would have been missing if they had worked independently. The EEC acted as one, for example, in negotiations under the General Agreement on Tariffs and Trade (GATT), and in reaching preferential trade agreements with 18 former African colonies under the 1963 Yaoundé Convention (see Chapter 9).

1961 as a prelude to full accession, which might have come sooner had it not been for the Greek military coup of April 1967. With the return to civilian government in 1974, Greece almost immediately applied for full membership, arguing that EEC membership would help underpin its attempts to rebuild democracy. The Community agreed, negotiations opened in 1976, and Greece joined in January 1981.

Map 3.1   *Growth of the EU, 1952–86*

KEY

■ Founder Members of ECSC 1952   ▢ Second Enlargement 1981–86

▢ First Enlargement 1973

Meanwhile, Spain and Portugal had both requested negotiations for associate membership in 1962, but both were dictatorships. A preferential trade agreement was signed with Spain in 1970 and with Portugal in 1973, but it was only with the overthrow of the Caetano regime in Portugal in 1974 and the death of Franco in Spain in 1975 that EEC membership for the two states was taken seriously. Despite the relative poverty of both countries, problems over fishing rights, and concern about Portuguese and Spanish workers moving north in search of work, the EEC felt that membership would encourage democracy in the Iberian peninsula and help link the two countries more closely to NATO and Western Europe. Negotiations opened in 1978–79 and both states joined in January 1986, the Ten thereby becoming the Twelve.

The doubling of membership had several political and economic consequences: it increased the global influence of the EEC, it complicated the Community's decision making processes, it reduced the overall influence of France and Germany, it altered the Community's relations with the United States and with developing countries, and – by bringing in the poorer Mediterranean states – it altered the internal economic balance of the EEC. Rather than enlarging any further, it was now decided to focus on deepening ties among the Twelve. Applications were made by Turkey (1987), Austria (1989), and Cyprus and Malta (1990), and although East Germany entered through the back door with German reunification in October 1990, there was to be no more enlargement until 1995.

Economic and social integration (1979–92)

By 1986 the EEC had become known simply as the European Community (EC). Its member states had a combined population of 322 million and accounted for just over one-fifth of all world trade. The EC had its own administrative structure and an independent body of law, and its citizens had direct (but limited) representation through the European Parliament. But progress towards integration remained uneven. The customs union was in place, but completion of the common market was handicapped by barriers to the free movement of people and capital, including different national technical, health, and quality standards, and varying levels of indirect taxation. It was also clear that there could never be a true single market without a common European currency, a controversial idea because it would mean a significant loss of national sovereignty and a significant move towards political union. These issues had now begun to concern EC leaders, who responded with the two critical initiatives: the launch of the European Monetary System, and the signature of the Single European Act.

The EEC treaty had mentioned the need to 'coordinate' economic policies, but had given the Community no specific powers to ensure this, so in practice coordination had been minimal. New momentum had been provided in 1969 by a change of leadership in France and West Germany: President Georges Pompidou was less averse than de Gaulle to strengthening EC ties and Chancellor Willy Brandt was in favour of monetary union. Turbulence in the international monetary system in the late 1960s gave the idea new urgency and significance, but EEC leaders disagreed about whether economic union or monetary union should come first (Urwin, 1995, p. 155). At a December 1969 summit in The Hague, Community leaders discussed the principle of economic and monetary union (EMU), and agreed to control fluctuations in the value of their currencies and to make more effort to coordinate national economic policies. In August 1971, however, the Nixon administration took the United States off the gold standard, and signalled the end of the Bretton Woods system of fixed exchange rates by imposing domestic wage and price controls and placing a surcharge on imports. This led to international monetary turbulence, which was exacerbated in 1973 by the Arab-Israeli war and the attendant global energy crisis. Because only West Germany, the Benelux countries, and Denmark were able to keep their currencies reasonably stable, the goal of achieving EMU by 1980 was shelved.

In 1979, a new initiative was launched in the form of the European Monetary System (EMS). Using an Exchange Rate Mechanism (ERM) based around an accounting tool known as the European currency unit (ecu), the EMS was designed to create a zone of monetary stability and to control fluctuations in exchange rates. The hope was that the ecu would become the normal means of settling debts among Community members, psychologically preparing them for the idea of a single currency. With this in mind, Commission president Jacques Delors decided in 1989 to take EMU a step further with the elaboration of a three-stage plan aimed at fixing exchange rates and turning the ecu into a single currency. His hopes were dashed, however, by speculation on the world's money markets, which caused Britain and Italy to pull out of the ERM, and Ireland, Portugal, and Spain to devalue their currencies. Ironically the crisis deterred speculation and reinforced currency stability, and EMU was back on track by 1994.

Meanwhile there was concern that progress towards the single market was being handicapped by inflation and unemployment, and by the temptation of member states to protect their home industries with non-tariff barriers such as subsidies. Economic competition from the United States and Japan was also growing. In response, a decision was reached at the 1983 European Council meeting in Stuttgart to refocus on the original core goal of creating a single market. The result was the signature in Luxembourg in February 1986 of the Single European Act (SEA), which came into force in July 1987. It had several goals, the most important of which was to complete all requirements for the single market by midnight on 31 December 1992. This involved agreeing and implementing nearly 300 new pieces of legislation aimed at the removal of all remaining physical barriers (such as customs and passport controls at internal borders), fiscal barriers (mainly in the form of different levels of indirect taxation) and technical barriers (such as conflicting standards, laws, and qualifications). This would create 'an area without internal frontiers in which the free movement of goods, persons, services and capital is assured'. The deadline came and went without all the new laws being adopted, but the single market went into force in January 1993 with the understanding that the backlog of legislation would be cleared as soon as possible.

The effects of the SEA were profound:

- It created the single biggest market and trading power in the world. Many internal passport and customs controls were eased or lifted, banks and companies could do business throughout the Community, there was little to prevent EC residents living, working, opening bank accounts and drawing their pensions anywhere in the Community, EC competition policy was given new prominence, and monopolies on everything from electricity supply to telecommunications were broken down.
- It gave Community institutions responsibility over new policy areas that had not been covered in the Treaty of Rome, such as the environment, research and development, and regional policy.
- It gave new powers to the European Court of Justice, and created a Court of First Instance to hear certain kinds of cases and ease the workload of the Court of Justice.
- It gave legal status to meetings of heads of government under the European Council, and gave new powers to the Council of Ministers and the European Parliament.
- It gave legal status to European Political Cooperation (foreign policy coordination) so that member states could work towards a European foreign policy and work more closely on defence and security issues.
- It made economic and monetary union an EC objective and promoted 'cohesion', meaning the reduction of the gap between the richer and poorer parts of the EC.

Despite the signing of the SEA, progress on opening up borders was variable, and there was no common European policy on immigration, visas, and asylum. Impatient to move ahead, the governments of France, Germany, and the Benelux states in 1985 signed the Schengen Agreement, under which all border controls were to be removed among signatory countries. All 27 EU member states have now signed the agreement, along with Iceland, Norway and Switzerland, but not all have introduced truly passport-free travel (Britain has stayed out of most elements of Schengen, claiming its special problems as an island state, and Ireland has had to follow suit because of its passport union with Britain), and the terms of the agreement allow the signatories to implement special controls at any time. Nonetheless, its signature marked a substantial step towards the removal of border controls.

With all this focus on economic issues, social problems were often overlooked by European leaders. The Treaty of Rome provided for the development of a Community social policy, but this was left in the hands of the member states and was narrowly defined, emphasizing improved working conditions and standards of living for workers, equal pay for equal work among men and women, social security for migrant workers, and increased geographical and occupational mobility for workers. As the economic links among EEC member states tightened, however, so their different levels of wealth and opportunity became more obvious. Even in the mid-1960s, per capita GDP in the Community's ten richest regions was nearly four times greater than in its ten poorest regions. With the accession of Britain, Greece, and Ireland the gap grew to the point where the richest regions were five times richer than the poorest (George, 1996, pp. 143–4).

Cohesion policy has since focused on working to close the gaps by helping the poorer parts of Europe, revitalizing regions affected by serious industrial decline, addressing long-term unemployment, providing youth job training, and helping the development of rural areas. The Commission gives economic assistance in the form of grants from what are collectively known as structural funds. These include the European Social Fund (ESF) (which concentrates on youth unemployment and job creation), the European Regional Development Fund (ERDF) (set up in response to the regional disparities that grew when Britain and Ireland joined the Community), and the Cohesion Fund (which compensates the poorest EU member states for the costs of tightening environmental controls, and provides help for transport projects). The structural funds accounted for just 18 per cent of EC expenditure in 1984 but by 2007 represented nearly 45 per cent of EU spending (see Chapter 5).

The SEA made cohesion a central part of economic integration, the assumption being that although the single market would create new jobs, this would not be enough. New attention was drawn to social policy in 1989 with agreement of the Charter of Fundamental Social Rights of Workers (the Social Charter), which promoted the free movement of workers, fair pay, better living and working conditions, freedom of association, and protection of children and adolescents. Social issues are now one of the core policy areas for the European Union, with many of the actions taken by the governments of the member states driven by the requirements of EU law. The latter has addressed issues as varied as health and safety at work, parental leave from work, public health, and programmes to help the disabled and the elderly.

From Community to Union (1992–)

The controversial idea of political integration was long left on the back-burner because it was felt that there was little hope of political union without economic union, and political union in turn demanded cooperation on foreign policy. False starts had been made with the European Political Community and an attempt in 1961 to draw up a political charter that would spell out the terms of political union (the Fouchet Plan; see Urwin, 1995, pp. 104–7). Agreement was reached in 1970 on European Political Cooperation (EPC), a loose and voluntary process revolving around regular meetings of the Community foreign ministers. It achieved some successes, such as a joint EC policy declaration on the Middle East and the signature of the Yaoundé Conventions on aid to poor countries, and was eventually given legal status with the SEA. But it was more reactive than proactive and often found European governments at odds with one another. The divisions were revealed by the 1990–91 Gulf crisis set off by the Iraqi invasion of Kuwait, when the Community as a whole issued demands to the Iraqi regime, and imposed an embargo on Iraqi oil imports, but few individual member states – other than Britain and France – played much role in the allied military response. The divisions were revealed again in 1998 when Britain was almost alone in supporting US threats of military action against Iraq.

Determined to reassert French leadership in the EC, President François Mitterrand had focused on the theme of political union at the Fontainebleau European Council in 1984, with the result that a decision was taken in Milan in June 1985 to convene an intergovernmental conference (IGC) on political union. The outcome was the Treaty on European Union, agreed at the European Council summit in Maastricht in December 1991 and signed by the foreign and economics ministers of the Community in February 1992. The draft treaty had included the goal of federal union, but Britain had balked at this so the wording was changed to 'an ever closer union among the peoples of Europe, in which decisions are taken as closely as possible to the citizen'. The treaty had to be ratified by the 12 member states before it could come into force, and although doubts were raised by lengthy political debates in Britain, France, and Germany, the biggest setback came with its rejection by Danish voters in a referendum in June 1992. It was only narrowly accepted by a referendum in France in September, so its content was further discussed by the European Council, and following agreement that the Danes could opt out of the single currency, common defence arrangements, European citizenship, and cooperation on justice and home affairs, a second Danish referendum was held in May 1993 and the treaty was accepted.

Like the Single European Act before it, the Treaty on European Union – usually known as the Maastricht treaty – made some significant changes to the contract among the member states of the EU:

- Reflecting the lengths to which the member states will occasionally go to reach compromises, a peculiar arrangement was agreed by which – instead of new powers being given to the European Community – three 'pillars' were created, and the whole structure was given the new label 'European Union'. The first pillar consisted of the three pre-existing communities (economic, coal and steel, and atomic energy), and the second and third pillars consisted of areas in which there was to be more formal intergovernmental cooperation: a Common Foreign and Security Policy (CFSP), and justice and home affairs. Final responsibility for the CFSP remained with the individual governments rather than being handed over to the EU. The pillar arrangement is a diplomatic sideshow that is marginal to an understanding of the EU today.

- A timetable was agreed for the creation of a single European currency by January 1999, confirming in essence the plan outlined by Commission president Jacques Delors in 1989.
- EU responsibility was extended into new policy areas such as consumer protection, public health policy, transport, education, and (except in Britain) social policy.
- There was to be greater intergovernmental cooperation on immigration and asylum, a European police intelligence agency (Europol) was to be created to combat organized crime and drug trafficking, a new Committee of the Regions was set up, and regional funds for poorer EU states were increased.
- New rights were provided for European citizens and an ambiguous European Union 'citizenship' was created which meant, for example, the right of citizens to live wherever they liked in the EU, and to stand or vote in local and European elections.
- New powers were given to the European Parliament, including a 'codecision procedure' under which certain kinds of legislation are subject to a third reading in the European Parliament before they can be adopted by the Council of Ministers.

Meanwhile enlargement was still on the agenda, the end of the cold war leading to a new focus on expansion to Eastern Europe. At its June 1993 meeting in Copenhagen, the European Council agreed a formal set of requirements for membership of the EU. Known as the Copenhagen conditions, they require that an applicant state must (a) be democratic, with respect for human rights and the rule of law, (b) have a functioning free market economy and the capacity to cope with the competitive pressures of capitalism, and (c) be able to take on the obligations of the *acquis communautaire* (the body of laws and policies already adopted by the EU). Deciding whether applicants meet these criteria has proved difficult, not least because of the problem of defining 'Europe' (see Chapter 2).

Throughout the 1980s, discussions about enlargement centred on other Western European states, if only because they came closest to meeting the criteria for membership. In order to prepare prospective members, negotiations began in 1990 on the creation of a European Economic Area (EEA), under which the terms of the SEA would be extended to the seven EFTA members, in return for which they would accept the rules of the single market. The EEA came into force in January 1994, but quickly lost relevance because Austria, Finland, Norway, and Sweden had applied for EC membership. Negotiations with these four applicants were completed in early 1994, and all but Norway (where a referendum once again went against membership) joined the EU in January 1995.

Map 3.2   *Growth of the EU, 1990–2007*

KEY

Existing Members

East Germany 1990

Third Enlargement 1995

Fourth Enlargement 2004–07

1. Slovenia
2. Croatia
3. Bosnia and Herzegovina
4. Serbia
5. Montenegro
6. Republic of Macedonia
7. Albania

Their accession left just three Western European countries outside the EU: Iceland, Norway and Switzerland. Iceland relies largely on the export of fish and does more than half its trade with the EU, and so has found the logic of joining the EU increasingly difficult to resist. Should it join, it would – with a population of just 300,000 people – be the smallest EU member state. In Norway, much of the early opposition to EU membership – based on factors such as fear of lowered environmental standards and concern about the power of large member states – has dissipated, and Norway continues to keep pace with economic and foreign policy developments in the EU, and to be impacted by EU developments through its membership of the EEA. Switzerland, which had considered applying for EC membership in 1992, rejected the EEA that same year and in 1995 found itself completely surrounded by the EU. Demands for the Swiss to open their highways to EU trucks and intra-EU trade increased the pressure for EU membership, but further discussion ended in March 2001 when a national referendum went heavily against EU membership.

Partly in preparation for anticipated eastern enlargement, but also to account for the progress of European integration and perhaps move the EU closer to political union, two new treaties were signed in 1997–2000. The first was the Treaty of Amsterdam, which was signed in October 1997 and came into force in May 1999. It fell far short of achieving political union to accompany the economic and monetary union promoted by the SEA and Maastricht, and the 15 leaders were unable to agree anything more than modest changes to the structure of EU institutions in preparation for enlargement. Policies on asylum, visas, external border controls, immigration, employment, social policy, health protection, consumer protection, and the environment were developed, cooperation between national police forces (and the work of Europol) was strengthened, and improvements were made to the arrangements for EU foreign policy. There was also agreement on the goal of a single European currency, and on the principle of eastern enlargement.

Less radical than either the SEA or Maastricht, the key goal of the Treaty of Nice – agreed in December 2000 and signed in February 2001 – was to make the institutional changes needed to prepare for eastward enlargement, and to make the EU more democratic and transparent. It proved to be a disappointment, though, doing little more than tinkering with the structure of the institutions, including increasing the size of the European Commission and the European Parliament, and redistributing the votes in the Council of Ministers. European leaders were taken by surprise in June 2001 when Irish voters rejected the terms of the treaty, its opponents arguing that it involved the surrender of too much national control, and being particularly concerned about the implications for Irish neutrality. A second vote was taken in Ireland in October 2002, following assurances that Ireland's neutrality on security issues would be respected, and – thanks in part to bigger turnout – the treaty was accepted by a 63 per cent majority. Nice came into force in February 2003.

Meanwhile, the EU took a dramatic step forward on the economic front with the final adoption of the single currency. A decision had been taken in 1995 to call it the euro, and the timetable agreed under Maastricht required participating states to fix their exchange rates in January 1999. Several so-called 'convergence criteria' were considered essential prerequisites: these included placing limits on national budget deficits, public debt, consumer inflation, and long-term interest rates. At a special EU summit in May 1998

Box 3.3   The failed European constitution

The Treaty of Nice came into force in February 2003, but the changes it introduced went largely unnoticed because there had already been broader discussions about the need to make the EU more democratic and to bring it closer to its citizens. At the Laeken European Council in December 2001 it was decided to establish a convention to debate the future of Europe, and to draw up a treaty containing a constitution designed to simplify and replace all the other treaties, to decide how to divide powers between the EU and the member states, to make the EU more democratic and efficient, to determine the role of national parliaments within the EU, and to pave the way for more enlargement.

The Convention on the Future of the European Union met between February 2002 and July 2003 under the presidency of former French president Valéry Giscard d'Estaing, with 105 representatives from the 15 EU member states and the 13 applicant Eastern European and Mediterranean countries, as well as representatives from each of the 28 national parliaments, and from the European Parliament. The convention considered numerous proposals, including an elected president of the European Council, a foreign minister for the EU, a limit on the membership of the European Commission, a common EU foreign and security policy, and a legal personality for the EU, whose laws would cancel out those of national parliaments in areas where the EU had been given competence. It took two European Council meetings (December 2003 and June 2004) to reach agreement on the draft treaty, which had then to be put to public referendums or government votes in every EU member state.

Lithuania became the first country to ratify through a parliamentary vote in November 2004, and Spain became the first to ratify through a national referendum in February 2005. But there were already clear signs of political and public resistance in several countries, the popular expectation being that the treaty was unlikely to survive a referendum in Eurosceptical Britain. But it was left to the French and the Dutch – both founding members of the European Union – to stop the process in its tracks, with negative votes in national referendums in May and June 2005 respectively. Several explanations for the votes were offered, including concerns in France about the economic effects of further integration, worries about increased immigration from Eastern Europe, and the unpopularity of the French and Dutch governments (which both favoured the treaty).

The negative votes led to widespread predictions of institutional collapse and loss of strategic direction, but the EU survived and continued to function, while worried discussions were held about the next step. At the European Council in June 2007 it was decided to save as many elements as possible of the constitution, and to reformulate them into a new treaty designed mainly to adjust the institutional structure of the EU to account for enlargement. As this book went to press, a new treaty of Lisbon had been agreed and signed, the goal being to have it ratified by all member states before the June 2009 European Parliament elections.

it was decided that all but Greece met the conditions, but public and political opinion in the member states was divided on which should or would fix their exchange rates. While inflation rates were low in the member states, unemployment rates were not, and the rate of industrial growth was slowing in several. There was also considerable public resistance to the idea of the single currency in several countries, notably Britain and Germany. In the event, all but Denmark, Sweden, and the UK adopted the euro, banknotes and coins began circulating in January 2002, and the 12 members of the euro zone abolished their national currencies in March.

At the same time, the identity of the EU on the global stage was undergoing something of a transformation. European leaders had been embarrassed by their divisions over the 1990–91 Gulf War, and then by their failure to provide leadership in responding to the violent breakup of Yugoslavia in 1991–95 (see Chapter 9 for more details). But EU policy succeeded in Eastern Europe, where it took the lead on post-cold war reconstruction, helping former Soviet bloc states to make the transition to democracy and free markets. Meanwhile, the role of the US in EU affairs was declining, as reflected in the fallout from the 2003 US-led invasion of Iraq, which may be shown by history to have been the event that pulled the EU out of the foreign policy lethargy into which it had fallen. EU governments were divided in their response – Britain, Italy and Spain led the support for the invasion, and France and Germany led the opposition – but far more significant was the unity of public opposition throughout the EU to the war, and US leaders were taken aback by the openness with which the US was criticized by hostile EU governments. The shape of the EU on the radar of international relations was given new clarity, new appreciation meanwhile grew for its remarkable powers in global trade, and new attention has since been paid to US–EU differences over the priorities of defence and security policy.

In May 2004, the EU undertook its most significant enlargement when ten Eastern European and Mediterranean states joined: Cyprus, the Czech Republic, Estonia, Hungary, Latvia, Lithuania, Malta, Poland, Slovenia, and Slovakia. Together their economies were smaller than that of the Netherlands, and they increased the population of the EU by less than 20 per cent; the real significance of the 2004 enlargement lay in the fact that the EU was no longer an exclusive club for wealthy west Europeans. The East was now included, and – for the first time – former Soviet republics (Estonia, Latvia, Lithuania) became part of the European Union. As well as providing an important symbolic confirmation of the end of the cold war division of Europe, the 2004 enlargement also promised to accelerate the process of transforming the economies and democratic structures of Eastern European countries. The trends continued in January 2007 when Bulgaria and Romania joined the EU, a development widely seen as a second phase of the 2004 enlargement. Croatia, Macedonia and Turkey have also been accepted as 'candidate countries' (meaning that negotiations on membership are under way), and little trouble is anticipated except in the case of Turkey (see Box 2.2).

Four out of five Europeans are now residents of the EU, and although there has been recent evidence of 'enlargement fatigue', and declining enthusiasm for further short-term expansion, at least 12 more countries qualify in principle for future membership. Even outside the EU they find it hard to resist the economic and political pull of their giant neighbour; not only are the cold war divisions of Western and Eastern Europe almost gone, but the distinction between the EU and Europe is also fading away. Slovenia joined the euro zone in January 2007, and Cyprus and Malta in January 2008, and other Eastern European states are expected to follow as soon as they are ready.

Conclusions

Europe has travelled a long and uneven road since the end of the Second World War. At that time, most European states were physically devastated, the suspicions and hostilities that had led to two world wars in the space of a generation still lingered, Western Europe found itself being pulled into a military and economic vacuum as power and influence moved outwards to the United States and the Soviet Union, and Eastern Europe came under the political and economic control of the Soviet Union. The balance of power in the west changed as an exhausted Britain and France dismantled their empires and reduced their militaries, while West Germany rebuilt and eventually became a dominant force in European politics. Intent on avoiding future wars, and concerned about being caught in big-power rivalry, Western European leaders began considering new levels of regional cooperation, pooling the interests of their states, and helping give the region new confidence and influence.

Beginning with the limited experiment of integrating their coal and steel industries, and building on an economic foundation and security shield underwritten by the United States, six European states quickly agreed a common agricultural policy, a customs union, and the beginnings of a common market. The accession of new members in the 1970s and 1980s greatly increased the size of the Community's population and market, pushing its borders to the edge of Russia and the Middle East. The global economic instability that followed the end of the Bretton Woods system and the energy crises of the 1970s served to emphasize the need for Western European countries to cooperate if they were to have more control over their own future rather than simply to respond to external events.

After several years of relative lethargy the European experiment was given new impetus by completion of the single market, and then by the controversial decision to stabilize exchange rates as a prelude to the abolition of national currencies and the adoption of a single European currency. At the same time, the European Union increasingly showed a united face to the rest of the world, with more cooperation on foreign and trade policy (along with some embarrassing disagreements along the way), and the seeds of a European defence capacity. The effects of integration have been felt in a growing number of policy areas, including agriculture, competition, transport, the environment, energy, telecommunications, research and development, working conditions, culture, consumer affairs, education, and employment.

The 2003 controversy over Iraq drew new attention to the place of the EU in the international system, while the 2004–06 eastern enlargement had an important impact on the personality of the EU, making it more truly an exercise in European integration. The failure of the European constitution proved a disappointment to many, but it had nothing like the deleterious effect on the functioning of the EU that pessimists predicted. As Europe looked back from the fiftieth anniversary of the signing of the Treaty of Rome in March 2007, it could draw much satisfaction from its achievements, but there was also cause for concern at the work that remained to be done, and at the doubts that remained to be overcome.

Chapter 4

The European Institutions

As the European Union has grown, so have the powers and the reach of its institutions. Unfortunately, their construction has been driven by short-term needs, internal competition, and political compromises, without much long-term sense of what the 'government' of the EU should eventually become. The result has been a fluid network of institutions that most observers of the EU, and most European political leaders, refuse to describe as a European government. The member states still hold most of the decision making powers, and are responsible for implementing EU policies on the ground. For some, the EU is best described using terms such as *multi-level governance*, and is best thought of as a powerful international organization. For others, it is reasonable to think of the EU as a full-fledged political system, and to study it by looking at its executive, legislative and judicial functions.

The EU institutions can be compared with the governing bodies of the member states, even if there are few direct equivalents. The College of Commissioners is something like a cabinet of ministers, but not quite. The European Parliament has some of the powers of a conventional legislature, but not all. The European Commission is a bureaucracy responsible for drafting and executing the laws and regulations of the EU, but it is also much more. The European Council and the Council of Ministers are like nothing found in most national governments, although they can be compared in some ways to an upper chamber of a legislature. The Court of Justice is the only institution to directly parallel those found at the national level – it has most of the features of a typical constitutional court.

To summarize very briefly, the work of the major institutions: the European Commission develops proposals for new laws and policies, on which final decisions are taken by the Council of Ministers and the European Parliament. Once a decision is made, the European Commission is responsible for overseeing implementation by the member states. Meanwhile, the Court of Justice works to ensure that laws and policies meet the terms and spirit of the treaties, while the European Council brings the leaders of the member states together at periodic summit meetings to guide the overall direction of European integration. This brief outline does not reflect the many subtle nuances of European decision making, nor does it convey the many informal aspects of EU government: the differing levels of influence exerted by member states; the political and economic pressures that drive the decisions of the member states; the key role played by interest groups, corporations, staff in the Commission, specialized working groups in the Council of Ministers, and the permanent representatives of the member states; and all the muddling through and incremental change that often characterize policy making in the EU, as in national systems of government.

This chapter looks at the five major institutions of the EU, describing how they are structured, showing how they fit into the policy process, and explaining how they relate to each other and to the member states. It paints a picture of a system that is often complicated, occasionally clumsy, and regularly misunderstood. It argues that the EU institutions are caught in a web of competing national interests, and that the tension between inter-governmental and supranational forces impacts them all. But in spite of the challenges to their identity and personality, they have taken on many of the features of a distinctive supranational European political system, and they are best understood as such.

A constitution for Europe

A constitution is a written document that describes the structure of a system of government, outlines the powers of the different governing institutions, describes limits on those powers, and lists the rights of citizens relative to government. Liberal democratic constitutions are usually fairly short, provisions are made by which they can be amended, and a constitutional court exists with the duty of providing interpretation by measuring the laws and actions of government against the content and principles of the constitution. Most importantly, they are permanent documents, and wholesale changes are made only on those rare occasions when a system of government has broken down and is in need of a thorough overhaul, as – for example – when France replaced the Fourth Republic with the Fifth Republic in 1958.

The European Union has functioned so far without a formal constitution, and has instead been guided by a series of treaties which together function as something like a constitution: Paris (now expired), the two Treaties of Rome, the Merger treaty, the Single European Act, Maastricht, Amsterdam and Nice (see Phinnemore and Church, 2005; Piris, 2006). Each has amended and built upon its predecessor, resulting in a mobile constitution, or one that is in a constant state of flux without ever reaching a final form. Although studies of EU law often talk of constitution building and the 'constitutionalization' of the EU legal order (see Mancini, 1991; Dehousse, 1998, Chapter 2; Shaw, 2000, Chapter 3), the reluctance of many European leaders to give up control and to recognize the EU as a new level of government has so far meant a refusal in political discussions to recognize the treaties as a constitution.

When American leaders decided to create the United States of America, they drew up a constitution that had four important features. First, it was a contract between people and government, outlining their relative roles, powers, and rights. Second, it was short and succinct, meaning that it could easily be read and understood by almost anyone. Third, it was ambiguous and provided few details on the specific powers of government, thereby allowing room for evolutionary change. Finally, there was provision for amendments to be made, but – by accident – loopholes ensured that the most important changes to the constitution were to come as a result of judicial interpretations provided by the US Supreme Court and new laws passed by the US Congress. These have changed many of the details of the structure of government, allowing the constitution more or less to keep up with prevailing political, economic and social values.

The treaties of the EU have had none of these advantages. Instead of being contracts between people and government, they have been contracts among governments. Instead of being short, they have been long and often complex, sometimes confusing even the legal experts. Instead of being ambiguous (and thus flexible), the obsession of European leaders with making sure that there is minimal room for misunderstanding has produced documents that have gone into considerable detail on the specific powers of EU institutions, the policy responsibilities of the EU, and the rights of citizens. And instead of being changed only by formal amendments, by judicial interpretation, or by changes in EU law, wholesale revisions have been introduced as a result of new treaties.

The European constitutional convention that met in 2002–03 might have taken the opportunity to undertake some fundamental spring-cleaning, and to follow the American model by producing a short, readable, and flexible document that would replace the treaties and give Europeans a better sense of what integration meant. It might also have taken the opportunity to introduce some stirring declarations, thereby encouraging Europeans to read it and to learn its key points. But where the authors of the US constitution were drawing up a virtually new political system from scratch, had relatively few opinions to take into account, and were dealing with just 13 largely homogeneous American states, the authors of the EU constitution were faced with the challenge of summarizing an accumulation of 50 years' worth of treaties, and had to take into account not only the views of 15 member states with often different values and priorities, but also of 12 candidate member states from Eastern Europe. The result was a draft treaty that was long (well over 300 pages), detailed, and controversial. It was approved by the leaders of the member states in June 2004 only after heated debate, doubts were raised from the beginning about whether it would survive the national approval process, and those doubts were confirmed when the constitution was rejected by Dutch and French voters in national referendums in 2005.

In spite of predictions that institutional chaos would follow, the EU continued to function quite normally, and in 2007 there was agreement among European leaders to preserve most of the elements of the constitution, and to reformulate it as the latest set of reforms to the treaties. Critics charged that the new Lisbon treaty was not that different in essence from the constitutional treaty, and that it had simply been dressed in different clothes in order to make it more politically palatable, and to avoid the need for national referendums. Signed in December 2007, Lisbon is designed to update some of the structural elements of the EU institutions to account for enlargement, but also has provisions to fine-tune structures and policies to account for changes in the political climate. As for the future, the EU has two choices: it can either try once again to agree a fixed and permanent constitution, with built-in arrangements for amendments and interpretation, or it can continue to work with the mobile constitution provided by the treaties. The latter option may be the most realistic as long as (a) the EU keeps growing and (b) there is no political or public agreement about what the EU will become. But as the external borders of the EU settle down and attitudes towards integration change, the agreement of a permanent document is all but inevitable.

The European Commission

The European Commission is the executive-bureaucratic arm of the EU, responsible for developing proposals for new laws and policies (see Box 4.1), for overseeing the execution of those laws and policies once they are adopted, and for promoting the general interests of European integration. Headquartered in Brussels, its staff work in multiple buildings around the city, and in regional cities around the EU and national capitals around the world. It is the most supranational of the EU institutions, encouraging member states to harmonize their laws, regulations and standards, and acting as the driving force behind many important EU policy initiatives, including the single market programme and the development of the euro.

Eurosceptics like to scorn the Commission, arguing that it is big, expensive, and powerful, that it meddles in the internal affairs of member states, that its leaders are not elected, and that it has too little public accountability. But the criticism is often misguided:

- Far from being big and expensive, it has just over 20,000 staff, only two-thirds of whom work actively on policy. This makes it smaller than the administration of a mid-sized city, and its administrative costs account for less than 3 per cent of the EU budget, or about €3.3 billion in 2007.
- It is not particularly powerful, being less a decision making body than a servant of the member states, charged with making sure that the broad goals of integration are converted into specific actions. Decision making power

Box 4.1   European Union law

A key difference between the EU and a conventional international organization is that the EU has a body of law which is applicable in all its member states, which supersedes national law in areas where the EU has 'competence' (that is, responsibility), and which is backed up by rulings from the Court of Justice. The creation of this body of law has involved the voluntary surrender of powers by the member states in a broad range of policy areas, and the development of a new level of legal authority to which the member states are subject.

The foundation of the EU legal order is provided by the treaties, which are the 'primary' sources of EU law (Lasok *et al.*, 2001, Chapter 4), out of which come the 'secondary' sources of EU law, the most important of which are the thousands of individual binding laws adopted by the EU, and which take five main forms:

- *Regulations* are the most powerful, and the most like conventional acts of a national legislature. They are directly applicable in that they do not need to be turned into national law, they are binding in their entirety, and they take immediate effect on a specified date. Usually fairly narrow in intent, regulations are often designed to amend or adjust an existing law.
- *Directives* are binding in terms of goals, but it is left up to the member states to decide what action they need to take to achieve those goals. For example, a 1988 directive on pollution from large industrial plants set targets for the reduction of emissions (how much, and by when), but left it up to the member states to decide individually how to meet those targets. Directives usually include a date by which national action must be taken, and member states must tell the Commission what they are doing.
- *Decisions* are also binding, but are usually fairly specific in their intent, and aimed at one or more member states, at institutions, or even at individuals. Some are aimed at making changes in the powers of EU institutions, some are directed towards internal administrative matters, and others are issued when the Commission has to adjudicate disputes between member states or corporations.
- *Recommendations* and *opinions* have no binding force. They are sometimes used to test reaction to a new EU policy, but they are used mainly to persuade or to provide interpretation on the application of regulations, directives and decisions.

Until the early 1990s the EU was adopting as many as 6,000–7,000 laws every year, but the number has since fallen to about 1,500–1,800. The fall-off was due in part to a deliberate policy by the Commission to focus more on the implementation of existing laws, and in part to the completion of the single market programme.

rests with the Council of Ministers, which is firmly under the control of the governments of the member states, and with the European Parliament, elected by the voters of the EU.

- Although Commission leaders are not elected, they are appointed by elected national government leaders, and to have them elected would be to give the Commission more of the power and independence that Eurosceptics so fear.
- It may sometimes appear secretive and anonymous, but its record is no worse than that of national bureaucracies and in some ways is better. It has so few staff and resources that it must rely heavily on input from outside agencies.

The Commission is headed by a College of Commissioners with 27 members (one from each of the member states – see Table 4.1). This serves a five-year term and functions as a European cabinet, making the final decisions on which proposals for new laws and policies to send on for approval. Each commissioner has a portfolio for which he or she is responsible (these include external relations, trade, the internal market, the environment, enlargement, competition, and fisheries). Commissioners are appointed by their national governments, but they are not national representatives, and they must swear an oath of office saying that they will renounce any defence of national interests. There are no formal rules on appointments, but nominees are discussed with the Commission president, and must be acceptable to other governments and to the European Parliament (for details on the process, see Spence, 2006, pp. 34–8). Under the terms of the Lisbon treaty, membership of the College will be reduced in 2014 to no more than two-thirds of the number of member states, with members chosen on a rotation from among the states.

The dominant figure in the Commission is the president, the person who comes closest to being the leader of the EU. The word 'leader' should be treated with some caution, though, because the president does not have the same political status as a head of government, and is more the chief bureaucrat of the EU. However, the president has much authority within the Commission: he or she can influence the appointment of other commissioners, has sole power over distributing portfolios, sets the agenda for the Commission, can launch major new policy initiatives, chairs meetings of the College, can reshuffle portfolios mid-term, and represents the Commission in dealings with other EU institutions and national governments.

As with all such positions, the powers of the office depend to some extent on the personality of the office holder. Following several early presidents who in the main did not make much of an impression, the administration of former French economics minister Jacques Delors in 1985–94 was a watershed (see Ross, 1995). Delors centralized authority, had firm ideas about a strong, federal Europe asserting itself internationally, and used this vision to champion the single market and single currency programmes. He was succeeded by Jacques Santer, former prime minister of Luxembourg, who avoided bold new initiatives, and focused instead on improving the implementation of existing laws and policies. The Santer College resigned en masse in January 1999

Table 4.1   *The European Commissioners, 2005–09*

Name	Member state	Portfolio
José Manuel Barroso	Portugal	President
Siim Kallas	Estonia	VP, Administrative Affairs, Audit and Anti-Fraud
Jacques Barrot	France	VP, Transport
Günter Verheugen	Germany	VP, Enterprise and Industry
Franco Frattini	Italy	VP, Justice, Freedom and Security
Margot Wallström	Sweden	VP, Institutional Relations, Communication Strategy
Benita Ferrero-Waldner	Austria	External Relations
Louis Michel	Belgium	Development and Humanitarian Aid
Meglena Kuneva	Bulgaria	Consumer Protection
Markos Kyprianou	Cyprus	Health
Vladimír Špidla	Czech Republic	Employment and Social Affairs
Mariann Fischer Boel	Denmark	Agriculture and Rural Development
Olli Rehn	Finland	Enlargement
Stavros Dimas	Greece	Environment
László Kovács	Hungary	Taxation and Customs Union
Charlie McCreevy	Ireland	Internal Market and Services
Andris Piebalgs	Latvia	Energy
Dalia Grybauskaitė	Lithuania	Financial Programming and Budget
Viviane Reding	Luxembourg	Information Society and Media
Joe Borg	Malta	Fisheries and Maritime Affairs
Neelie Kroes	Netherlands	Competition
Danuta Hübner	Poland	Regional Policy
Ján Figel'	Slovakia	Education, Training, Culture and Youth
Janez Potočnik	Slovenia	Science and Research
Joaquín Almunia	Spain	Economic and Monetary Affairs
Leonard Orban	Romania	Multilingualism
Peter Mandelson	UK	Trade

following charges of nepotism and incompetence directed against some of its members. Santer was replaced by former Italian prime minister Romano Prodi, who oversaw the passage of the treaties of Amsterdam and Nice, the holding of the constitutional convention, the arrival of the euro, and the 2004 enlargement. Prodi was replaced in 2005 by José Manuel Barroso, the incumbent prime minister of Portugal, who was faced with fighting public

Table 4.2   *Presidents of the European Commission*

Term	Name	Ideology	Country
1958–67	Walter Hallstein	Christian Democrat	West Germany
1967–70	Jean Rey	Centrist	Belgium
1970–72	Franco Maria Malfatti	Christian Democrat	Italy
1972	Sicco Mansholt	Centrist	Netherlands (interim)
1973–76	François-Xavier Ortoli	Gaullist	France
1977–80	Roy Jenkins	Socialist	Britain
1981–84	Gaston Thorn	Socialist	Luxembourg
1985–94	Jacques Delors	Socialist	France
1995–99	Jacques Santer	Christian Democrat	Luxembourg
1999	Manuel Marín	Socialist	Spain (interim)
1999–2004	Romano Prodi	Centrist	Italy
2004–	José Manuel Barroso	Social Democrat	Portugal

apathy towards the EU, improving relations with the US, and dealing with the fallout from the collapse of the constitutional treaty (see Table 4.2).

There are few formal rules regarding how the president is appointed (for details on recent appointments, see Nugent, 2001, pp. 63–8). It has become normal for the leaders of the member states to decide the appointment at the European Council held in the June before the term of the incumbent Commission ends, settling on someone acceptable to all of them and to the European Parliament. Appointed for renewable five-year terms, the president will usually be someone with a strong political reputation, a strong character, proven leadership abilities, and a philosophy toward the EU that is acceptable to all major EU leaders.

Below the College, the Commission is divided into directorates-general (DGs) and services – which are equivalent to national government ministries – and deal with matters as varied as agriculture, competition, economic and financial affairs, external relations, regional policy, humanitarian aid, and personnel issues. Every DG is responsible for a particular policy area, has its own director-general, and is tied to a commissioner. The Commission also works closely with a series of several hundred advisory, management and regulatory committees made up of national government officials (in a phenomenon known as *comitology*), and with expert committees made up of national officials, specialists appointed by national governments, corporate interests, and special interest groups.

The general task of the Commission is to ensure that EU policies are advanced in light of the treaties (for details, see Edwards and Spence, 1997, Chapter 1). It does this in five ways.

- *Powers of initiation.* The Commission makes sure that the principles of the treaties are turned into laws and policies. Proposals can come from a commissioner or a staff member of one of the DGs, may be a response to a ruling by the Court of Justice, may flow out of the requirements of the treaties, or may come out of pressure exerted by member state governments, interest groups, the European Council, the European Parliament, and even private corporations. A new piece of law will begin life as a draft written by officials in one of the DGs. It will then work its way up through the different levels of the DG, being discussed with outside parties (such as interest groups or corporations), and with other DGs, being amended along the way. The draft will finally reach the College of Commissioners, which can accept a proposal, reject it, send it back for redrafting, or defer making a decision. Once accepted, it will be sent to the European Parliament and the Council of Ministers for a decision. The process can take anything from months to years, and Commission staff will be involved at every stage.

- *Powers of implementation.* Once a law or policy is accepted, the Commission is responsible for making sure that it is implemented by the member states. It has no power to do this directly, but instead works through national bureaucracies, using its power to collect information from member states, to issue written warnings, and to take to the Court of Justice any member state, corporation, or individual that does not conform to the spirit of the treaties or follow subsequent EU law. The Commission adds to the pressure by publicizing progress on implementation, hoping to embarrass the laggards into action.

- *Acting as the conscience of the EU.* The Commission is expected to rise above competing national interests and to represent and promote the general interest of the EU. It is also expected to help smooth the flow of decision making by mediating disagreements between or among member states and other EU institutions.

- *Management of EU finances.* The Commission makes sure that all EU revenues are collected, plays a key role in drafting and guiding the annual budget through the Council of Ministers and Parliament, and administers EU spending.

- *External relations.* The Commission has been given the authority by the member states to represent the EU in dealings with international organizations such as the United Nations and the World Trade Organization (Smith, 2006). It is also a key point of contact between the EU and the rest of the world; more than 140 governments have opened diplomatic missions in Brussels accredited to the EU, while the EU has opened more than 130 offices in other parts of the world, staffed by Commission employees. The Commission also vets applications for full or associate membership from aspirant member states, and oversees negotiations with an applicant.

Box 4.2 Intergovernmental conferences

The extent to which decision making in the EU is still intergovernmental rather than supranational is reflected in the way that many of the big decisions of recent years have come out of intergovernmental conferences (IGCs), convened outside the formal framework of the EU's institutions to allow negotiations among the governments of the member states. Even as the powers of those institutions have grown, so the IGC has become an increasingly common event on the EU calendar; there have been nine IGCs since 1950, but seven of them have been held since 1985.

The first IGC was opened in May 1950, was chaired by Jean Monnet, and led to the creation of the ECSC and the signing of the Treaty of Paris. The second was opened at Messina in April 1955, and led to the creation of the EEC and Euratom and the signing of the Treaties of Rome. Perhaps because national leaders were focused on building the three Communities and the common market, because of the intergovernmental nature of Community decision making in the early years, and because of the fallout from the energy crises of the 1970s, it was to be another 27 years before another IGC was convened. Concerned about the lack of progress on integration and Europe's declining economic performance in relation to the United States and Japan, the third IGC was launched in September 1985, and by December had outlined the framework of what was eventually to become the Single European Act.

Two more IGCs met during 1991 to look at political union and monetary union, their work resulting in the Treaty on European Union. A sixth IGC was launched in 1996 with institutional reform and preparations for eastward enlargement at the top of its agenda, the product of which was the Treaty of Amsterdam. Institutional reform was also on the agenda of the IGC that led to the 2000 Treaty of Nice, widely regarded as a disappointment. The eighth IGC in 2003 reviewed the draft of the new European constitution, which was itself designed to 'promote new forms of European governance'. The ninth IGC in 2007 finalized the details of the Lisbon treaty.

The IGCs since 1985 have been negotiated by a combination of national government ministers and permanent representatives, and have continued to symbolize the extent to which decision making on the big initiatives of the EU still rests with the member states. While there is nothing in the founding treaties about IGCs, they have become a normal part of the calendar of European integration, and most have resulted in important decisions on the development of the EU.

The Commission has been a productive source of initiatives for new laws and policies, and is much more accessible and open than, say, the Council of Ministers. It has been at the core of European integration since the beginning, and while it has not always made the best use of the resources it has available, its staff on the whole is professional and hardworking, and the criticisms made against the Commission by Eurosceptic media and politicians are often unfair and misinformed.

The Council of Ministers

The Council of Ministers is the key decision making branch of the EU, is responsible for the coordination of key EU policies, is the primary champion of national interests, and is arguably the most powerful of the EU institutions. Yet it is also the institution about which most Europeans know the least: its meetings attract little media coverage and it has been the subject of much less academic study than the Commission or Parliament. When Europeans think about the activities of the EU, they tend to first think of the Commission, forgetting that the Commission can only propose, and that the Council of Ministers actually makes the final decisions. In many ways, its powers make the Council more like the legislature of the EU than the European Parliament, although new powers for Parliament in recent years have made the two bodies into 'co-legislatures'.

Once the Commission has proposed a new law or policy, it is discussed and amended by the Council of Ministers and the European Parliament. Headquartered in the Justus Lipsius Building in Brussels, the Council (formally the Council of the European Union) is one of the most intergovernmental of EU institutions. It consists of national government ministers, who meet in one of nine technical councils (or 'configurations'), the membership depending on the topic under discussion. The most important of these is the General Affairs and External Relations Council (GAERC), which brings together the EU foreign ministers to deal broadly with internal and external relations, and to discuss politically sensitive policies and proposals for new laws. Economics and finance ministers meet together as the Economic and Financial Affairs Council (Ecofin), agriculture ministers as the Agriculture and Fisheries Council, and so on. The relevant European commissioner will also attend in order to make sure that the Council does not lose sight of broader EU interests. How often each council meets depends on the importance of its area. The GAERC, Ecofin and the Agriculture and Fisheries Council meet monthly because of the amount of work on their agendas, but the councils dealing with other issues meet perhaps only two to four times each year. Most meetings last no more than one or two days, and are held in Brussels.

Between meetings of ministers, national interests in the Council are protected and promoted by Permanent Representations, or national delegations of professional diplomats, which are much like embassies to the EU. Expert staff from the delegations meet regularly in the powerful Committee of Permanent Representatives (Coreper), whose critical role in EU policy making is routinely overlooked. Coreper acts as a link between Brussels and the member states, conveys the views of the national governments, and keeps capitals in touch with developments in Brussels. Most importantly, it prepares Council agendas, oversees the committees and working parties set up to sift through proposals, decides which proposals go to which council, and makes many of the decisions

Table 4.3　*Rotation of presidencies of the Council of Ministers*

2007	1st half – Germany	2011	1st half – Hungary
	2nd half – Portugal		2nd half – Poland
2008	1st half – Slovenia	2012	1st half – Denmark
	2nd half – France		2nd half – Cyprus
2009	1st half – Czech Republic	2013	1st half – Ireland
	2nd half – Sweden		2nd half – Lithuania
2010	1st half – Spain	2014	1st half – Greece
	2nd half – Belgium		2nd half – Italy

(Bulgaria is not scheduled for its first presidency until 2018, and Romania until 2019.)

about which proposals will be accepted and which will be left for debate by ministers (see Hayes-Renshaw and Wallace, 2006, pp. 72–82).

Direction is given to the deliberations of the Council and Coreper by the presidency of the Council of Ministers, which is held not by a person, but by a member state. Every EU member state has a turn at holding the presidency for a spell of six months, the baton being passed in January and July each year (see Table 4.3). The state holding the presidency sets the agenda for European Council meetings (and for the EU as a whole), arranges and chairs meetings of the Council of Ministers, chairs at least one meeting of the European Council, promotes cooperation among member states, runs EU foreign policy for six months, acts as the main voice of the EU on the global stage, coordinates member state positions at international conferences and negotiations in which the EU is involved, and (along with the president of the Commission) represents the EU at meetings with the president of the United States, and at the annual meetings of the G8 group of major industrialized countries. (For details on some recent presidencies, see Elgström, 2003.)

There are both advantages and disadvantages to the rotating presidency. Among the advantages: it allows the leaders of the member states to convene meetings and launch initiatives on issues of national interest, to bring those issues to the top of the EU agenda, and – if they do a good job – to earn prestige and credibility. It also allows the leaders of smaller states to negotiate directly with other world leaders and helps the process of European integration by making the EU more real to the citizens of the country holding the presidency. Among the disadvantages: as the EU has grown, so has the workload of the presidency, and some of the smaller states have found themselves struggling to find the necessary leadership. As membership of the EU has expanded, so has the cycle of the presidency. With 15 member states, each had a turn at the helm only once every seven and a half years, but with 27 members that has grown to thirteen and a half years.

One of the provisions contained in the draft constitutional treaty – and carried over into the new Lisbon treaty – is to abolish the arrangement by which member states hold the presidency, and to instead have an individual elected by the European Council to run the Council for a term of two and a half years, renewable once. If the change is approved, the election will use the qualified majority system (see below), and the person elected will have to be approved by the European Parliament. The idea is to provide an individual who can set the agenda and become the focus of political attention, and to eliminate the constant change in the 'leadership' of the EU. Britain, France, and Germany have all favoured the idea, but smaller states have been less enthusiastic, fearing a loss of influence. There have also been concerns about the complications that might arise out of having two leaders of the EU – the president of the Commission and the president of the Council.

Once the European Commission has proposed a new law, it is sent to Parliament and the Council of Ministers for debate and for a final decision on adoption or rejection. The more complex proposals will usually go first to one or more specialist Council working parties, which will look over the proposal in detail, identifying points of agreement and disagreement, and responding to suggestions for amendments made by Parliament (for more detail, see Hayes-Renshaw and Wallace, 2006). The proposal will then go to Coreper, which looks at the political implications, and tries to clear as many of the remaining problems as it can, ensuring that the meeting of ministers is as quick and as painless as possible. The proposal then moves on to the relevant Council for a final decision. Ministers prefer to reach a consensus whenever they can, and to avoid a formal vote. Even when a vote is called, the countries in the minority may simply acquiesce (Dinan, 2005, p. 253). If an issue goes to a vote, however, ministers have three options:

- *A simple majority.* This is used mainly if the Council is dealing with a procedural issue or working under treaty articles, but as the SEA and Maastricht broadened the number of issues and areas in which a qualified majority vote could be used, the use of majority voting declined.
- *Unanimity.* This was once needed where a new policy was being introduced or an existing policy framework was being amended. Its use has been increasingly restricted, though, and it is now needed only on major constitutional issues, on matters of political sensitivity, or if the Council wants to change a Commission proposal against the wishes of the Commission.
- *A qualified majority vote (QMV).* This is needed for almost every other kind of decision where ministers have failed to reach a consensus. Instead of each minister having one vote, each is given several votes roughly in proportion to the population of his or her member state, for a total of 345 (see Table 4.4). To be successful, a proposal must win a triple majority of at least 255 votes (just under 74 per cent of the votes), from a majority of

Table 4.4   *Votes in the Council of Ministers*

Germany	29	Belgium	12	Lithuania	7
UK	29	Hungary	12	Latvia	4
France	29	Portugal	12	Slovenia	4
Italy	29	Austria	10	Estonia	4
Spain	27	Bulgaria	10	Cyprus	4
Poland	27	Sweden	10	Luxembourg	4
Romania	14	Slovakia	7	Malta	3
Netherlands	13	Denmark	7		
Greece	12	Finland	7		
Czech Republic	12	Ireland	7	Total	345

states (in some cases a two-thirds majority), and with the votes in favour representing states with a combined population that is at least 62 per cent of the EU total.

Because the Council of Ministers is a meeting place for national interests, the keys to understanding how it works are terms such as *compromise*, *bargaining*, and *diplomacy*. The ministers are often leading political figures at home, so they are motivated by national political interests. Their views are also ideologically driven, and their authority will depend to some extent on the strength and stability of the governing party or coalition at home. All these factors combine to pull ministers in different directions, and to deny the Council the kind of structural regularity enjoyed by the Commission.

The European Parliament

The European Parliament (EP) is the junior member in the EU decision-making system, mainly because (unlike conventional legislatures) it cannot introduce laws or raise revenues (these are powers of the Commission), and it shares the powers of amendment and decision with the Council of Ministers. Parliament also has a credibility problem: it is the most democratic of EU institutions, because it is the only one that is directly elected by voters in the member states, but few EU citizens know what it does, and they have not yet developed the same kinds of psychological ties to the EP as they have to their national legislatures.

Despite its handicaps, Parliament has shrewdly used its powers to play a more active role in running the EU, and has been entrepreneurial in suggesting new laws and policies to the Commission. It has also used arguments about democratic accountability to compel the other institutions to take it more seriously. Where it once mainly reacted to Commission proposals and Council

Table 4.5   *Seats in the European Parliament, 2007–09*

	2007	2009		2007	2009		2007	2009
Germany	99	99	Portugal	24	22	Lithuania	13	12
United Kingdom	78	72	Czech Republic	24	22	Latvia	9	8
France	78	72	Hungary	24	22	Slovenia	7	7
Italy	78	72	Sweden	19	18	Estonia	6	6
Spain	54	50	Austria	18	17	Cyprus	6	6
Poland	54	50	Bulgaria	18	17	Luxembourg	6	6
Romania	35	33	Slovakia	14	13	Malta	5	5
Netherlands	27	25	Denmark	14	13			
Greece	24	22	Finland	14	13			
Belgium	24	22	Ireland	13	12	Total	785	736

votes, it has become more aggressive in launching its own initiatives and making the other institutions pay more attention to its opinions. It has also won more powers to amend laws and to check the activities of the other institutions, with the result that it now has equal standing with the Council of Ministers on deciding which proposals for new laws will be enacted and which will not.

The European Parliament is the only directly elected international legislature in the world. It has a single chamber, and the 785 members of the European Parliament (MEPs) are elected by universal suffrage by all eligible voters in the EU for fixed, renewable five-year terms. The number of seats is divided up among the member states roughly on the basis of population, so that Germany has 99 while Malta has just five. This formula means that bigger countries are under-represented and smaller countries over-represented, so while Germany, Britain, France, and Italy each have one MEP per 800,000 citizens, the ratio for Belgium, the Czech Republic, Hungary, and Portugal is about 1:425,000 citizens, and for Malta and Luxembourg it is about 1:80,000. For the 2009 elections, the distribution will be adjusted, mainly in order to bring down the total membership to 736 (see Table 4.5).

Absurdly, Parliament's buildings are divided among three cities: while the administrative headquarters are in Luxembourg, and parliamentary committees meet in Brussels for about two to three weeks every month (except August), the parliamentary chamber is situated in Strasbourg, and MEPs are expected to meet there in plenary sessions (meetings of the whole) for about three or four days each month except August. Since committees are where most of the real bargaining and revising takes place, and since 'additional' plenaries can be held in Brussels, few MEPs actually attend the Strasbourg plenaries, preferring to spend most of their time in Brussels. This arrangement comes courtesy of the French government, which stubbornly insists that Strasbourg must remain the site for plenary sessions, undermining the credibility of the EP while inflating its budget (see Judge and Earnshaw, 2003, pp. 158–63).

The EP is chaired by a president, who presides over debates during plenary sessions, decides which proposals go to which committees, and represents Parliament in relations with other institutions. The president must be an MEP, and is elected by other MEPs for two-and-a-half-year renewable terms (half the life of a Parliamentary term). The president would probably come out of the majority party group if there were one, but since no one group has ever had a majority (see Chapter 6), he or she is chosen out of one of the bigger party groups as a result of inter-party bargaining. To help with the task of dealing with many different party groups in Parliament, the president works with the chairs of the different party groups in the Conference of Presidents, which draws up the agenda for plenary sessions and oversees the work of parliamentary committees.

Like most national legislatures, the EP has standing and ad hoc committees which meet in Brussels to consider legislation relevant to their area or to carry out parliamentary inquiries (see Judge and Earnshaw, 2003, pp. 177–96). The committees range in size from 28 to 86 members, and have their own hierarchy, which reflects levels of parliamentary influence over different policy areas: among the most powerful are those dealing with the environment and the budget. Seats on committees are distributed on the basis of a mixture of the balance of party groups, the seniority of MEPs, and national interests. For example, there are more Irish and Danish MEPs on the agriculture committee than on committees dealing with foreign and defence matters.

Although it cannot introduce legislation, Parliament's powers to influence and amend EU law have grown. As well as the advisory and supervisory powers set out in the treaties, Parliament has several essentially negative powers: the Commission tries to anticipate the EP's position while drawing up a proposal, Parliament can delay or kill a proposal by sitting on it, and it also has the power to dismiss the Commission. Unfortunately, the concern of member states with preserving their powers over decision making in the Council of Ministers has created a complex legislative process:

- By the Treaty of Rome, Parliament was given a *consultation procedure* under which it was allowed to give a non-binding opinion to the Council of Ministers before the latter adopted a new law in selected areas, such as aspects of transport policy, citizenship issues, the EC budget, and amendments to the treaties. The Council could then ask the Commission to amend the draft, but the Commission had no obligation to respond. The procedure is now rarely used.
- The SEA introduced a *cooperation procedure* which gave Parliament the right to a second reading for certain laws being considered by the

Council of Ministers, notably those relating to aspects of economic and monetary policy.

- Maastricht created a *codecision procedure* under which Parliament was given the right to a third reading on bills in selected areas, thereby sharing powers with the Council in these areas. Maastricht also extended Parliament's powers over foreign policy issues by obliging the presidency of the European Council to consult with the EP on the development of a common foreign and security policy.

The Treaty of Amsterdam significantly increased the powers of Parliament by abolishing the cooperation procedure on everything except certain issues related to economic and monetary union (over which the member states wanted to retain control), and increasing the number of areas to which the codecision procedure applied from 15 to 38; these now include public health, movement of workers, vocational training, the structural funds, transport policy, education, customs cooperation, consumer protection, and the environment.

In addition to these legislative powers, Parliament also has joint powers with the Council of Ministers over fixing the EU budget, so that the two institutions between them constitute the 'budgetary authority' of the EU – they meet biannually to adopt a draft and to discuss amendments. The EP can ask for changes to the budget, ask for new appropriations for areas not covered (but cannot make decisions on how to raise money), and ultimately – with a two-thirds majority – can reject the budget.

Finally, Parliament has several supervisory powers over other EU institutions, including the right to debate the annual programme of the Commission, to put questions to the Commission, and to approve the appointment of the College of Commissioners. The most substantial of Parliament's powers is its ability – with a two-thirds majority – to force the resignation of the College of Commissioners through a vote of censure. While this power has never been used, Parliament came close in January 1999 after charges of mismanagement and nepotism were directed at two members of the College. Anticipating a vote of censure, the Santer Commission resigned just before the findings of an EP investigation were published in March. In October 2004, Parliament blocked the appointment of the new Italian Commissioner Rocco Buttiglione, who had expressed controversial views on homosexuality and women.

The European Court of Justice

The Court of Justice is the most underrated of the five major institutions of the EU, and the one that has been subject to the least political analysis. While the Commission and Parliament attract most of the media and public attention, and become embroiled in the biggest political controversies, the Court has quietly gone about its business of clarifying the meaning of European law. Its activities have been critical to the progress of European integration, and its role just as significant as that of the Commission or Parliament, yet few Europeans know what it does, and its decisions rarely make the headlines.

The job of the Court is to make sure that national and European laws – and international agreements being considered by the EU – meet the terms and the spirit of the treaties, and that EU law is equally, fairly, and consistently applied throughout the member states. It does this by ruling on the 'constitutionality' of EU law, giving opinions to national courts in cases where there are questions about the meaning of EU law, and making judgments in disputes involving EU institutions, member states, individuals, and corporations. In so doing, the Court gives the EU authority and makes sure that its decisions and policies are consistent and fit with the agreements inherent in the treaties. EU law takes precedence over the national laws of member states where the two come into conflict, but only in areas of EU competence. Hence the Court does not have powers over criminal law or family law, but has instead made most of its decisions on the kind of economic issues in which the EU has been most actively involved, having less to do with policy areas where the EU has been less active, such as education and health.

Based in a growing cluster of buildings in the Centre Européen on a plateau above the city of Luxembourg, the Court is the supreme legal authority of the EU, and the final court of appeal on all EU laws. It made its most basic contribution to the process of integration in 1963 and 1964 when it declared that the Treaty of Rome was not just a treaty, but was a constitutional instrument that imposed direct and common obligations on member states, and took precedence over national law. The Court has also established important additional precedents through decisions such as *Costa* v. *ENEL* [1964], which confirmed the primacy of EU law, and the *Cassis de Dijon* case of 1979, which greatly simplified completion of the single market by establishing the principle of mutual recognition: a product made and sold legally in one member state cannot be barred from another (see Chapter 7). Other Court rulings have helped increase the powers of Parliament, strengthened individual rights, promoted the free movement of workers, reduced gender discrimination, and helped the Commission break down the barriers to competition.

The Court of Justice has 27 judges, each appointed for a six-year renewable term of office. In order to keep the work of the Court running smoothly, the terms are staggered, so that about half the judges come up for renewal every three years. The judges are theoretically appointed by common agreement among the governments of the member states, so there is technically no national quota. However, because every member state has the right to make one nomination, all 27 are effectively national appointees. The persistence of the quota emphasizes once again the role of national interests in EU decision making.

Apart from being acceptable to the other member states, judges must be independent, must be legally competent, and must avoid promoting the national interests of their home states. Some judges have come to the Court with experience as government ministers, some have held elective office, and others have had careers as lawyers or as academics; whatever they have done in their previous lives, they are not allowed to hold administrative or political office while they are on the Court. They can resign from the Court, but they can only be removed by the other judges (not by member states or other EU institutions), and then only by unanimous agreement that they are no longer doing their job adequately.

The judges elect one of their own to be president by majority vote for a three-year renewable term. The president presides over Court meetings, is responsible for distributing cases among the judges and deciding the dates for hearings, and has considerable influence over the political direction of the Court. Despite his or her critical role in furthering European integration, the president – Vassilios Skouris of Greece since 2003 – never becomes a major public figure in the same mould as the president of the Commission.

To speed up its work, the Court is divided into chambers of five, seven or thirteen judges, which make the final decisions on cases unless a member state or an institution asks for a hearing before the full Court. To further ease the workload, the judges are assisted by eight advocates-general, advisers who review each of the cases as they come in, and deliver a preliminary opinion on what action should be taken and on which EU law applies. The judges are not required to agree with the opinion, or even to refer to it, but it gives them a point of reference from which to reach a decision. Although advocates-general are again appointed in theory by common accord, one is appointed by each of the Big Five member states, and the other four are appointed by the smaller states. One of the advocates-general is appointed First Advocate-General on a one-year rotation.

The Court of Justice has become busier as the reach of the EU has widened and deepened. In the 1960s it was hearing about 50 cases per year and making about 15–20 judgments, but now it hears about 400–550 cases per year, and makes about 400–700 judgments. As the volume of work grew during the 1970s and 1980s, it was taking the Court up to two years to reach a decision on more complex cases. To move matters along, a subsidiary Court of First Instance was created in 1989, to be the first point of decision on less complicated cases. If cases are lost at this level, the parties involved may appeal to the Court of Justice. There are 27 judges on the lower Court – one from each member state – and it uses the same basic procedures as the Court of Justice. To further ease the workload, the EU Civil Service Tribunal was created in 2004 to take over from the Court of First Instance any cases involving disputes between the EU institutions and their staff. It has seven judges appointed for six-year renewable terms.

The work of the Court falls under two main headings:

- *Preliminary rulings.* These make up the most important part of the Court's work, and account for about 40–60 per cent of the cases it considers. If a matter of EU law arises in a national court case, the national court can ask for a ruling from the European Court on the interpretation or validity of that law. Members of EU institutions can also ask for preliminary rulings, but most are made on behalf of a national court, and are binding on the court in the case concerned.
- *Direct actions.* These are cases where an individual, company, member state, or EU institution brings proceedings against an EU institution or a member state. For example, a member state might have failed to meet its obligations under EU law, so a case can be brought by the Commission or by another member state. The Commission has often taken member states to Court charging that they have not met their single market obligations. Private companies can also bring actions if they think a member state is discriminating against their products.

  Direct actions can also be brought against the Commission or the Council to make sure that EU laws conform to the treaties, and to attempt to cancel those that do not. The defendant is almost always the Commission or the Council because proceedings are usually brought against an act they have adopted. Others can be brought against an EU institution that has failed to act in accordance with the terms of the treaties. The European Parliament brought one such action against the Council of Ministers in 1983 (Case 13/83), charging that the Council had failed to agree a Common Transport Policy, as required under the Treaty of Rome. The Court ruled that while there was an obligation on the Council, no timetable had been agreed, so it was up to the member states to decide how to proceed.

Unlike all the other EU institutions, where English is becoming the working language, the Court works mainly in French, although a case can be heard in any official EU language at the request of the plaintiff or defendant. Court proceedings usually begin with a written application, describing the dispute and the grounds on which the application is based. The President assigns the case to a chamber, and the defendant is given one month to lodge a statement of defence, the plaintiff a month to reply, and the defendant a further month to reply to the plaintiff. The case is then argued by the parties at a public hearing before a chamber of judges. Once the hearing is over, the judges retire to deliberate, and – having reached a conclusion – return to Court to deliver their judgment.

Court decisions are supposed to be unanimous, but votes are usually taken by a simple majority. All decisions are secret, so it is never publicly known who – if anyone – dissented. The Court has no direct powers to enforce its judgments, so implementation is left mainly to national courts or the governments of the member states, with the Commission keeping a close watch. Maastricht gave the Court of Justice new powers by allowing it to impose fines, but the question of how the fines would be collected was left open, and the implications of this new power are still unclear.

The European Council

The European Council is often described as an extension of the Council of Ministers, but it is quite different both in terms of its powers and its composition. More a process or a forum than a formal institution (although it would have become a full institution under the constitution), it consists of the heads of government of the EU member states, their foreign ministers, and the president and vice-presidents of the Commission. This group meets at least twice each year at summit meetings, and provides strategic policy direction for the EU. The Council is something like a steering committee or a board of directors: it discusses the broad issues and goals of the EU, leaving it to the other EU institutions to work out the details.

The Council was created in 1974 in response to a feeling among some European leaders that the Community needed better leadership, and a body that could take a more long-term view of where the Community was headed. It immediately became an informal part of the Community decision making structure, although its existence was only finally given legal recognition with the Single European Act. Maastricht elaborated on its role, but did not provide much clarity beyond noting that the Council would 'provide the Union with the necessary impetus for its development and shall define the general political guidelines thereof'.

The Council has since been an important force for integration, with many of the most important initiatives of recent years coming out of Council discussions, including the launch of the European Monetary System in 1978, and the discussions that led to all the most recent European treaties. Council summits have also issued major declarations on international crises, reached key decisions on institutional changes (such as the 1974 decision to begin direct elections to the European Parliament), and given new clarity to EU foreign policy. But the Council has also had its failures, including its inability to speed up agricultural or budgetary reform, or to agree common EU responses to crises in Iraq and the Balkans.

The European Council makes the key decisions on the overall direction of political and economic integration, internal economic issues, foreign policy issues, budget disputes, treaty revisions, new member applications, and institutional reforms (such as the changes that were made under the Treaty of Nice). The summits achieve all this through a combination of brainstorming, intensive bilateral and multilateral discussions, and bargaining. The results depend on a combination of the quality of organization and preparation, the leadership skills of the presidency (which convenes and chairs each summit), and the ideological and personal agendas of individual leaders. The interpersonal dynamics of the participants is also important: for example, the political significance of the Franco-German axis was long a key part of the mechanics of decision making (although less so since eastward enlargement has diluted the voting and political power of the Big Two). Leaders who have been in office a long time or who have a solid base of political support at home or who have a record of progressive positions on Europe will be in a different negotiating position from those who do not.

Regular summits of the Council are held in June and December every year, with additional meetings held when necessary. Meetings are chaired by the leader of the member state holding the presidency of the Council of Ministers, and in the past took place either in the capital of that country, or in a regional city or town; they now almost all take place in Brussels. Organization is left largely to the presidency, which usually sees the summits as an opportunity to showcase the priorities of that member state. The agenda is driven in part by the ongoing priorities of the EU, but also by the particular priorities of the member state. The goal is to agree a set of Conclusions of the Presidency, an advanced draft of which is usually awaiting the leaders at the beginning of the summit, and provides the focus for discussions.

Officially, the Council has no set agenda, but there has to be some direction, so it is usual for senior officials from the country holding the presidency to work with the Council of Ministers to develop an agenda. The items on the agenda depend on circumstances: national delegations normally have issues they want to raise, there must be some continuity from previous summits, and leaders will often have to deal with a breaking problem or an emergency that needs a decision. Some issues (especially economic issues) are routinely discussed at

---

Box 4.3   Specialized EU institutions

As the EU has grown, so has the number of institutions and specialized agencies created to deal with specific aspects of its work. They now include the following:

- *European Economic and Social Committee* (based in Brussels, created 1958). Allows employers, workers and other sectional interests to meet and express their views.
- *European Investment Bank* (Luxembourg, 1958). An autonomous institution that encourages 'balanced and steady development' by granting loans and giving guarantees.
- *European Centre for the Development of Vocational Training* (Thessaloniki, Greece, 1975). Promotes vocational training in the EU.
- *Court of Auditors* (Luxembourg, 1977). The EU's financial watchdog, charged with carrying out annual audits of the accounts of EU institutions.

- *European Environment Agency* (1993, Copenhagen). Collects information which is used to help develop environmental protection policies, and to measure the results.
- *Translation Centre* (Luxembourg, 1994). A self-financing office that helps most of these specialized agencies with their translation needs.
- *Committee of the Regions* (Brussels, 1994). Allows representatives of local units of government to meet and discuss matters relating to regional and local issues.
- *European Agency for Safety and Health at Work* (Bilbao, Spain, 1995). Provides information in support of improvements in occupational safety and health.
- *European Monitoring Centre for Drugs and Drug Addiction* (Lisbon, 1995). Provides information on drugs and addiction that can be used in anti-drug campaigns.
- *European Medicines Agency* (London, 1995). Promotes public and animal health through the evaluation and supervision of medicines for human and veterinary use.
- *Community Plant Variety Office* (Angers, France, 1995). An independent office responsible for implementing EU plant variety rights.
- *Office for Harmonization in the Internal Market* (Alicante, Spain, 1996). Responsible for the registration and administration of EU trademarks and designs.
- *European Central Bank* (Frankfurt, 1998). Ensures monetary stability by setting interest rates in the euro zone (see Box 7.3).
- *European Police Office (Europol)* (The Hague, 1999). Promotes EU police cooperation by managing a system of information exchange targeted against terrorism, drug-trafficking, and other serious forms of international crime.
- *European Food Safety Authority* (Parma, Italy, 2002). Provides independent scientific advice on issues relating to food safety.
- *European Aviation Safety Agency* (Cologne, 2003). Promotes civil aviation safety in the EU.
- *European Maritime Safety Agency* (Lisbon, 2004). Promotes maritime safety and pollution prevention.
- *European Railway Agency* (Valenciennes/Lille, France, 2004). Promotes an integrated and competitive European rail network.
- *European Agency for the Management of Operational Cooperation at the External Borders* (Warsaw, 2004). Coordinates cooperation among member states on the management of the EU's external borders.
- *European Network and Information Security Agency* (Heraklion, Greece, 2004). Provides advice and expertise on issues relating to information security.
- *European Centre for Disease Prevention and Control* (Stockholm, 2005). Works to strengthen Europe's defences against infectious disease.
- *Community Fisheries Control Agency* (Vigo, Spain, 2005). Monitors the uniformity and effectiveness of enforcement of the Common Fisheries Policy.
- *European Chemicals Agency* (Helsinki, 2006). Manages the registration and evaluation of chemicals.
- *European Fundamental Rights Agency* (Vienna, 2007). Provides help and expertise on the implementation of EU fundamental rights law and policy.

every summit. The Commission may also promote issues it would like to see discussed, and an active presidency might use the summit to bring items of national or regional interest to the attention of the heads of government.

Preparations for each summit begin as soon as a member state takes over the presidency in January or July, monthly meetings of the foreign ministers try to resolve potential disagreements, and as the date for the summit approaches, the prime minister and foreign minister of the state holding the presidency become increasingly involved. Some summits are routine, and result in general agreement among leaders; others see deep differences in opinion, with some member states perhaps refusing to agree a common set of conclusions.

The summits themselves usually run over a period of two days, beginning with informal discussions over breakfast, and moving into details at plenary sessions held in the morning, afternoon, and – if necessary – evening. Overnight, officials from the presidency and the Secretariat of the Council of Ministers will work on the draft Conclusions, which will be discussed at another plenary on the morning of the second day, and – if necessary – at a final session in the afternoon. The summit then normally ends with the public release of the Conclusions. The Council tries to take its decisions on the basis of unanimity, or at least of consensus, but the occasional lack of unanimity may force a formal vote, and some member states may want to attach conditions or reservations to the Conclusions.

The summits are always major media events, and are surrounded by extensive security, a need that became particularly obvious with the street demonstrations against globalization during the June 2001 summit in Goteborg, Sweden. Enormous symbolism is attached to the outcomes of the summits, which are measured according to the extent to which they represent breakthroughs, or show EU leaders to be bogged down in disagreement. Failure and success reflect not only on the presidency, but on the whole process of European integration. The media attention devoted to summits is often enough in itself to concentrate the minds of participants and to encourage them to agree, although this did not apply to the December 2003 summit: intended to reach agreement on the draft constitution, its failure was seen in part as a reflection on the erratic Italian presidency and the leadership of prime minister Silvio Berlusconi. By contrast, when the German presidency was able to broker agreement at the June 2007 European Council on the treaty that would replace the failed constitution, this was seen as a reflection on the new influence of the Merkel government.

Conclusions

The European Union has built a wide network of administrative bodies since its inception. Among them, they are responsible for making general and detailed policy decisions, developing and adopting laws, overseeing the implementation of laws and policies by the member states, ensuring that those laws and policies meet the spirit and the letter of the treaties, and overseeing activities in a variety of areas, from environmental management to transport, consumer protection, drug regulation, and police cooperation. In many ways they fit the standard definition of a confederal system of administration: a general system of government coexisting with local units of government, each with shared and independent powers, but with the balance in favour of the local units (in this case, the member states). Except for the European Parliament, EU citizens do not have a direct relationship with any of the EU institutions, instead relating to them through their national governments.

Despite concerns in some of the member states about the federalization of Europe, the institutions still lack many of the features of a conventional federal government. For example, there is no European army or air force, no elected European president, no European tax system, no European foreign and defence policy, and no single postal system. Furthermore, the focus of decision making still rests with the European Council and the Council of Ministers, both of which are intergovernmental rather than supranational. Finally, the European Union is still ultimately a voluntary arrangement, and lacks the powers to force its member states to implement European law and policy. The withdrawal of one of its members would not be regarded as secession.

Nonetheless, while debates rage about the finer points of the decisions reached by the EU institutions, the national governments of the member states have transferred significant powers to these institutions. Particularly since the passage of the Single European Act, the activities of the Commission, the Council of Ministers, Parliament, and the Court of Justice have had a more direct impact on the lives of Europeans, and government in Europe is no longer just about what happens in national capitals and regional cities, but also about what happens in Brussels, Luxembourg and Strasbourg.

The relationships among the five major institutions – and between them and the governments of the member states – changes constantly as the balance of power is adjusted and fine-tuned. Out of a combination of internal convenience and external pressure is emerging a new layer of government that is winning more powers as the member states cautiously transfer sovereignty from the local and national levels to the regional level. In the two chapters that follow, we will see what this has meant for the member states and for the citizens of Europe.

Chapter 5

The EU Policy Process

So much responsibility for making policy has been transferred from the exclusive domain of national governments to the EU institutions that the EU has – in this sense at least – come to look in many ways like a European superstate. EU institutions are at the heart of discussions about policy priorities, many of the actions of national governments are determined by new laws adopted by the EU, and in some areas – notably trade and agricultural policy – the member states now take part in the policy process mainly as voting members of the European club. Collectively, the EU institutions and the governments of the member states working within those institutions have become powerful and productive policy entrepreneurs and policy makers – certainly more powerful than can be said of any conventional international organization.

The implications have been controversial. How much can EU member states still do alone, and how much is now part of the remit of EU institutions? How are the interests of European citizens represented? How far do national interests still drive the work of the EU institutions? Is the EU policy process as elitist and as undemocratic as its critics often charge? Many Europeans are unclear about what integration has meant for their home states, and continue to champion the cause of separate national identities and residual powers for their home governments. But there are others who argue that the pooling of powers has been beneficial and efficient, and not a cause for concern: national identities and interests can be preserved, they argue, even in the face of common policies and joint institutions.

However we now understand the EU, its member states relate to each other quite differently from the way they did before the process of European integration began. As they have integrated their economies, agreed universal standards and regulations, and developed common policies on a wide range of issues, so the differences among them have declined and the effects of integration have become deeper and more complex. But just what this has meant for Europe poses a puzzle for Europeans and non-Europeans alike. For the most part, the EU is still regarded as an association of sovereign states, and few observers have yet woken up to the fact that those states will often act as one in their dealings with the rest of the world. They may occupy individual seats in the United Nations and the World Trade Organization, for example, but they usually agree joint positions on important foreign policy issues, and vote together. True, they still fight rearguard actions at home in the interests of preserving their national identities, but whatever the doubts about the wisdom and consequences of integration, the EU states have been pushed irresistibly by internal and external pressures into making policy together on a wide range of issues.

The previous chapter looked at how the European institutions work and make decisions. This chapter develops that story by looking at the changing balance of policy responsibilities between the EU and the member states, at the key pressures on the EU policy process and at the underlying features of that process, and at how the policy process has changed the relationship between the parts and the whole. It then looks at the political implications of the EU budget, before ending with some general conclusions about the impact of integration on the member states of the EU.

The changing balance of power

European society – like all societies – is in a constant state of flux. Political, economic, and social relationships among Europeans undergo continuous alteration, the pressures for change coming from different sources; where once it was war, economic competition, and political alliances, more recently it has been regional integration and changes in communications, technology, and economic activity. As noted in Chapter 1, the state system with which we are all familiar today dates back barely two centuries, and was preceded by political arrangements that were themselves constantly changing, and that led routinely to the redrawing of the political boundaries between different communities. A quick flick through an historical atlas of Europe shows how the boundaries of states have changed, and continue to change even today: Germany has not long been reunified, Czechoslovakia split apart only in 1993, and the breakup of Yugoslavia has not yet ended: Montenegro became Europe's newest state in 2006, and as this book went to press discussions continued about the future status of Kosovo. New questions have been raised meanwhile about possible independence for Scotland.

Before the Second World War, Europe held the balance of global political, military, and economic power, and the world's major powers included Britain, Germany, and France. The international system was defined in large part by the competition among mainly European powers for political, economic, and military advantage. This all changed after 1945, when Europe found itself squeezed militarily and ideologically between the two superpowers and saw the focus of economic power shifting to new centres, notably the United States and Japan. As discussed in Chapter 3, the need to save Europe from itself combined with the need to build economic and military security in the postwar world to encourage Western European elites to call for a new regional community, and for cooperation rather than competition. Where the relationship among European states before the war had been driven by competition, now it was driven by cooperation.

As late as the 1960s and 1970s, European states still related to each other as sovereign states with strong and independent national identities. They had their own bodies of law, they pursued their own distinctive sets of policies, and travellers were reminded of the differences when they crossed national borders and had to show their passports. There were controls and limits on the movement of people, money, goods, and services, and citizens of one state who travelled to another felt very much that they were 'going abroad'. The nation state was dominant, and was both the focus of mass public loyalty and the source of primary political and administrative authority. Italians were clearly Italians, the Dutch were clearly Dutch, and Poles were clearly Poles – at least this is what most Europeans wanted to believe, or were encouraged to believe by circumstances.

The situation today is quite different, and the relationship between the EU and its member states has been transformed. There has been a transfer of authority from the member states to the European Union, and an agreement to share or pool the exercise of power in a variety of policy areas. The member states have remained the essential building blocks in this process, but they have moved far beyond the simple cooperation normally associated with international organizations, and have built a new layer of powerful institutions underwritten by a common body of laws.

In those policy areas where the governments of the member states have agreed to shift 'competence' (that is, policy authority) to the EU, national leaders now reach most key decisions through negotiation with their counterparts in the other member states, typically in the meeting rooms of the Council of Ministers and the European Council. Debates on the meaning of the treaties have combined with day-to-day discussions within the Commission and the Council of Ministers to encourage national leaders to work towards multinational compromises, and towards a European consensus. As this has happened, so it has become more difficult for leaders to define and pursue 'national interests', and they have been obliged to think more in terms of European interests. Increasingly, national and European interests have become indistinguishable from one another. At the same time, ordinary Europeans are reminded less often of their national differences, and the borders that once divided the member states have become so porous that in some places they have become little more than lines on a map demarcating different administrative units.

Two critical and competing influences have come to bear on the process. First, spillover has pushed the EU into an expanding set of policy interests, starting from a base of promoting economic integration and moving into a network of related areas, ranging from transport to communications, labour relations, policing, research and development, financial services, the environment, and foreign and security policy. Second, the brakes have been applied by the ongoing debate about subsidiarity, the principle that decisions should be taken at the lowest level possible for effective action. It was first raised in the European context in 1975 when the European Commission – in its response to the Tindemans report (see Chapter 6) – argued that the Community should be given responsibility only for those matters that the member states were no longer capable of dealing with efficiently. There was little further discussion until the mid-1980s, when member states opposed to increasing the power of the Commission began quoting the principle. It was finally brought into the mainstream of discussions about the EU by Article 3b of Maastricht:

> In areas which do not fall within its exclusive competence, the Community shall take action, in accordance with the principle of subsidiarity, only if and in so far as the objectives of the proposed action cannot be sufficiently achieved by the Member States and can therefore, by reason of the scale or effects of the proposed action, be better achieved by the Community.

The pressures of spillover and subsidiarity have reduced the ability of national governments to make policy and law according to national interests and priorities. Responsibilities have instead shifted to the European level, leaving national legislatures weaker and more marginalized in a process that has sometimes been described (pejoratively) as 'creeping federalism'. National legislatures once had almost complete authority to make laws as their members saw fit, within the limitations created by constitutions, public opinion, the powers of other government institutions, and the international community. They now find themselves limited to those policy areas in which the EU is less active, while reacting in other areas to the requirements of EU law and the pressures of regional integration.

It is debatable just how responsibilities are now divided up between the EU and the member states (see Box 5.1). In the realm of 'high politics' (a concept rarely defined, but usually understood to mean the universal, the persistent, or the most pressing concerns of government, such as economic and foreign policy) the balance still tends to lie with the member states, but they have less freedom of movement than before. The existence of the single market means that almost every aspect of economic policy is now influenced in some way by European policy, while the adoption of the euro has ensured that there are now few elements of monetary policy (both inside and outside the euro zone) that are not mainly driven by Europe rather than by the member states (see Chapter 7). But the member states still have the bulk of control over tax policy, and they still have their own budgets, which are far bigger (per capita) than the EU budget.

Box 5.1   The division of policy authority

Over time, the competence of the EU institutions has grown at the expense of the member states. At first, the only powers transferred were those agreed under the terms of the European Coal and Steel Community. But even in this limited area there was the promise of change to come: the Treaty of Paris gave the ECSC the power to ensure the rational use of coal resources (a precursor to environmental policy), to promote improved working conditions (a precursor to social policy), and to promote international trade (a precursor to trade and foreign policy). The logic of spillover was clearly at work from the outset, and the EU institutions have since been given competence over a broader set of policy issues, the authority of the member states declining along the way.

Most of the policy areas for which the EU has formal competence today are outlined in the treaties, the assumption being that all other policy areas remain the responsibility of the member states. But there is much ambiguity built in to the system, and there is no clear distinction between exclusive and nonexclusive competence, with the result that authority in most areas is divided, the balance of power in some areas tending towards the EU, and in other areas towards the member states:

Areas in which the balance lies with the EU	*Areas in which authority is shared*	*Areas in which the balance lies with the member states*
agriculture	culture	broadcasting
competition	employment	citizenship
consumer protection	energy	criminal justice
cross-border banking	export promotion	defence
cross-border crime	foreign relations	education
customs	information networks	elections
environment	overseas aid	health care
EU transport networks	regional development	land use
monetary policy	small and medium	local transport
(euro zone)	enterprises	policing
fisheries	social issues	postal services
immigration	vocational training	tax policy
trade		welfare
working conditions		

Thanks to a combination of formal agreements, expediency, and the often irresistible effects of policy spillover, it is safe to say that almost all policy areas are now influenced in some fashion by decisions taken at the level of the EU.

On international issues, meanwhile, the EU still has some way to go before it can claim a common foreign policy, and the member states still have much freedom in their relationships outside Europe and in the way they define and express their defence interests. But the EU is becoming a more distinctive and assertive actor on the world stage, and its effects are now measured jointly as much as individually, even if Eurosceptics still like to point to its failures and its disagreements. In one aspect of foreign policy – trade relations – the EU takes common positions and has flexed its economic muscle to notable effect; the separate sets of national economic interests still pursued by member states such as Britain and France in their former colonies have – as a result – become relatively unusual.

In the realm of 'low politics' (matters that are both more sectional and further down the agendas of most national governments, such as the environment, culture, and transport), the shift has been more clearly toward the EU. The political stakes are not so great, and so there has been a greater willingness by governments to pool or shift responsibility, and less concern among voters. And in many cases, the logic of policy integration has been clear; thus the building of trans-European transport and energy networks makes economic sense, environmental problems are often better dealt with by member states working together rather than in isolation, and the pressures of the single market have led to cooperation on employment policy, worker mobility, education, regional policy, and justice and home affairs.

All these changes have reordered the way in which Europeans regard one another, and approach their understanding of the division of policy interests. There are still many reminders of the differences among Europeans, and nationalism remains an issue, especially among minorities and those most actively opposed to integration. But increased individual mobility has allowed Europeans not just to visit other member states on vacation, but to live in – and even 'emigrate' to – those states. Europeans are slowly transferring their loyalty from individual states to a more broadly defined European identity, and are thinking of themselves less as Germans or Belgians or Slovaks and more as Europeans. It has been a slow process, to be sure, but recent Eurobarometer polls have found that about 55–60 per cent of Europeans often or sometimes think of themselves as European in addition to their own nationality, and that about 60 per cent feel proud to be European. Thus, inevitably, they will see policy priorities less in distinctive national terms and more in communal European terms.

Critics of integration have long argued that one of the greatest dangers posed by integration is the homogenization that comes as member states lose their individuality in the move towards Europe-wide standards and regulations. They argue that authority is shifting from national governments mandated by the people towards a European superstate that lacks such a mandate. But this depends upon how the EU is understood; if it is a European federation, then many problems remain. But if it is a confederation, in which citizens have the closest ties to their home states, and national governments set the pace of regional integration, then there is little to complain about (see Chapter 6 for more discussion). And rather than lead to a homogenized Europe, integration

Box 5.2   The rise of regional identity

Ironically, as the nation states of Europe have been busy cooperating on the construction of the European Union, so national minorities within these states have become more visible, more vocal, and more demanding of greater independence. In other words, as there has been macro-level integration, so there has been a degree of micro-level disintegration. These pressures were present long before the creation of the European Economic Community, but they have grown in recent decades at least in part because of the impact that regional integration has had on national identity. The effect has been to remind us that Europe is not just a region divided into three dozen nation states, but into more than 100 different nationalities. They run the gamut from the Dutch and English in the maritime north, to Portuguese and Cantabrians on the Atlantic coast, Alsatians and Franconians in the northwest, Bavarians, Swiss, and Styrians in the Alpine regions, Castilians, Andalusians, and Ligurians in the west-central Mediterranean, Serbs and Croats in the Balkans, Czechs, Slovaks, and Ruthenians in the east, Poles and Lithuanians in the northeastern plains, and Lapps, Finns, and Karelians in the northern Baltic (see Fernández-Armesto, 1997, for more details).

In some cases – such as the Cornish in England, Galicians in Spain and Lombards in Italy – these nations have been fully integrated into the larger states of which they are part. In others, integration has never been complete, secessionist movements have been active, and there have been calls for greater self-determination and even independence. This is particularly true in Britain, where Scotland, Wales and Northern Ireland have had regional assemblies since 1998–99, and a large segment of public opinion in Scotland is in favour of independence. There are similar demands for independence or devolution from Bretons and Corsicans in France, Basques in the Spanish-French borderland, Catalans in Spain, and Walloons in Belgium.

The status of national minorities has traditionally been a domestic matter for individual national governments, but European integration has helped redefine the relationship between the parts and the whole. As the member states lose their distinctive political identity, so the cultural identity of minorities is strengthened and the pressure for disintegration – or, at least, devolution – grows. It is possible that greater self-determination will lessen the demand among nationalists for complete independence, and that we will simply see a reassertion of cultural differences within the member states. It is also possible, however, that self-determination will lead to independence for minorities within the European Union, and a redrawing of administrative boundaries along cultural lines.

has actually helped promote a reassertion of cultural differences as Europeans have grown to better understand and appreciate the variety of the regions in which they live (see Box 5.2).

Indeed it is often argued that a Europe of the regions may come to rival or even replace a Europe of the states. In the interests of correcting economic imbalances, and prompted by growing demands for greater decentralization, European states began to regionalize their administrative systems in the 1960s, and as a result regions have emerged as important actors in politics and policy (Keating and Hooghe, 1996). They have come to see the EU as an important source of investment and of support for minority cultures, and in some cases this has given more confidence to nationalist movements (such as those in Scotland and Catalonia), as they feel less dependent on the support of the state governments. It has also reduced the overall importance of interstate relations within the EU, and drawn new attention to inter-regional relations. The logical conclusion is that forces of this kind will lead to Europe centralizing and decentralizing at the same time, with the member states as we know them today squeezed in the middle.

The policy environment

Public policies are the deliberate actions (or inactions) of government in response to the needs of society. When governments or political leaders run for office, they do so on a platform of explanations about what they see as the most important problems and challenges facing society, and of promises about what they will do in response. The actions they take while in office, and those they opt to avoid, collectively constitute their policies. If the different pressures on government – such as public opinion, economic changes, and external influences – are described as the inputs into the political process, then policies can be described as the end results, or the outputs.

Policies exist at many different levels, from the local community to towns, cities, counties, states, the national level, and – in the case of the EU – the multinational level. Policies are adopted and pursued not just by governments, but by political parties, the media, lobbies, and individual government institutions. Within every policy community there are multiple sub-communities with their own separate and often conflicting policy interests, and this is no less true at the EU level than at the national level; European policy is influenced by the major institutions (such as the Commission, Parliament, and the Council of Ministers), the directorates-general within the Commission, the regional and national policy interests pursued by member states, and the cross-national policies pursued by groups with shared interests, such as the environmental lobby, farmers, corporations, workers, labour unions, and parties within the European Parliament.

The influences that create and impact policies at the national level are many and complex, but at the level of the EU those complexities are compounded, coming from sources that are internal and external to the EU institutions, formal and informal, predictable and unpredictable, expected and unexpected, and structured and unstructured. They include the following:

- *Treaty obligations.* The treaties outline the general goals and principles of European integration, as well as some of the more specific tasks of the EU institutions. So, for example, Maastricht said that the general goals of the EU were (among others) to 'promote economic and social progress ... the strengthening of economic and social cohesion ... [and] to assert its identity on the international scene'. These are broad and ambiguous goals, but they set the foundations for policy, which must be turned into specific actions, mainly in the form of new laws.
- *Pressures to harmonize.* The need to bring national laws and policies into alignment has been central to avoiding economic and social differences among the member states, and to ensuring the smooth functioning of the single market. It accounted, for example, for most of the early laws on environmental policy, which were designed to remove the barriers to the single market created by different environmental standards.
- *Legislative pressures.* Many new proposals for policy and law come out of requirements or assumptions built into past laws. This is certainly the case with laws that include within them an obligation for amendment or review after a specified period of time, and is particularly true of the EU's framework directives, which set general goals with the assumption that more laws – known as daughter directives – will be developed later that will provide more detail and focus.
- *Policy evolution and spillover.* Policy is rarely static, and the principles and goals of EU policy are constantly redefined as greater understanding emerges about the causes and effects of problems, as technological developments offer new options for addressing old problems, as the failure of existing policies demands new approaches, as the balance of interests changes within the member states, and as the political, economic, and social priorities of European integration evolve.
- *Institutional pressures.* While the Commission has a monopoly over the development of new proposals for law, it is subject to various formal and informal pressures, including suggestions from the European Council regarding the broad goals of EU policy, 'invitations' from the European Parliament (EP) and the Council of Ministers to develop new proposals, suggestions or demands from the EP or the Council of Ministers for changes in Commission proposals, and the impact of rulings by the Court of Justice on the content and nature of EU law.
- *International law.* The EU as a unit has signed numerous international treaties on behalf of the member states, most of which impose specific obligations on the EU. This means the development of new laws and policies to respond to those obligations, and the development of common positions taken during negotiations on the progress of implementation.
- *Political initiatives.* Individual national leaders, working alone or in combination with others, have always been at the core of important policy

initiatives. Thus the early steps on building a European foreign policy came out of a decision by European leaders to organize regular meetings among the foreign ministers of the member states, much of the headway on security policy in the late 1990s was made because of initiatives taken by Tony Blair of Britain and Jacques Chirac of France (see Chapter 9), and it was agreement among European leaders in early 2007 that led to the revival of the defunct constitutional treaty as the Lisbon treaty.

• *Public opinion.* Although the EU is often described as elitist and undemocratic, neither the EU institutions nor the leaders of the member states have been able to ignore public opinion. It has been important, for example, in the development and agreement of new treaties and in the debate over the constitution. And even if voters have not always been able to express their opinions on new treaties through national referendums, the unwillingness or failure of governments to hold referendums has itself drawn attention to public opinion and has often sparked vigorous debates about Europe.

• *Internal pressures.* As integration has proceeded, so problems have presented themselves that have been internal to Europe, common to multiple member states, and potential barriers to successful integration. These have included, for example, ongoing concerns about unemployment, which have exercised EU governments for many years, or the need to monitor the movement of criminals around the EU, which has set off an active programme of policy and legal responses in the field of justice and home affairs.

• *External pressures.* Problems and demands have also come from outside the EU, and have often demanded the concerted and united response of all member states. In addition to the sometimes obvious and sometimes more subtle impact of pressures from the EU's major allies (such as the United States) and its competitors (such as China), policy has also responded to economic problems in other parts of the world, to trade imbalances and disputes, or to disagreements with other countries.

• *Emergencies or crises.* These have been a part of the policy calendar from the beginning, ranging from the collapse of the European Defence Community to the empty-chair crisis, the dispute over the budget in the 1980s, the EU's failures in the Balkans in the 1990s, the 2003 fallout with the United States over Iraq, and the collapse of the constitutional treaty. Each event has been followed by much hand-wringing, but has also ultimately drawn new attention to policy needs.

These multiple influences have created a complex and sometimes disorderly policy environment in which it is often difficult or impossible to be sure of the provenance of policy initiatives, or of the key actors involved in the development and implementation of policy initiatives.

The policy cycle

In an ideal world, public policy would be developed rationally, problems would be prioritized, options would be carefully researched and weighed, spending would be carefully planned, and the best solutions would be implemented, monitored, and evaluated. But modern society is too complex to make such an ideal possible, it is often impossible to undertake a meaningful cost benefit analysis of the options available, political pressures skew the outcomes of policy, and studies of policy routinely emphasize the scarcity of real organization. The result is that policy is often driven by compromise and opportunism, and is often simply a matter of muddling through from one problem to another (Lindblom, 1959). In an attempt to try and impose some order for the purposes of better understanding how public policy evolves, it is common to approach policy analysis using a process model involving a logical progression of steps. This implies that there is considerably more order to the policy process than exists in reality, but at least it offers a way of working through the maze.

Problem identification and agenda-setting

Before a policy choice can be made, there must be political agreement on the definition of a problem, and a decision must be made to add that problem to the list of policy concerns that are considered part of the remit of government. In a democracy, the development of the policy agenda is normally driven by a combination of the individual preferences and priorities of elected officials and their advisers, the struggles for power among political institutions (mainly the executive and the legislature), and the combined pressures of public opinion and media attention.

To the extent that there is a European agenda (see Peters, 2001), it is formed and driven mainly by the European Council, which outlines broad policy goals and sparks new policy initiatives. It was the Council, for example, that decided to draft and agree the Single European Act and the Maastricht, Amsterdam, Nice and Lisbon treaties, that has issued major declarations on international crises, that has reached key decisions on EU institutional changes, and that has given new momentum to EU foreign policy. But it must be remembered that the 27 prime ministers, chancellors and presidents who meet as the Council are ultimately national political leaders, and that they are torn between protecting national interests and pursuing the European interest. The pressures and influences to which they are subject come from many different sources: public opinion, treaty obligations, recommendations from consultative committees, the personal initiatives of individual leaders, tension among member states, the need to harmonize laws, international treaty requirements, discussion papers, specialist reports, and changes in the outside world.

There are at least three important differences between agenda-setting at the national and at the European level:

- Elected leaders at the national level often add issues to the policy agenda in response to public and media opinion, or – more cynically – in order to win legislative votes or build support for the next national election. At the EU level, however, there is no European 'public' in the sense that there is a large body of citizens demanding change at the European level. Furthermore, there is no elected European government that is constantly looking to its standing in the polls or to the outcome of an election. Thus policy is heavily driven by pressures internal to the process of European integration, and by leaders rather than by citizens. This leads to the common – and sometimes reasonable – assertion that the EU policy process is elitist. But this is a charge that applies equally to policy making at the national level (see Dye and Zeigler, 2000).
- The European agenda is pulled in different directions by the often competing motives and interests of the EU institutions. So while the Commission and the Court of Justice take a supranational approach to agenda-setting, the European Council and the Council of Ministers are more interested in protecting national interests, Parliament's choices are driven by voter interests, and the whole edifice is underwritten by a struggle for power and influence among the institutions.
- The complexity and variety of the needs and priorities of the member states make it more difficult to identify pan-European problems and to tease out the common causes of such problems, to build political support for a unified response, or to anticipate the potential effects of policy alternatives. This is particularly true in regard to policy issues on which there is less of a European consensus, such as foreign policy, where the member states bring different values and priorities to bear.

It is also important to appreciate that while we may talk of the 'European agenda', it is little more than the accumulation of narrower agendas being pursued by all the actors with an interest in the European policy process: the key EU institutions, the sub-institutional agendas of directorates-general within the Commission, the national agendas of individual member states, regional agendas pursued by groups of member states (poorer states will have different needs from richer states, agricultural states will have different needs from industrial states, and so on), and cross-national agendas pursued by like-minded groups in multiple states, such as the environmental lobby, farmers, multinational corporations, and workers and labour unions. Each of these in their own way will limit, redirect, or broaden the cumulative policy interests of the European Union.

Formulation and adoption

Once a problem or a need has been recognized, a response must be formulated and adopted. In the case of the EU, this usually involves debating the options at meetings of the European Council, developing proposals for new laws and new budgetary allocations, drafting work programmes or action programmes, publishing discussion papers, or making public announcements. Whichever response is chosen, it might be reasonable to expect that some kind of methodical analysis would be conducted in which the causes and dimensions of a problem are studied and all the options and their relative costs and benefits are considered before the most efficient policy alternative is chosen (see Dye, 2002, p. 17). However, this rational policy model rarely works in practice, because understanding of the value preferences of Europeans is incomplete, as is the information about policy alternatives and about costs and benefits. As a result, most EU policy is designed and applied incrementally, intuitively, or in response to emergencies or changes in public opinion.

In national systems of government, policy is usually formulated by the executive, the legislature, or government departments. In the case of the EU, the major focus of policy formulation is the Commission, which not only has a monopoly on the drafting of new laws and policies, but also has a pivotal position as a broker of interests and a forum for the exchange of policy ideas (Mazey and Richardson, 1997). The Commission does not function in a policy vacuum, however, and its proposals are routinely amended as a result of lobbying by interest groups or national governments, as a response to internal and external emergencies and crises, and as they are discussed by consultative committees, the Council of Ministers and the European Parliament. According to the Commission's own calculations, about 30 per cent of its proposals come in response to the international obligations of the EU, about 20–25 per cent come as a follow-up to resolutions or initiatives from the other European institutions, about 20 per cent involve the updating of existing EU laws, and 10–15 per cent arise out of obligations under the treaties or secondary legislation (Commission of the European Communities, 2001b, p. 6).

Once a new law or policy has been proposed by the European Commission, it must formally be adopted before it goes into effect. The final say over adoption comes out of a complex interplay involving Parliament, Coreper, the Council of Ministers, the Commission, and the member states, with the Court of Justice providing legal interpretation when necessary. Changes introduced by the Single European Act and by the Maastricht, Amsterdam and Nice treaties have provided new powers to Parliament, which – in most areas – has now become a 'co-legislature' with the Council of Ministers.

Figure 5.1   *The European policy structure*

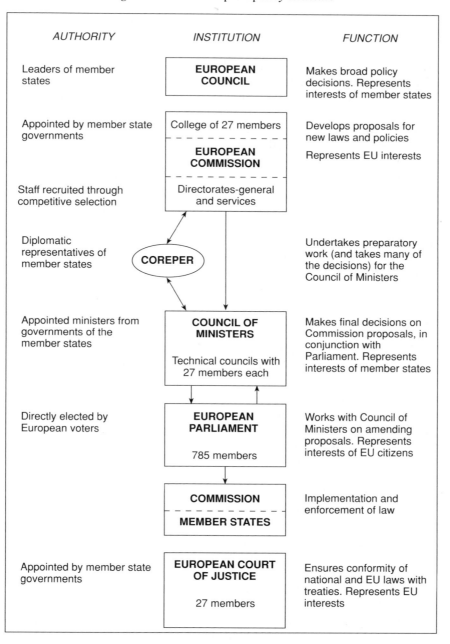

Implementation

Arguably the most important step in the policy cycle is implementation, the point at which the goals and objectives of government result – or fail to result – in real change for the governed. Unfortunately, implementation has so far proved a relatively weak part of the EU policy process, and several structural problems have made it difficult always to be sure about the extent to which EU laws and policies are actually implemented in the manner in which they were intended by their authors, or make a difference in the lives of Europeans. This has been a matter of growing concern for EU institutions, within which there has been an expanding debate on how to improve implementation. The Commission itself blames non-conformity between national and EU law on the existence of two or more legal systems in several member states (notably those with a federal structure), and the difficulties that arise in amending national laws because of the effect they have on provisions in a variety of other areas, such as agriculture, transport and industry (Commission of the European Communities, various years).

The implementation of public policies is normally left to bureaucracies. However, the bureaucracy of the EU – the Commission – is small and has no powers directly to enforce European law, and so must work instead to ensure implementation through the bureaucracies of the member states. The Commission occasionally convenes meetings of national representatives and experts to monitor progress, and also carries out its own investigations using its contacts in national government agencies. Most of the time, however, the Commission must rely on other sources, including the governments of member states (who will occasionally report on other governments that are not being as aggressive as themselves in implementing law), whistleblowing by interest groups, the media and private citizens, the European Parliament (which since 1983 has required that the Commission submit annual reports on the failure of member states fully to implement Community legislation) and the European ombudsman (who has the power to conduct inquiries into charges of bad administration against Community institutions, except the Court of Justice and Court of First Instance).

Useful though they may be as a means of drawing attention to problems that the Commission might otherwise have missed, complaints are not an entirely reliable measure, and the system suffers at least four drawbacks. First, it is ad hoc and unstructured. Second, many of the problems drawn to the attention of the Commission are found not to be infringements because there is no relevant legal base (Commission of the European Communities, 1998, p. 49). Third, the number of complaints is influenced by the political culture of different member states, and by their varied relationships with the EU. The fact that a large number of complaints are registered in a particular member state may reflect less a problem with implementation than a high level of interest in the effects of EU law. Finally, complaints are difficult to prioritize – they may not necessarily be made about the most serious or the most urgent cases.

Evaluation

The final stage in the policy cycle is to determine whether or not a law or policy has worked. This is difficult unless specific goals were set and unless national bureaucrats can be trusted to report accurately to the Commission on the results of policies. In many cases it is almost impossible to know which actions resulted in which consequences or whether the results are being accurately reported. This is particularly true in the case of the EU, where it is difficult always to distinguish the effects of national and local government actions from those of EU law. Nonetheless, evaluation in the EU is conducted by a combination of the Commission, the Council of Ministers, the European Council, the European Parliament, and reports from member states, interest groups, and individuals.

Features of the policy process

All societies have particular characteristics that influence the nature of the policy process. In democracies, for example, the process is more complex than in authoritarian systems, simply because so many more opinions and influences must be taken into consideration. With its own complexity and peculiarities, the EU has a unique combination of features that colour the way in which policy is made and implemented.

Compromise and bargaining

In a democratic society, all politics is a matter of compromise. Individuals cannot all have things their own way, because there are always others who will disagree with their analysis of a problem and their suggested prescriptions. The fewest compromises are needed in unitary systems of government with majoritarian political parties (such as Britain, Portugal or Spain), where the focus of political power rests with a national government dominated by a single political party. More compromises are needed in federal systems such as Belgium and Germany, where there is a division of powers between national and sub-national government, or in member states governed by coalitions (such as Bulgaria, Finland, or Hungary). With a political arrangement such as the EU, however, where the power structure is still not clearly defined, where political relationships are still evolving, and where the 'government' is effectively a coalition of the representatives of the member states, the entire policy process revolves around compromise.

Some policy initiatives, such as the single market, have been less difficult to address than others because they have enjoyed a high degree of political support. The costs to national sovereignty were relatively low, while the potential benefits to national economies were relatively high. But in other areas, the member states have fought hard to protect national interests, forcing sometimes unhappy compromises. The creation of the Common Agricultural Policy, for example, was based around compromise, with France winning concessions on agriculture in return for concessions given to German industry. Similarly, the negotiations leading up to Maastricht were riddled with compromises and package deals, notably over the timetable for the development of the euro. The adoption of the euro was itself a compromise, with every member state given the option of either joining or not.

Political games

A major approach to public policy analysis is offered by game theory, which studies situations in which two or more actors compete against each other for influence, their positions being influenced by what they think other actors will do. In the process of seeking compromises, runs the argument, politics is typically reduced to a struggle for power and influence, with one person or group trying to win concessions from – or pressing their views on – others. Such struggles take place even in the smallest and most local of communities in human society, but they are magnified in the EU by its sheer size and by the extent to which member states and institutions compete with each other, unconstrained (so far) by the presence of a constitution. Peters (1992, pp. 106–7) describes three sets of interconnected games in the EU:

- A national game among member states trying to extract as much as possible from the EU while giving up as little as possible. This was the case even with the six founding members, but as the EU has expanded in size, so the game has become more complex and intense, because the stakes and the payoffs have been much greater, while the EU has become more politically, economically, and socially diverse.
- A game played out among EU institutions trying to win more power and influence relative to each other. Once just an experiment in combining coal and steel industries, European integration has spilled over into almost every area of policy, and the EU has grown to cover almost all of Europe. As the stakes have been raised, so the EU institutions have jockeyed with each other for a greater role.
- A bureaucratic game in which the directorates-general in the Commission have their own organizational cultures and are competing for policy space. Again, this has been driven in large part by the growing policy responsibilities of the EU, the new resources available to the Commission, and

the natural inclination of bureaucracies to justify their importance and to compete for influence.

Multi-speed integration

The old 'Community method' – by which all the member states were obliged to proceed at the same pace and to adopt and implement the same laws and policies (see Lindberg and Scheingold, 1970) – has been replaced by what has been variously known as 'multi-speed' integration, Europe *à la carte*, 'variable geometry', or 'enhanced cooperation'. These are all terms for an arrangement that allows different member states to opt in or out of different elements of European policy. For example, Britain was allowed to opt out of the Social Charter (see Chapter 6), only 15 member states have so far made the switch to the single currency, not all member states have removed border controls as planned under the Schengen Agreement, and traditionally neutral states such as Ireland and Finland have preferred not to participate in attempts to build a common European defence policy. The Treaty of Amsterdam imposed conditions that limited the scope of the application of 'enhanced cooperation', while Nice required a minimum of eight member states to take part in any plan, removed the right of each member state to veto the plan, and provided for the possibility of enhanced cooperation in foreign policy.

Formal versus informal

The EU has found itself subject to a combination of policy pressures that have been both formal and informal. Wallace (1990, pp. 54–5) defines formal integration as the deliberate actions taken by policy makers to create and adjust rules, to establish and work through common institutions, to regulate, encourage or inhibit social and economic flows, and to pursue common policies. He defines informal integration as patterns of interaction that develop without the intervention of deliberate government decisions, following the dynamic of markets, technology, communications, and social exchange, or the influence of mass movements. Wallace also distinguishes between proactive and responsive integration, the former having deliberate and explicit political aims, while the latter reacts to economic and social change.

If all EU member states had similar political agendas, similar economic and social structures, similar levels of wealth and productivity, and the same sets of standards and regulations, integration would be relatively straightforward and would lean towards the formal and the proactive. However, the member states have different structures, policies, values and levels of wealth, so they approach integration from different perspectives. Concerned with avoiding a multi-speed Europe, national leaders have often had to react to the unforeseen effects of integration, and so have found themselves being driven by informal

Box 5.3   Europeanization

The term 'public policy' is often associated with national government responses to national issues, and yet policy is made at many different levels. Of particular interest since the 1970s has been the internationalization of public policy, through which national governments have been influenced by pressures coming out of international relations, most notably by trade and globalization. Nowhere has the process of internationalization gone as far as it has in the EU, where the harmonization of European law and policy has given rise to the phenomenon of Europeanization, which has in turn spawned a large number of new analytical studies of the EU policy process.

Europeanization is usually defined as the process by which laws and policies in the member states have been brought into alignment with EU law and policy. One key set of assessments of Europeanization (Graziano and Vink, 2007, pp. 7–8) defines it as 'the domestic adaptation to European regional integration', or the process whereby administrations in the member states adapt to the requirements of EU law and policy, or the process of integration 'feeds back' into national political systems. The changes have seen differences in national laws and regulations being reduced by the agreement of European laws and regulations (see Page, 2003). But it is more than just about laws and policies; it can also be applied to understanding the meaning of 'Europe', to the new opportunities made available to interest groups by changing administrative structures and processes, to the general project of unifying Europe, and even to our understanding of the borders of Europe.

Opinion is divided on just how far the process of Europeanization has gone, and it is not always clear how far the pressures that have led to policy change have been clearly European, as opposed to coming out of initiatives driven by the member states or out of international pressures such as globalization. Opinion is also divided as to whether the concept is all that useful, or whether it has simply become fashionable to employ it. Part of the problem is that there is no universally accepted definition, and it is routinely reinterpreted to fit with the arguments made by individual scholars and analysts. But this is a problem common to most concepts in the social sciences. For now, at least, Europeanization is an important tool for understanding the EU policy world.

pressures. For example, while the process of integration has been focused on harmonizing standards, laws and regulations, it has also obliged European leaders in some areas to agree to proceed through mutual recognition (if something is good enough for one state, it is good enough for them all).

Incrementalism

Policy making in a democratic society is inevitably cautious, because neither public nor political opinion will typically tolerate radical change, and many competing interests have to be taken into account. Lacking the time and resources to investigate all the options available, policy makers tend to build on precedent, adjusting and fine-tuning what has gone before rather than bringing about wholesale change (Lindblom, 1959). This has been particularly true at the European level, because of concerns over the loss of national sovereignty, the absence of a consensus about the wisdom of European integration, and the need for constant compromise. The EU has occasionally agreed relatively dramatic policy initiatives (such as the Single European Act, Maastricht, the launch of the euro, and eastern enlargement), but none of these changes have come without much deliberation and debate, and most EU policy making is based on the development and elaboration of existing policies. Because there are so many counterweights and counterbalances in the policy process, member states and EU institutions can rarely take the initiative without conferring first with other member states or EU institutions. For the most ardent supporters of integration, the process has sometimes slowed to a crawl; for Eurosceptics, meanwhile, it has usually been moving much too quickly.

Spillover

Critics of the EU have charged that it has tried to become involved in too many policy areas, and that institutions such as the Commission have become too powerful and even somewhat imperious. What they often fail to realize, though, is that the EU institutions have often been driven by forces beyond their control: as functionalists have argued, the 'invisible hand' of integration has been at work, the launch of new initiatives often revealing or creating new problems or opportunities, which in turn can lead to pressures for additional supporting initiatives. This policy spillover has been one of the enduring features of policy making in the EU, the prime example coming from efforts to complete the single market. The task of removing barriers to the free movement of people, money, goods, and services could not be achieved either easily or quickly, and involved making many of the adjustments – anticipated or not – that opened up the European market. This meant moving into new areas of policy that were never anticipated by the founding treaties, including social issues, working conditions, and the environment.

This combination of features has created a policy process that is complex, constantly changing, and still not yet fully understood. New attention has been paid by scholars and commentators in the last two decades to trying to better understand the different institutions of the EU, and the EU's activities in specific areas of policy. (Interestingly, there has been an inverse relationship between the attention paid to a policy area and its achievements on the ground; thus there have been more studies of foreign and security policy, where the EU record has been mixed, than of environmental, agricultural and trade policy, where the impact and achievements of the EU have been more substantial.)

But there are still few studies of the broader policy process and of the ways in which policy making at the European level has changed the relationship among member states, and between member states and Europe as a whole (for one notable exception, see Richardson, 2006). At least part of the fault for this can be laid at the dominating influence of international relations (IR) theory in attempts to understand the EU. Scholars of IR are not typically interested in public policy, but focus instead on alliances and the balance of power. As the methods, models and approaches coming out of comparative politics and public policy play a greater role in attempts to understand the EU, so – presumably – will our understanding of the European policy process.

The politics of the budget

The budget is one of the biggest influences on policy at any level of government, because the choices that a government makes regarding how and where to raise and spend money affect both the policy choices it makes and the effectiveness of the policies it pursues. It is typically less a question of how *much* is raised and spent than of *how* and *where* that money is raised and spent. The revenue and spending of the European Union is no exception, and the budget has frequently set off controversies that have resulted in member states being at odds with one another and with the EU institutions. The level of controversy is surprising considering the relatively small size of the EU budget: just under €130 billion ($180 billion) in 2007, or just over 1.2 per cent of the combined GDP of the member states (see Figure 5.2). Some of the biggest battles have concerned the relative amounts given and received by each member state, and the balance between national contributions and the EU's own sources of revenue. To the extent that the EU has had to rely on national contributions, it has been more subject to political leverage by the member states. To the extent that it has been able to develop its own sources of revenue, the EU institutions have been able to build more independence.

The European Economic Community – like most international organizations – was originally funded by national contributions. Each member state made a payment roughly in proportion to the size of its population, thus France, Germany, and Italy each contributed 28 per cent of the budget, Belgium and the Netherlands 7.9 per cent, and Luxembourg 0.2 per cent. In an attempt to win more independence for itself, the Commission in 1965 suggested that the revenue from tariffs placed on imports from outside the EC should go directly to the Community, thereby providing it with its 'own resources'. At the same time, Parliament began pushing for more control over the budget as a means of gaining more influence over policy. Charles de Gaulle thought that the Commission already had too much power, and it was these proposals (combined with France's opposition to reform of the Common Agricultural

Figure 5.2   *The European Union budget*

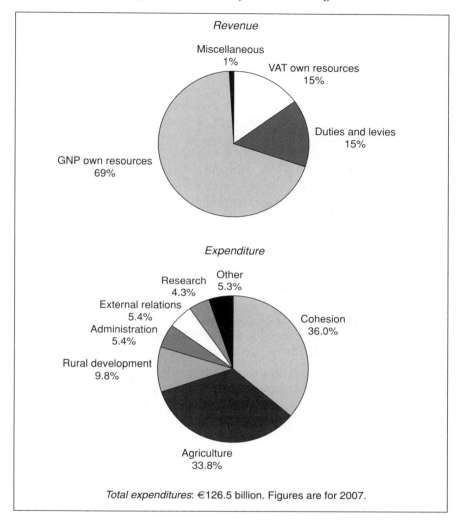

Total expenditures: €126.5 billion. Figures are for 2007.

Policy) that led to the 1965 empty-chair crisis when France refused to take part in EEC business (see Dinan, 2004, pp. 104–5).

Pressure for budgetary reform persisted regardless, and changes in the early 1970s led to an increase in the proportion of revenues derived from the Community's own resources: customs duties, levies on agricultural imports, and a small proportion of value-added tax (VAT). But there were two problems with this formula: it took little account of the relative size of the economies of member states, and the amounts raised were insufficient to meet the needs of the Community, which was not allowed to run a deficit or to borrow to meet shortfalls. By the early 1980s, the Community was nearly bankrupt, and it was obvious that either revenue had to be increased or spending had to be restructured or cut.

Matters came to a head over the insistence by the then new British prime minister, Margaret Thatcher, that Britain's contributions be recalculated. Arguing that Britain bore an unfair share of the Community budget, and received an inadequate amount in return, she generated alarm at her first European Council appearance in 1979 by bluntly telling her Community partners: 'I want my money back.' Her campaign continued through the early 1980s, tied to her demands for a reform of the Common Agricultural Policy. After much acrimonious debate, a complex deal was reached in 1984 by which Britain's contributions were cut, its rebates were increased, and the overall budget was recalculated in preparation for the accession of Spain and Portugal. More reforms agreed in 1988 resulted in the system of revenue raising we find today:

- The budget cannot be greater than 1.24 per cent of the combined GNP of the member states, and cannot be in deficit.
- About 69 per cent of revenues come from national contributions based on national GNP levels, with each member state paying a set amount in proportion to its GNP.
- Revenues from VAT account for about 15 per cent of revenues.
- About 15 per cent of revenues come from customs duties on imports from non-member states and from agricultural levies.

The effect of the changes has been to make the richer states the biggest net contributors, while the poorer states have been the biggest net recipients. When the Commission published its Agenda 2000 proposals in 1997, aimed at preparing for eastward enlargement and reform of the Common Agricultural Policy and the regional funds, it stirred up a hornets' nest of debate about the future of the budget. Several countries that were net contributors – including Austria, Germany, the Netherlands, and Sweden – began pressing for a re-examination of the budget, suggesting that contributions be capped at 0.3 per cent of national income. This caused particular nervousness among net recipients such as Greece and Spain, which were concerned that they would have to take on a greater burden of funding rebates.

In terms of spending, the EU budget has raised a separate set of political problems. Like almost every budget, EU expenses consist of a combination of mandatory payments over which it has little or no choice (such as agricultural price supports) and discretionary payments (such as spending on regional or energy policy) regarding which there is more flexibility. EU spending is about equally divided between the two:

- In 2007, about 36 per cent of spending went on cohesion policy: development spending on poorer regions of the EU, including spending under the

European Social Fund aimed at helping offset the effects of unemployment, and investments in agriculture. The proportion of EU expenditures in this area has almost tripled since the mid-1970s.

- About 34 per cent of spending went to agricultural subsidies and supports to fisheries, and a further 10 per cent to rural development. Thanks to reforms in agricultural policy (see Chapter 7), the proportion of EU spending that goes to agriculture has fallen substantially from its peak during the 1970s, when it accounted for nearly 75 per cent of the budget.
- Just over 5 per cent went to administrative costs for the EU institutions. Critics of the EU routinely and misguidedly argue that the EU institutions spend far more than they actually do, and this has become one of the great myths of Euroscepticism. Recent Eurobarometer polls have found that between a quarter and one-third of Europeans think that administrative overheads are the single biggest item on the EU budget.
- Most of the balance (about €19 billion, or 15 per cent of the total) went to all the other policy areas in which the EU was active, including transport, energy, the environment, consumer policy, education, research and development, and foreign policy activities.

The EU budget is only partly a reflection of the policy areas in which the member states have agreed to transfer competence to the EU institutions. Looking at the figures, one could easily conclude that Europe was not much more than an exercise in social, agricultural, and regional development. But it must be remembered that much of the work of the EU involves little or no operational cost; for example, the entire single market programme has been based largely on the development of new laws and policies. The same is true of competition policy, environmental protection (where most of the costs are borne by national and local government or private business), trade matters, and fiscal policy. It must also be remembered that the member states have their own domestic budgets to invest in agriculture and in the kind of development supported by EU cohesion policy. So, in this sense, the EU budget is little more than a modest complement to the work of the member states.

Conclusions

While debates rage about the powers and nature of the European Union, with both support for and resistance to the expansion of EU powers and responsibilities, there is no question that its member states have lost powers to the EU and now have less policy independence than they did even twenty years ago. Integration has changed the relationship among EU member states at several levels: there has been a reduction in social differences, a harmonization of standards, laws and regulations, and removal of the physical and fiscal barriers that have differentiated the member states from one another.

There is also an emerging consensus that cooperation in a variety of other areas makes better sense than independent action, which can lead to unnecessary competition and duplication of effort. It is still too early to talk about a federal relationship among the member states, and between them and the EU institutions, but the trend is undoubtedly in that direction. Several levels of government are being created, all with independent powers. How far European cooperation will go depends on how we choose to define subsidiarity, but while this is moving higher up the agenda of EU negotiations, the definition of which issues are best dealt with at the level of the member state and which at the level of Europe remains fluid.

The member states still have a large measure of control over domestic policy, in a wide variety of important areas, from foreign policy to defence policy, tax policy, education, criminal justice, and health care. Compared, for example, to the American case, where the states now have only residual responsibilities in a modest selection of areas, and whose independence from national government in Washington DC is largely symbolic, the member states of the EU are still powerful, independent actors. This is unlikely to last indefinitely, however. Internal political and economic pressures have meant a gradual surrender of powers by the member states, a steady accumulation of responsibilities by the EU institutions, and – increasingly – the sense that Europe is governed both from Brussels and from 27 national capitals.

External pressures are also bound to continue to tighten the definition of Europe. Most of the rest of the world has not yet woken up to the implications of European integration, and to the idea that the 27 member states of the EU can and should be seen as a political and economic unit, that is exerting its global influence ever more effectively. Non-Europeans still treat Europeans mainly as citizens of individual member states, but this is slowly changing. As it does, it will give Europeans themselves a greater sense that they can be both European *and* British or Italian or Greek or Czech or Lithuanian. This in turn will give a tighter definition to the concept of Europe.

Chapter 6

The EU and its Citizens

The Maastricht treaty famously claimed that the goal of European integration was to create 'an ever closer union among the peoples of Europe, in which decisions are taken as closely as possible to the citizen'. But even the most enthusiastic supporters of the EU concede that it has been less a popular movement for change than a process begun and sustained by elites. The argument that the average European has few opportunities directly to influence the work of the EU has become serious enough to earn its own label: the democratic deficit.

'What about us?' the European public might reasonably ask. 'Does anyone in Brussels or our national capitals care what we think?' It sometimes seems as though the work of the EU goes on despite public opinion, which is often confused, sometimes doubtful, and in some cases actively hostile towards integration. Many of the key decisions on Europe are taken as a result of negotiations among national political leaders, who often refuse to put those decisions to a democratic test through a national referendum. Popular control over the European Commission and the European Court of Justice is only indirect, and although voter interests are directly represented in the European Parliament, it is one of the weaker European institutions.

To make matters worse, most Europeans are puzzled by the European Union. Its character and personality are hard to pin down, it is engaged on a journey to an unknown destination, the media often misrepresent the way it works, the Commission has done a mixed job of explaining what the EU does, and most academic writing on the EU makes the European project sound dull and legalistic. The result is confusion and apathy – as reflected, for example, in the poor turnout at European elections. The European Council decided as long ago as 1984 to promote 'a people's Europe' aimed at making Europe more 'real' to its people, and changes to the treaties have made the EU institutions more 'transparent' (more open to scrutiny), but the argument that popular enthusiasm can be generated by public policy is fundamentally flawed.

But there is a counter-argument to all this: the interests of citizens are represented by their national governments in the meeting rooms of the European Council and the Council of Ministers, and the powers and influence of the European Parliament are growing. The European Commission is no less transparent or responsive than national bureaucracies, and is so short-staffed that it actually makes more use of input from ordinary citizens, interest groups and corporations than do most of its national counterparts. And in many respects the democratic deficit in the EU is no bigger than the deficit in the member states, where citizens often complain that they are insufficiently consulted.

This chapter asks what integration has meant for Europeans, and for the nature of democracy in the European Union. It begins with an assessment of public attitudes towards integration, examining the relationship between public opinion and the decisions taken by national leaders, and discussing the problem of the democratic deficit. It then looks at the channels through which Europeans can express their opinions on EU policy – including elections, referendums, and interest groups – and asks how effective they have been, and what kinds of changes need to be made to bring Europe closer to its citizens.

Public opinion and Europe

The EU has a survey research programme known as Eurobarometer, which measures public opinion on a wide variety of issues relating to European integration, ranging from views on the general process to those on specific policies. Surveys over the last 30 years have found a waxing and waning of enthusiasm for the EU: support grew from 50 per cent in 1980 to a peak of 71 per cent in 1990, but fell in Germany after reunification, and then more widely throughout the EU in the wake of the controversy over Maastricht. By 2000–04, only 48–50 per cent of Europeans thought that membership was a 'good thing', although the number had recovered by 2007 to nearly 60 per cent (Eurobarometer polls 54 (2001), 61 (2004), and 67 (2007)).

There has also been first a decline and then a recovery in the number of people who believe that their country has benefited from membership, from 58 per cent in 1990 to 47 per cent in 2004 to 59 per cent in 2007. Among those most convinced of the benefits are the majority of Eastern European member states (Bulgaria and Hungary excepted) and older member states that have most clearly seen the economic benefits of membership, such as Ireland, Greece, and Spain. Eurosceptical Denmark is surprisingly enthusiastic (with four out of five Danes seeing benefits), stalwarts Germany and France are surprisingly lukewarm (just over half of respondents feel there have been benefits), and Britain predictably helps bring up the rear (see Figure 6.1).

Clearly, opinion about the EU is mixed, and there are several probable explanations for this. First, integration is still a relatively new issue for the average European. True, the Treaty of Rome was signed back in 1957, and work was under way on the construction of the common market in the 1960s and 1970s, but it has only been since the early 1990s that the effects of integration have really begun to have much of a direct impact on the lives of Europeans, who have been slow to appreciate its implications, and have

Figure 6.1 *Public opinion on EU membership*

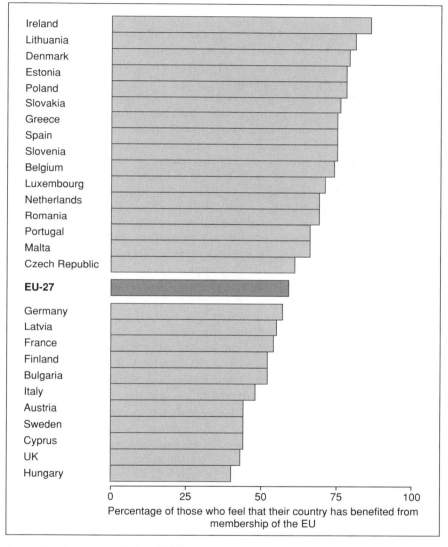

Source: Eurobarometer 67, June 2007.

only recently begun to think in much depth about the costs and benefits of integration, or to learn more about how the EU works.

Second, the actions of national and EU leaders are often at odds with the balance of public opinion. Take the issue of enlargement, for example: only 44 per cent of EU citizens supported the idea in 2000 while 35 per cent were opposed, and only 26 per cent saw it as a priority for the EU while 62 per cent did not. Undeterred, the Commission continued to negotiate with aspirant members, and 12 of them joined in 2004–07. In a similar vein, support for the euro strengthened in the lead-up to the final switch in 2002, but it was still lukewarm, with only 55 per cent in favour, 37 per cent against, and 8 per cent undecided. Equally undeterred, the leaders of 12 member states gave up their national currencies and switched to the euro, in every case failing to put the issue to a public referendum.

Although public opinion is occasionally overlooked, there is reason to question the extent to which it is well informed, and thus can be relied upon. The average European admits to knowing little about how the EU functions or what it does (see Box 6.1), which raises questions about the credibility of the views of many of those surveyed by Eurobarometer or other polls. And there have been several cases where polls have found initial majority opposition to an initiative, only to find it later replaced by majority support. Take, for example, the debate over the euro. Two years after its adoption, Europeans still had mixed views (47 per cent support and 44 per cent opposition). However, by 2006 there had been a switch to 60 per cent support, and nowhere was the change of heart more clear than in Germany: polls in the mid-1990s found that more than 60 per cent of Germans were opposed to the euro and unwilling to surrender the Deutschmark, but by 2006 two-thirds of Germans supported the euro (Eurobarometer, Flash EB 153, November 2003; Eurobarometer 66, December 2006). On some issues at least, the EU's political leaders can reasonably claim to be ahead of public opinion.

The third problem is that national leaders, European institutions, the media and academic experts have done a less than perfect job of explaining the implications, costs, and benefits of integration. To be fair, integration is a complex process that is constantly changing, and the implications of the changes have not always been fully understood even by policy makers – every new step has produced unanticipated effects (the single market programme being a prime example) and the switch to the euro was a leap into the unknown. But there has been no constitution to which citizens can refer for clarification, the treaties confuse as much as they illuminate, academics seem to be much more interested in what is wrong with the EU than what is right with it, and coverage in the Eurosceptical media misleads by emphasizing the negative at the expense of the positive.

Finally, and perhaps most fundamentally, there is the issue of the democratic deficit. This has been defined as 'the gap between the powers transferred to the Community level and the control of the elected Parliament over them' (Williams, 1991, p. 162), and as 'the shift in decision-making powers from the national to the EU level, without accompanying strengthening of parliamentary control of executive bodies' (Archer, 2000, p. 58). These definitions imply that the democratic deficit could be narrowed by giving the European Parliament greater powers, or by giving national legislatures greater control over EU institutions, but the problem is much broader, and a better

Box 6.1   The knowledge deficit

No matter how much the European Commission tries to make Europe seem more real to its citizens, and no matter how often the European Council talks about the importance of transparency, one critical reality remains: the average European knows little about how the EU works. This has been made clear by the results of Eurobarometer surveys, in which respondents are asked how much they know about the EU, its policies, and its institutions, and to give themselves a score out of 10, with 10 meaning they know a great deal and 1 meaning they know little. In 2002, no less than 71 per cent of respondents gave themselves (failing) scores of 5 or less, and the average for the sample worked out at 4.48. Just 2 per cent gave themselves scores of 9 or higher (Eurobarometer 58, Autumn 2002). The results were even worse in 2006, when 76 per cent gave themselves scores of 5 or less, and the average worked out at 4.10 (Eurobarometer 66, December 2006).

Those who feel they know the most include managers, university graduates, Europeans who use the media regularly, and those in the age range of 25–54. Those with the lowest levels of knowledge include manual workers, retirees, and people with a high school education or lower. In descending order, Luxembourgers, Danes, the Dutch, Austrians, Slovakians and Swedes felt they knew the most in 2006 (all above 4.7), while those who scored themselves lowest were Italians, Belgians, Bulgarians, French, Spaniards, Hungarians, and Britons (all 4.0 or below). It is interesting to note that Eurosceptic Danes scored themselves so high, while the French admitted to knowing so little.

When tested on the specifics in 2004, 55 per cent of respondents incorrectly thought that the EU was created just after the First World War, 50 per cent did not know that Members of the European Parliament were directly elected by voters, and 48 per cent incorrectly thought that the president of the European Commission was elected to that position. Meanwhile, nearly one in three Europeans had never even *heard* of the Council of Ministers, and about one in five had never heard of the European Commission, the Court of Justice, or the European Central Bank. Meanwhile, reflecting popular prejudices, one in four Europeans thought that the biggest item on the EU budget was the cost for officials, meetings, and buildings. (As we saw in Chapter 5, administration actually accounts for just over 5 per cent of EU spending, while cohesion and agriculture account for 70 per cent.) (All results from Eurobarometer 61, Spring 2004.)

These are not encouraging figures. It will be difficult for Europeans to develop a sense of belonging to the European Union if they continue to know so little about it, and as long as they know so little, they will continue to misunderstand its work, raising questions about the extent to which polling on the EU can be relied upon, and perpetuating the elitist qualities of EU decision making. Ironically, the lack of public knowledge persists despite attempts by the Commission to make its work more accessible through printed and audiovisual media and the internet.

definition of the democratic deficit might be the gap between the powers of European institutions and the ability of European citizens to influence their work and decisions.

The deficit takes several forms:

- The leaders of the member states, meeting as the European Council, reach decisions on important policy matters without always referring to their electorates. Less than half the EU-15 member states asked their citizens whether they wanted to join the European Community or the European Union, for example (in contrast to the newest eastern and Mediterranean members, where referendums were held in nine of the 12 countries). The Maastricht treaty was negotiated largely behind closed doors, poorly explained to the European public and – despite the important changes it made to the structure and goals of the EU – was put to the test of a referendum in only three member states (Denmark, France, and Ireland), one of which (Denmark) said no, and another of which (France) said yes only by a narrow margin. Amsterdam and Nice were equally poorly explained, and equally poorly tested.

- Despite its powers over proposing and developing new European laws, the Commission is subject to little direct or even indirect public account-ability. Appointments to the College of Commissioners must be approved by Parliament, but otherwise they are made without reference to voters. The president of the Commission is appointed as a result of a game of musical chairs run by the leaders of the member states, represents the views of the EU in several international forums without a mandate from the people, and has tenure that is subject to the whims of national leaders rather than the opinions of European citizens. Furthermore, there is little opportunity for citizens to take part in or contribute to the deliberations of the Commission, and only limited (albeit improving) opportunity for the European Parliament to hold it accountable for its initiatives and decisions.

- Most meetings of the Council of Ministers and the permanent repre-sentatives in Brussels are closed to the public, despite the fact that many important decisions on the content of new laws and policies, and on their acceptance or rejection, are taken there. Ministers and representatives take the kinds of decisions that – at the national level – are taken by members of elected assemblies, who are held accountable for their actions at elections, by the media, and in the court of public opinion.

- The European Parliament – the only democratically elected institution in the EU system – lacks several of the powers of a true legislature: it cannot raise revenues or introduce new laws, and it has only a limited ability to hold the Commission accountable for its decisions. It has worked hard to win new powers for itself, but most of the important decisions on EU law and policy are still taken elsewhere.

- The Court of Justice is the institution that best champions the cause of individual Europeans, being the final court of appeal for anyone who feels they have been hurt by European law, by its non-appliance, or by contradictions between European and national law. However, Europeans have no direct say in appointments to the Court, nor will they until the kind of legislative confirmation that is used for courts in many member states is adopted by the EU, and nominees to the Court of Justice and the Court of First Instance are investigated and confirmed by the European Parliament.

• The formal rights of Europeans relative to the EU institutions are modest: they have the right to vote in European elections, to petition Parliament or the European ombudsman (see below) if they feel their rights or interests have been violated, to access the documents of EU institutions (within certain limits), and to diplomatic representation outside the EU by any member state, provided their own country has no local representation.

The democratic deficit has contributed to a psychological barrier between Europeans and the EU, undermining the development of the ties that must exist between leaders and citizens in order for a system of government to work. True, most national systems of government also suffer from their own forms of democratic deficit, but the perception (at least) is that the problem is significantly worse in the EU, and that it has helped create a troubling distance between Europeans and the EU institutions. It is hardly surprising that the anti-European media are able to generate public distrust and resentment towards these institutions, which often appear distant and mysterious. This is most obvious in the case of the Commission. Although it is a small and productive institution with a small budget, and can only propose and oversee the implementation of new laws, it is often misrepresented by Eurosceptics as powerful, overpaid, unaccountable, and secretive. It is helped little by the fact that most of its staff occupy a series of anonymous buildings spread around the suburbs of Brussels, and that access to those buildings by ordinary Europeans is restricted.

The European Commission is well aware of the problems, and made some candid admissions in a White Paper published in 2001 on the issue of governance:

> Europeans ... increasingly distrust institutions and politics or are simply not interested in them. The problem ... is particularly acute at the level of the European Union. Many people are losing confidence in a poorly understood and complex system to deliver the policies that they want. The Union is often seen as remote and at the same time too intrusive ... [The EU] must start adapting its institutions and establishing more coherence in its policies so that it is easier to see what it does and what it stands for. A more coherent Union will be stronger at home and a better leader in the world ... Reform must be started now.

The paper also defended the work of EU institutions, noting that there is a perception that the EU cannot act effectively where a clear case exists (such as on unemployment, food safety scares, and security concerns on EU borders), that even where the EU acts effectively it does not get fair credit for its actions, that people do not see that improvements in their quality of life often come from European rather than national initiatives, that '"Brussels" is too easily blamed by Member States for difficult decisions that they themselves have agreed or even requested', and that many Europeans 'do not know the difference between the [EU institutions, and do not] understand who takes the decisions that effect them and do not feel the Institutions act as an effective channel for their views and concerns' (Commission of the European Communities, 2001a, pp. 3, 7). Unfortunately, rather than making specific suggestions for change, the paper made the usual mistake of talking in generalities and employing bureaucratic notions of better involvement, more openness, greater flexibility, 'partnership arrangements', 'a more systematic dialogue', and 'policy coherence' – whatever these mean.

The democratic deficit has been the topic of a scholarly debate dating back many years (see, for example, Andersen and Eliassen, 1995; Chryssochoou, 2000), but opinion is divided on whether or not it is the problem it seems. Franklin (1996, p. 197) once described the lack of proper democratic account-ability in the EU as 'a crisis of legitimacy', and this is a view still widely held. But Jolly (2007) argues that the suggestion that increasing the powers of the European Parliament can help remedy the deficit is based on the flawed assumption that the citizenry of Europe can be compared to the citizenries of individual member states, and that there is a European demos – or people – that cares about such matters. Much also depends upon how the EU is understood. If it is a federation, or has aspirations to become one, then the necessary links between citizens and EU institutions are indeed weak. But if it is a confederation, then the links are unusually strong. In a confederal system the links are expected to be no more than indirect: national governments answer to their citizens, and in turn represent them in the meeting chambers of the central authority. If this is accepted as a description of how the EU works, then the extent of the problem of the democratic deficit must be called into question.

The people's Europe

It took more than thirty years for political leaders to begin paying much attention to the question of how Europeans related to the process of integration. A report was drawn up in 1975 at the request of the European Council by Leo Tindemans, prime minister of Belgium, looking into the steps that might be taken to achieve a more integrated Europe that was 'closer' to its citizens. But nothing more was done until June 1984, when the EEC heads of government, meeting in Fontainebleau and spending most of their time agreeing reforms to the Community budget, briefly turned their attention to the idea of a 'people's Europe'. Pietro Adonnino, a former Italian MEP, was hired to chair a committee to put forward suggestions on how the EEC might be brought more closely in touch with its citizens.

The committee endorsed arrangements that had already been made for a European passport: national passports were phased out after 1986 and replaced by a standardized burgundy-coloured European passport bearing the words 'European Community' (later 'European Union') in the appropriate national language, and the name and coat of arms of the holder's home state. It also endorsed arrangements for a European flag, adopting the banner used since 1955 by the Council of Europe, the design of which – a circle of 12 gold stars on a blue background – is credited to Paul Levy, director of information for the Council (Bainbridge and Teasdale, 1995, pp. 188–9). The flag has since become a potent symbol of Europe – it can be seen flying on public buildings, shops and hotels throughout the EU, and is omnipresent at meetings of EU leaders. (It was popularly thought until the early 1990s that the 12 stars represented the 12 member states but the number was coincidental and the design has not been changed as membership of the EU has grown.) Meanwhile the European Commission created an annual 'Europe Day' (9 May, the anniversary of the Schuman Declaration), and adopted as the official European anthem the 'Ode to Joy' by Friedrich von Schiller, sung to the final movement of Beethoven's Ninth Symphony.

The Single European Act incorporated more of the Adonnino recommendations, the most important of which was the easing of restrictions on the free movement of people. At the time of the Treaty of Rome it was understood that an open labour market would be an essential part of a single market, but while all Community citizens were given the right to 'move and reside freely' within all the member states, this was subject to 'limitations justified on grounds of public policy, public security or public health'. Since integration in the early days was economically driven, priority was given to making it easier for people who were economically active to move from one state to another. Limits were placed on migration, initially because governments wanted to protect themselves against the possibility of a shortage of skilled workers, and then because of the lack of opportunities in the target states (Barnes and Barnes, 1995, p. 108).

Changes under the SEA allowed residents of the EU-15 to move and live anywhere in the EU, provided they were covered by health insurance and had enough income to avoid being a 'burden' on the welfare system of the country to which they moved (see Chapter 7 for more discussion). The removal of restrictions on movement has since helped make Europeans more mobile, and the number of non-nationals living in member states has risen. There were 5

Box 6.2   Euroscepticism

Public and political opinion on both the process of European integration and on the work of the European institutions is divided, but this is no surprise: all political endeavours in democratic systems will have their supporters and their opponents. Although the majority of Europeans support the process and feel that Europe has benefited from the work of the EU, there are many who disagree, and who advocate opinions ranging from wholesale reform of the process to its abandonment. Known variously as Eurorealists or Eurosceptics, critics of the EU believe that it is a harmful development, and regret the shift of sovereignty away from the member states to the EU institutions. Although the scale of criticism has not increased much in recent years, the Eurosceptic debate has become more visible thanks in part to its growing prominence in media debates about Europe, and it has played a greater role both in domestic politics – with the rise of minor parties opposed to European integration, and splits within mainstream parties between Europeans and anti-Europeans – and in the broader debate about integration, where it has had a critical role in opposition to treaty reforms, enlargement, and new policy initiatives.

The arguments put forward by Eurosceptics vary from country to country, and by issue and time, but they have included some or all of the following: that the European institutions have become too powerful and lack adequate transparency or democratic accountability; that integration is leading to the creation of a European superstate that is out of touch with citizens; that the EU is promoting unpopular policies (for the political left, for example, this means too much of an emphasis on free markets, and for the political right it means too much power in the hands of workers); that too many decisions are taken by European leaders without sufficient reference to citizens; that national sovereignty and identity are threatened by integration; that the demands of Europe are unsustainable for more fragile economies; that the EU institutions are elitist, and even – in more extreme cases – that there is a conspiracy among European leaders to move ahead without reference to citizens (for an example of Eurosceptic thinking, see Booker and North, 2005).

Euroscepticism is not a well-defined ideology so much as a set of related positions based on opposition to European integration. Taggart and Szczerbiak (2004) distinguish between hard and soft forms. The former is based on principled objections to the transfer of power to European institutions, it is relatively easy to see, and is most obvious in the case of those who argue for the withdrawal of their countries from the EU, and in the case of political parties whose platform is opposition to the EU, such as the People's Movement in Denmark and the UK Independence Party in Britain. Soft Euroscepticism is based on opposition to the direction being taken by the EU and a further expansion of its powers, and is both harder to see and more widespread than hard Euroscepticism.

million immigrants in 1950, 10 million in 1970, and there are probably more than twice that number today, although tracking has become more difficult as restrictions have been lifted. The flow of immigration was initially from south to north, and most of those moving were workers from Mediterranean states looking for higher-paying jobs, and then sending for their families to join them. Immigration flows today are more complex because there has been an increase in the movement of students, professionals, managers, and retirees. Where Europeans once moved involuntarily for economic reasons (and they still do, as shown by the number of Eastern Europeans moving west since 2004 in search of better-paid jobs), more are now moving voluntarily and for a variety of different reasons – they may be looking for a different cultural environment in which to live, looking to be educated in a different country, retiring to warmer parts of the EU, being posted by their employer, or looking for a new start in a new country.

Tourism has played an important role in making Europeans more mobile. Most Europeans could once afford to travel only within their own countries, but the advent of cheap mass tourism since the late 1960s has led to a marked increase in the numbers of people taking holidays in other member states. Day trips, weekend breaks, stays of one or two weeks, timeshares, package holidays, the purchase of holiday homes and extended visits for those who can afford the time have all combined to increase the ease and comfort with which Europeans travel around the continent. Language differences still pose a psychological barrier, but the easing of restrictions on movement has combined with the introduction of the euro to make other member states seem less 'foreign' to Europeans.

All these demographic shifts have been helped by another element of the Adonnino report that was formalized by the SEA: arrangements for the mutual recognition of professional qualifications. The Commission at first tried to work on each profession in turn, to reach agreement on the requirements, and then propose a new law. But this was time-consuming, and in 1991 a general systems directive was adopted by which the member states agreed to trust the adequacy of qualifications that required at least three years of professional training in other member states. The list of mutually recognized professions has since grown, and now includes accountants, librarians, architects, engineers, and lawyers. The Commission has meanwhile published a comparative guide to national qualifications for more than 200 occupations, helping employers work out equivalencies across the member states.

An important element in worker mobility is education and youth training, where the EU has been active in encouraging educational exchanges and addressing the critical issue of language training. The EU Lifelong Learning Programme (LLP), which replaces an earlier programme called Socrates, helps promote cross-border education through sub-programmes called Comenius (primary and secondary school partnerships), Erasmus (higher education) and Leonardo da Vinci and Grundtvig (vocational education). Since 1999 the Bologna process has improved the portability of qualifications with the goal of creating a European higher education area within which university education is compatible, comparable and transferable, and of making European higher education more attractive and internationally competitive. Bologna includes a European Credit Transfer and Accumulation System (ECTS) under which study at any university in the EU is translated into a common credit system, thus helping open up the educational options available to students in Europe. Almost every European country, along with Turkey and Russia, has signed on to the process.

The inability to speak other languages poses a practical barrier to the free movement of workers, and also stands as a potent reminder of the differences among Europeans. In addition to the 23 official languages of the EU – Bulgarian, Czech, Danish, Dutch, English, Estonian, Finnish, French, German, Greek, Hungarian, Irish, Italian, Latvian, Lithuanian, Maltese, Polish, Portuguese, Romanian, Slovak, Slovene, Spanish, and Swedish – Europeans must also deal with many local languages and dialects, and languages spoken within the EU by large numbers of nationals from non-EU states (notably Turks and Arabs). Almost all secondary school pupils in the EU learn at least one foreign language, although some have a better record than others. The rise of English as the lingua franca of Europe has been notable and inexorable, helped by its use in international commerce, entertainment, and sport; an estimated 85 per cent of secondary school pupils in the EU-25 were learning English as a second language in 2004, the most active English learners being in Austria, Denmark, Finland France, Germany, Greece, Latvia, the Netherlands, Spain and Sweden (where more than 95 per cent of students take English classes). Meanwhile, only 23 per cent of Germans are learning French, and only 18 per cent of French students are learning German (Eurostat, 2007, p. 91).

While tourism, the removal of technical barriers to movement and the promotion of language training all contribute to free movement, integration will never be able to do much about the social and psychological barriers posed by differences in the routine of daily existence. Americans can readily travel from one state to another in search of jobs or to improve the quality of their lives, and will find their daily routine changing little; they will find the same shops, the same banking system, the same money, the same programmes on television, and so on. By contrast, Europeans not only face different languages, but must also deal with a host of new norms and rules, including everything from different social customs to different sets of road signs and traffic regulations, different procedures for renting or buying a home, taking out car insurance or opening a bank account, and a new array of products on the shelves of local supermarkets. It is psychologically difficult enough for an American family to uproot itself and move hundreds of miles away, but the challenge of acculturation in the EU is much greater. An Italian moving to Denmark or a Swede moving to Hungary may eventually learn how things are done locally, but there is a limit to how much new EU laws and policies can help.

Another of the changes introduced by Maastricht was the promotion of European citizenship, although this is not what it seems. 'Citizenship' in democracies is usually defined as full and responsible membership of a state, and has been described by some social scientists as including the right to equality before the law, the right to own property, the right to freedom of speech, and the right to a minimum standard of economic and social welfare. But these are all rights that legal non-citizens of democracies also enjoy. What usually makes a citizen different from a non-citizen in practical terms is that a citizen can vote and run for elective office in his or her home state, can serve on a jury in that state, is eligible to serve in the armed forces of that state (although some countries allow non-citizens to serve), cannot be forcibly removed from that state to another, has the right to receive protection from the state when outside its borders, is recognized as a subject of that state by other governments, and must usually obtain the permission of other governments to travel through or live in their territory. More intangibly, citizens feel a sense of 'belonging' to their home state.

According to Maastricht 'every person holding the nationality of a member state shall be a citizen of the Union', but this is less substantial than it sounds. A step in the direction of real citizenship was taken with the agreement that citizens of a member state finding themselves in need in a non-EU country where their home state had no diplomatic representation could receive protection from the diplomatic and consular authorities of any EU state that had a local office. Another step was taken with the easing of restrictions on voting and running for elective office: citizens of one member state living in another can vote and stand for municipal and European Parliament elections (but not for national elections).

Another change introduced by Maastricht under the 'People's Europe' initiative was the creation of a European ombudsman. If a legal resident of the EU feels that any of the EU institutions (other than the Court of Justice and the Court of First Instance) is guilty of 'maladministration', and can make a compelling case, the European Parliament must ask the ombudsman to review the complaint, and if necessary carry out an investigation. Appointed for a five-year term that runs concurrently with the term of Parliament, the ombudsman is expected to be both impartial and independent of any government. Since the first ombudsman was appointed in 1995, the Commission has been the target of most of the complaints, which have included charges that it has failed to carry out its responsibilities as guardian of the treaties, that it lacks sufficient transparency, and that it has abused its power. The number of complaints has grown over the years, which is probably less a sign that things are getting worse than a sign that more people are becoming aware of the work of the ombudsman.

Participation and representation

Making Europe more 'real' to Europeans poses one set of challenges, but giving them a meaningful say in how it makes its decisions poses quite another. The realization by the citizens of the member states that they belong to a larger joint enterprise in which it is in their interest to participate must come from them. They need to understand the implications of integration, they must see and directly experience its benefits, and they must feel that they can have a real impact on the way it evolves. Of course, if the EU is a confederation then direct links between EU institutions and Europeans are unnecessary: the people hold their national governments accountable, which in turn represent their interests at the European level. But this is no more than an ideal, because not only do Europe's national leaders often pursue narrow political interests, but they often reach agreements on European policy in the face of public opposition.

As 'Europe' becomes a more important issue in national politics, as more Europeans take advantage of the removal of internal borders and travel restrictions, and as voters figure policies on Europe into their calculations about choosing among competing national political parties and leaders, so Europeans will have more influence on policies and positions adopted in the meeting rooms and hallways of the Commission, the Council of Ministers, and the European Council. Until this happens, there are three other channels through which they can influence the outcome of European policy decisions: voting in European elections and referendums, and supporting the work of interest groups.

European elections

Held every five years since 1979, elections to the European Parliament (EP) give Europeans the opportunity to decide the make-up of the EP, which has an increasingly effective role in making European law. Voters must be 18 years of age and must be citizens of one of the EU member states. Since Maastricht, they have been allowed to vote in whichever country they have residence, and even to run for the EP wherever they live, regardless of citizenship. To vote they must make a declaration to the local electoral authority and meet local qualifications; to run for office they must meet qualifications in their home state. The minimum age for candidates varies from 18 to 25 years, depending on the country of residence, and there are also different rules on how candidates qualify; some member states do not allow independent candidates, some require candidates to pay deposits, others require them to collect signatures, and so on.

Every member state uses multi-member districts and variations on the theme of proportional representation (PR), either treating their entire territory as a single electoral district (Germany, Spain, Poland and most of the smaller EU states) or dividing it up into several Euro-constituencies (Britain, France, Italy, Belgium, and Ireland). Seats are then divided among parties according to their share of the vote. PR has the advantage of reflecting more accurately the proportion of the vote given to different parties, but it also results in many small parties being elected to Parliament. Also, PR leads to voters being represented by a group of MEPs of different parties, and constituents may never get to know or develop ties with a particular MEP.

Once elected, MEPs sit not in national blocks but in cross-national ideological groups with roughly similar goals and values. By the rules of the EP, a group must have at least 20 members, who must be elected from at least one-fifth of member states. No one party group has ever had enough seats to form a majority, so groups must work together in order to achieve a majority. The balance of power and the order of business is also affected by frequent changes in the number and make-up of party groups. Three groups have developed a particular consistency over time – the Socialists on the left, the Liberals on the centre-right, and the European People's Party on the right – but they have always had to share power with a cluster of smaller parties with a variety of values and opinions (see Box 6.3).

Unfortunately, turnout at EP elections is low, compromising the credibility and political influence of Parliament. From a modest peak of 63 per cent in 1979, figures fell to just under 57 per cent in 1994, then took a relatively sharp fall to just over 49 per cent in 1999, tailing off to just under 46 per cent in 2004. Belgium and Luxembourg usually have the highest turnout (85–92 per cent), but in most member states fewer than half of all voters now cast ballots. Several countries started out on a high note upon joining the EU, only to see their voters lose enthusiasm: thus Portugal fell from 72 to 39 per cent, Austria from nearly 70 to 42 per cent, and Finland from 60 to 40 per cent. Optimists expected that the figures in 2004 for new members in their first flush of membership would be high, but they turned out to be among the worst ever: less than 42 per cent turned out in most countries, and just one in five in Poland and Slovakia (see Figure 6.2).

There are several explanations for this state of affairs, the most compelling of which is the relative significance of 'first-order' and 'second-order' elections (Reiff and Schmitt, 1980; Hix, 2005, pp. 180–4). Voters give priority to national elections, because they determine who controls the national executive and legislatures, which in turn make the decisions that are most immediate and relevant in the lives of citizens. National elections are also hard-fought and attract the most media attention. By contrast, European elections are seen as second-order elections because there is less at stake; there is no potential change of government involved, they draw much less media attention, and most Europeans either know very little about what Parliament does, or are confused or badly informed about European issues.

Box 6.3   Parties in the European Parliament

The 2004 European elections brought 160 different parties to the EP, many of which consisted of as few as one or two members. Since there is little that these parties can achieve alone, it is in their interests to build alliances with other parties, and thus they have formed cross-European party groups. Some of these have been marriages of convenience, but most have built more consistency and focus with time (for details, see Bardi, 2002; Corbett *et al.*, 2005, Chapter 5). Moving from left to right on the ideological spectrum, the party groups in 2007 were as follows:

- *European United Left-Nordic Green Left (GUE-NGL).* One of the least consistent of the party groups, it is made up mainly of German, Italian, and Czech leftists.
- *Socialist Group (PSE).* This is the main left-wing group in Parliament, and currently the second largest, with a few ex-communists on the left but dominated by more moderate social democrats. It has members from all but two EU states, with France, Spain, and Germany sending the biggest contingents.
- *Alliance of Liberals and Democrats for Europe (ALDE).* Consistently the third largest group in the EP, the ALDE contains members from all but five member states. Difficult to pinpoint in ideological terms, most of its members sit in or around the centre, and its biggest national blocs are from Britain, Italy, France and Romania.
- *Greens-European Free Alliance (Greens-EFA).* Has seen substantial growth in recent years, with new additions to its numbers after the 2004 elections making it the fifth biggest party group in the EP. Pursues a variety of issues related to social justice.
- *European People's Party and European Democrats (EPP-ED).* The major right-wing group in Parliament, the EPP overtook the socialists in 1999 to become the biggest party group, with MEPs from every EU member state. The delegations from Germany, the UK, Spain, and Italy are the largest.
- *Union for Europe of the Nations (UEN).* A small group of centre-right MEPs driven by opposition to Maastricht and federalism, and who have so far refused to link up with their most natural ally, the EPP. Most of its members come from Poland and Italy.
- *Independence/Democracy Group (ID).* Created after the 2004 elections, this consists of self-described 'EU critics, eurosceptics, and eurorealists'. It opposes a European superstate and political centralization.
- *Identity, Tradition and Sovereignty Group (ITS).* The most conservative and nationalist party group, ITS was formed in 2007 when the accession of Bulgaria and Romania gave it enough MEPs to apply for group status.

Figure 6.2   *Turnout at European Parliament elections, 2004*

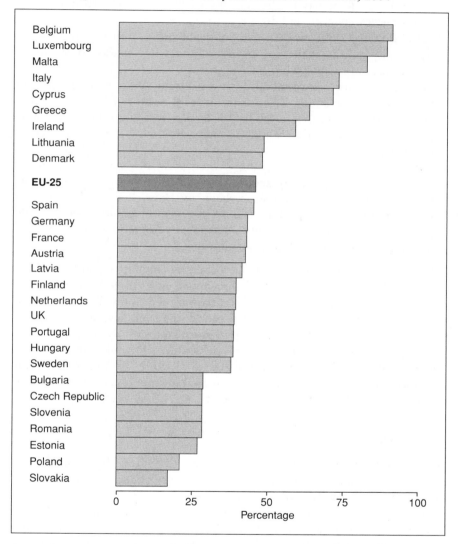

Source: European Parliament website, http://www.europarl.europa.eu. Bulgarian elections were held in May 2007 and Romanian elections in November 2007, and their turnout figures are not included in the EU average.

Among the other explanations for low turnout:

- EU voters have developed relatively few psychological ties to the European Parliament, which may be the best known of all the EU institutions, but still seems anonymous and distant to most.
- MEPs do not become well-known political figures, so there is little of the personality politics at the European level that often sparks voter interest and turnout in national elections.
- Low turnout mirrors a general downward trend in national elections in many EU member states. Where turnout at EP elections fell by 13 per cent between 1979 and 1999, it fell by 10–14 per cent over roughly the same period in (for example) France, Germany, Ireland, and the Netherlands (Corbett, 2001).
- Turnout is often a reflection of how voters view their home governments and national political issues, and many will use their vote to send a message to national politicians. This is exacerbated by the way most political parties run as national parties, rather than as members of genuine Europe-wide party groups. So if voters are not interested by national politics, they are less likely to turn out at European elections.

One of the suggestions made by the Adonnino committee that has not yet been implemented was for the establishment of a uniform electoral procedure for European elections. The idea was first outlined in the Treaty of Paris, repeated in the Treaty of Rome and raised again on several subsequent occasions, but little has been achieved in practical terms. Even the definition of the word 'uniform' in this context is debatable, and while a decision was taken at the 1974 Paris summit that the goal would be met if European elections were secret, direct, based on universal suffrage and held on the same day, this has not been the end of the story.

Referendums

National referendums allow European voters to express their opinions on narrow (but usually important) topics. Not every country uses them, and they have only been used for selected issues, but they have come to play an increasingly important role in the process of European integration, and there has been increased moral and political pressure for their use. Some have been little more than tools for political manipulation, as when Britain held a referendum in 1975 that was ostensibly about whether or not Britain should stay in the Community following renegotiation of the terms, but was actually designed to settle a division of opinion about Europe within the government (Nugent, 2006, p. 483). Others have had a significant impact on the course of European integration, as when the terms of Maastricht and Nice were amended following their rejection in referendums in, respectively, Denmark and Ireland. Voters are so rarely given the opportunity to express their views on EU matters that referendums are often used to express opinions on the EU and European integration more generally, rather than just the issue at hand.

Most referendums have fallen into one of two major categories:

- *Whether or not to join the EU*. These have been held only by newer members of the EU, beginning with the votes held in Denmark, Ireland, and Norway in 1972. A majority of Danes and Irish approved, but a majority of Norwegians disapproved, and said no in a second referendum in 1994. The Swiss also said no to EU membership in a referendum in 2001. All three countries that joined the EU in 1995 held referendums, as did nine of the ten countries that joined in 2004 (the exception was Cyprus). The results were all positive for membership, but levels of enthusiasm varied: the Slovaks, Lithuanians, and Slovenians were the most supportive, with 90–92 per cent majorities in favour, while in Finland, Sweden, and Malta, bare majorities of just over 50 per cent said yes. The only example of a territory leaving the EU came in 1982, when the 53,000 voters of Greenland – which had joined in 1973 as part of Denmark – opted to leave.

- *Whether or not to accept a new treaty*. This has only been a recent phenomenon, and only in a select few countries. Denmark held a vote on the Single European Act in 1986, mainly because the government wanted to outmanoeuvre parliament, which had voted against ratification. Most Danes (56.2 per cent) said yes on that occasion, but a bare majority of 50.7 per cent turned down Maastricht in 1992, and 54 per cent of Irish voters turned down the Treaty of Nice in 2001. The negative votes gave Europeans pause for thought, and resulted in changes to the treaties. New referendums in both countries subsequently went in favour of the treaties. The Danish vote on Maastricht also drew attention to the elitist nature of EU decision making, and obliged European leaders to think more about public opinion. Referendums were also held in 1998 in Denmark and Ireland on the terms of the Amsterdam treaty, and both were positive. Undoubtedly the most politically significant referendums to date were those in the Netherlands and France in 2005 on the constitutional treaty, when – respectively – 61 per cent and 55 per cent voted no. The French vote was particularly newsworthy, given that France has been a staple of European integration from the beginning.

Just as important as the result of some of these votes has been the symbolism often attached to the *absence* of referendums. The issue of adopting the euro was particularly controversial, and was put to a vote in just two countries, Denmark and Sweden, where the outcomes were both negative. Meanwhile, none of the 15 governments that adopted the euro have held a referendum, often for fear of a similar result. The Blair administration in Britain promised a referendum when the time was right, but never did, again mainly for fear of a negative vote; the Eurobarometer 61 poll (2004) found 61 per cent of Britons opposed to adopting the euro. Soon after coming to office, Gordon Brown found himself in trouble over the issue of the Lisbon treaty, claiming that it was significantly different from the constitutional treaty and thus did not merit a referendum, but failing to convince his critics.

Interest groups

While national leaders promote national agendas, non-governmental organizations (NGOs) – or interest groups – have cut across national frontiers to promote the shared sectional interests of groups of people in multiple member states. In addition to the EU bodies that represent these interests, such as the European Economic and Social Committee and the Committee of the Regions (see Box 4.3), the last 20–25 years have seen the growth of hundreds of NGOs that represent the views of a large number of groups of people with a stake in EU policy and law. Many are an outgrowth of pre-existing national groups, others have been set up specifically to respond to European issues, and many have opened offices in Brussels in order to be close to the Commission and the Council of Ministers. Studies in the 1990s indicated that there were nearly 700 groups working to influence decisions taken at the European level, and that about two-thirds of them had existed since 1980 or earlier. Just over 60 per cent were business groups, 21 per cent dealt with public interest issues and 16 per cent were professional organizations (Aspinwall and Greenwood, 1998).

The growth in interest group activity at the European level has paralleled the growth in the power and influence of the EU institutions, or the 'European-ization' of policy areas that were once the preserve of national governments (Mazey and Richardson, 1996, p. 200). The groups have not always simply followed the evolution of the EU, going wherever new opportunities for influence have presented themselves, but have often been actively involved in pushing the EU in new directions. Business leaders, for example, were champions of the single market, arguing that competition among European corporations was a handicap to their ability to take on the Americans and the Japanese. At the same time, the European Commission has encouraged interest group activity; it uses groups as a source of expert knowledge and to test the viability of new laws, and also uses them to monitor the compliance records of member states: most groups are only too happy to blow the whistle on their home governments if they are not implementing EU law.

Historically, business and labour groups have been the most active, mainly because the process of integration was for so long driven by economic issues (Greenwood, 2003). As the EU won new powers over competition policy, mergers, and the movement of workers, so business and labour groups made greater efforts to influence the Commission and the Council of Ministers. Not only are individual corporations represented either directly or through lobbying firms in Brussels, but several cross-sectoral federations have been created to represent the interests of a broader membership. These include BusinessEurope (formerly the Union of Industrial and Employers' Confederations of Europe (UNICE)), which represents 39 national business federations from 33 countries, the European Round Table of Industrialists (which brings together the chief executives of major European corporations such as British Airways, Renault, Bayer, Fiat, Philips, Volvo, and Nokia), and the EU Committee of the American Chamber of Commerce (which represents American firms active in Europe).

Labour is also represented in Brussels, notably through groups such as the European Trade Union Confederation (ETUC), whose membership consists of more than 80 European-level industry federations and national labour federations from 36 countries, including Britain's TUC, France's CGT, and Germany's DGB. Professional interests are represented by groups such as the Council of European Professional and Managerial Staff (EUROCADRES), and by associations representing everything from architects to dentists, journalists, opticians and vets. Several Brussels-based interest groups include member organizations from outside the EU, a reflection of how much the EU has come to matter to business and labour throughout Europe.

Groups representing public interests, such as consumer issues and the environment, have also become more active as the EU has become more involved in matters about which they care. Until the 1970s, environmental groups focused their attentions on national governments, because they had different priorities, and because most environmental policy in Western Europe was still made at the national level. As the Community became more active on the environment in the mid-1980s, it became a more profitable target for interest group pressure. The new emphasis given to EU-level activities was reflected in the opening of offices in Brussels by such groups as Friends of the Earth, Greenpeace, and the World Wide Fund for Nature, while many other groups employed full-time lobbyists. As environmental groups became more active, so did groups representing the industrial perspective on environmental issues, such as the European Chemical Industry Council (Cefic), Eurelectric (representing national electricity supply associations), and the European Crop Protection Association.

Increased access to EU policy makers led in turn to a more systematic approach among environmental groups to lobbying at the European level, and a clear trend towards approaching domestic environmental problems as EU-wide problems. The complexity of those problems encouraged domestic groups to work more closely together and to form transnational coalitions, the best known of which is the European Environmental Bureau (EEB). Founded in 1974 with the encouragement of the Commission, the EEB is an umbrella body for national interest groups in the EU, and acts as a conduit for the representation of those groups in the EU institutions, particularly the Commission. The Bureau now claims to represent more than 140 national environmental groups with a combined membership of 25 million (for more information, see McCormick, 2001, pp. 116–22).

The methods that European-level groups use are similar to those used by groups at any level: promoting public awareness in support of their cause, building membership numbers in order to increase their influence and credibility, representing the views of their members, forming networks with other interest groups, providing information to the EU institutions, meeting with EU lawmakers in an attempt to influence the content of law, and monitoring the implementation of EU law at the national level.

Aspinwall and Greenwood (1998) argue that the representation of interests at the European level has become more diversified and specialized, and that European groups are becoming protagonists: they now try to influence policy rather than simply to monitor events, using increasingly sophisticated means to attract allegiance. A symbiotic relationship has developed between the Commission and interest groups, with the former actively supporting the work of many groups and giving them access to its advisory committee meetings, and the latter doing what they can to influence the content and development of policy and legislative proposals as they work their way through the Commission.

The activities of interest groups have helped offset the problem of the democratic deficit by offering Europeans channels outside the formal structure of EU institutions through which they can influence EU policy. They have also helped focus the attention of the members of interest groups on how the EU influences the policies that affect their lives, have helped draw them more actively into the process by which the EU makes its decisions, and have encouraged them to bypass their national governments and to focus their attention on European responses to shared and common problems.

Conclusions

The European Union has helped redefine the relationship among Europeans. Where they have long identified themselves in national terms, and have been tied economically, legally and culturally to one nation state or another, the reduction of the barriers to trade and to the movement of individuals over the past decade has encouraged Europeans to think of themselves as part of a larger entity with broader interests. Common policies have resulted in key powers over the lives of individual Europeans shifting to Brussels, so that an increasing number of Europeans feel the effect of decisions made at the EU level. Personal mobility has increased and, cultural barriers aside,

Europeans have taken more interest in neighbours who have long been considered as 'foreign' rivals and occasionally a direct threat to their own national interests.

However, while this horizontal integration has been taking place, the vertical ability of Europeans directly to influence the European Union has lagged. Integration has been driven by the priorities and the values of the leaders of the member states, who have made most of their decisions with limited reference to their citizens. The result has been the creation of a European governing structure that is only indirectly accountable to the views of the people who live within it. European law is proposed and implemented by a European Commission whose leadership is not accountable to European voters. Key decisions on the adoption of new laws and policies are taken by national representatives meeting in closed session as the Council of Ministers. The only institution that directly represents European citizens – the European Parliament – is denied the power to propose new laws, and must share the power to adopt new laws with the Council of Ministers.

Europeans are divided about the wisdom of integration, with only half of them agreeing that membership has been a 'good thing' for their country, and most of them admitting that they do not understand how the EU works. As European institutions struggle to sell the concept of integration to the citizens of the member states, they are handicapped by the absence of effective channels of accountability, and by the perpetuation of the democratic deficit. Changes made under the people's Europe programme and as a result of new treaties have made Europe more real to its citizens, but uniform passports, a European flag, and student exchange programmes fall far short of the kinds of changes needed to make Europeans feel as though they are truly connected to the EU. The democratic deficit can only be addressed by a wholesale reform of the EU institutions aimed at making them accountable to the citizens of Europe instead of to the leaders of the member states. But this is something that few national leaders would willingly contemplate even if their citizens were more enthusiastic than they appear to date.

Chapter 7

Economic Policy

Economic issues have dominated the life and work of the European Union. Beginning with the experiment in pooling coal and steel production, and moving through the customs union, the Common Agricultural Policy, exchange rate stability, the single market, and the single currency, the EU agenda has been driven since the beginning by matters involving trade, tariffs, markets, currencies, competition, and labour mobility. It has only been relatively recently that the agenda of integration has broadened to include a wider variety of policy issues, from social affairs to the environment (addressed in the next chapter).

The priority given to economic integration was made clear from the outset in three of the primary goals of the Treaty of Rome: a customs union in which all obstacles to trade among EEC members would be removed and a common external tariff agreed for all goods coming into the EEC; a single market in which there was free movement of people, money, goods, and services; and a Common Agricultural Policy by which farmers were paid guaranteed prices for their produce, agricultural markets were stabilized, and food supplies were assured. The customs union was completed without much fanfare with the agreement in 1968 of a common external tariff, but non-tariff barriers to trade among the member states persisted, including variations in technical standards and quality controls, different health and safety standards, and different rates of indirect taxation. Prospects for the single market seemed to move beyond reach in the mid-1970s as recession encouraged member states to protect their national markets. Meanwhile, the Common Agricultural Policy soaked up Community spending, and led to massive overproduction by European farmers.

By the 1980s it had become clear that urgent action was needed to reverse the EC's relative economic decline, and a boost had to be given to the single market programme in order to respond to foreign competition. A first step was taken in 1985 with the signing of the Schengen Agreement, offering a fast-track for the removal of border controls. In 1986 came the signature of the Single European Act, aimed at removing the final barriers to the completion of the single market by the end of 1992. Finally, there were faltering attempts to build exchange rate stability, which led in 1999 to the creation of the single European currency, and in 2002 to the final switch in 12 member states to the euro.

The changes wrought by these three ventures have redefined the character of Europe and the policy reach of the EU. There is now all but free movement of people, money, goods and services among the western EU states, with greater freedoms being extended to the eastern states. The EU's external security regime has expanded in response to concerns about the dismantling of internal borders. European corporations have engaged in an aggressive programme of cross-border mergers and acquisitions. The EU has supported the building of a system of trans-European networks aimed at integrating the transport, energy supply, and telecommunications sectors of the member states. The place of the euro in the international monetary system has expanded, and with it the global influence of the EU. And in 2000 the Lisbon Strategy was launched, aimed optimistically at making the EU the most competitive and dynamic economy in the world within ten years. Progress on that goal has been mixed, but the expanded size and reach of the European marketplace has – regardless – created a new economic superpower whose global role cannot be ignored.

The single market

At its summit in Brussels in February 1985, the European Council agreed that it was time to refocus on one of the original goals of the European Community: the completion of a single market in which there would be no barriers to trade. This project had been so central to the identity and the purpose of the Community that throughout the 1960s and 1970s it was known interchangeably as the Common Market. At the core of the single market were the 'four freedoms', or the removal of barriers to the free movement of:

- *People*: legal residents of Community member states should be allowed to live and work in any other member state and have their professional qualifications recognized.
- *Money*: currency and capital should be allowed to flow freely across borders, and Community residents should be able to use financial services in any member state.
- *Goods*: businesses should be able to sell their products throughout the Community, and consumers should be free to buy those products in any member state without incurring costs or penalties.
- *Services*: every kind of service – from architecture to banking, insurance, legal aid, medicine and beyond – should be available in any member state, regardless of the home base of the provider.

In spite of its political prominence, worryingly little progress had been made on the single market, mainly because the member states continued to go their own ways on economic policy, protecting national markets and corporations, and working independently to deal with high unemployment, low investment, and slow growth. National monopolies in transport and communications more often bought services and products from national sources rather than seeking more competitive options outside their borders. Technical standards varied across the Community, adding a potent block to trade in merchandise. Member states had laws requiring foreign firms active within their borders to buy goods with local content. And a host of border and customs controls persisted, along with varying rates of value-added tax (see Neal and Barbezat, 1998, pp. 9–11).

When Jacques Delors became president of the European Commission in 1985, movement on the single market was at the top of his agenda. Trade and industry commissioner Lord Cockfield was charged with drawing up a White Paper outlining the changes that needed to be made (Commission of the European Communities, 1985). This in turn became the basis of the Single European Act (SEA), which was signed in February 1986 and came into force in July 1987. Unlike the debates that were later to surround the development of the treaties of Maastricht, Nice, and Amsterdam, the SEA was a relatively uncontroversial document. Even the arch-Eurosceptic Margaret Thatcher was supportive: 'At last, I felt, we were going to get the Community back on course, concentrating on its role as a huge market, with all the opportunities that would bring to our industries' (Thatcher, 1993, p. 556). (She was later to change her mind.)

The fundamental goal of the SEA was to remove the remaining non-tariff barriers to the single market by the end of 1992. These barriers took three main forms:

- *Physical barriers.* The most obvious of these were customs and border checks. Member states still controlled the movement of people (they were particularly concerned about illegal immigrants – see Box 7.1), collected taxes on alcohol, tobacco, and luxury goods, enforced different health standards, controlled banned products, and tried to prevent the spread of animal and plant diseases. Not only were these checks expensive, inconsistent, and time-consuming, but they interfered with the free flow of people, goods, and services. They were also a psychological barrier to integration, reminding Europeans that they still lived in a region of independent nation states.
- *Fiscal barriers.* The major problem here was different levels of indirect taxation, such as excise duties and value-added tax (VAT, a form of consumption tax); these distorted competition, created artificial price differences, and posed a handicap to trade. Rates of VAT in the 1980s varied between 12 and 22 per cent, and variations in the levels of excise duties reflected different levels of national concern about human health; thus French smokers in the 1980s paid nearly twice as much for cigarettes as those in Spain, Irish smokers four times as much, and Danish smokers

Box 7.1   Illegal immigration and terrorism

Just as the United States has long been a magnet for immigrants from Mexico and Latin America, so the EU has the same kind of attraction for workers from Eastern Europe, the Balkans, Turkey, North Africa, and the Middle East. But with restrictions on the numbers allowed in legally, immigration has gone underground, and the smuggling of people into the EU has become a major industry, with an estimated value of several billion euros annually. Run mainly by organized crime, the smuggling has grown as a result of a combination of the opening up of Eastern Europe and the removal of internal borders among Schengen signatories. There are estimates that as many as half a million people are arriving in the EU each year, entering from North Africa, the Balkans, Eastern Europe, and Russia via Spain, Italy, Austria, Germany, and Finland. Most of the illegal immigrants are Afghans, Albanians, Bangladeshis, Iranians, Iraqis, or Kurds. Once inside the EU, many claim to be refugees and apply for asylum (see Guiraudon, 2004).

For its part, terrorism was a problem for Europeans long before Americans were made aware of its harsh brutality in September 2001. Multiple groups were at work in Europe as early as the 1960s and 1970s, ranging from Irish, Basque, and Corsican separatists to the Red Brigades in Italy, and the Red Army Faction and the Baader-Meinhof group in Germany. The cross-border control of terrorists had been discussed as early as 1975 by senior officials from justice and home affairs ministries, meeting biannually as the Trevi Group to exchange information. They gradually expanded their interests to take in other security threats, such as those posed by organized crime and football hooligans. A particular concern was the relative ease with which terrorists could enter the Community from third countries through those member states with the weakest border controls, such as Greece or Portugal. The threat of terrorism has obviously achieved a new prominence and notoriety since the terrorist attacks on the United States, although the EU (the bombings in Madrid and London notwithstanding) has been less of a target than the United States and US interests overseas.

In order to help deal with concerns arising from the removal of internal border checks, member states have agreed common measures on visas, immigration, extradition, and political asylum, and have improved cooperation among national police forces, to which end the European Police Office (Europol) was created in 1995, and began operations in 1998. Based in The Hague, Europol was initially defined as an intelligence service, responsible for gathering and analyzing information about drug trafficking in support of the work of national police forces. Its interests have since expanded to include terrorism, illicit trafficking in radioactive and nuclear materials and in people, illegal immigration, money laundering, and organized crime, not only from internal sources, but from Turkey, Poland, Russia, and Colombia. Modelled in part on Interpol, the worldwide police organization, Europol cannot carry out investigations or bring prosecutions. It is building a computer base of information that can be accessed by its liaison offices in the member states, and by national police forces in the interests of building cooperation across borders (see Occhipinti, 2003, 2004).

six times as much. Agreement was reached in the 1990s on an EU-wide VAT system, although this has not yet resulted in the elimination of rate variation. Much more difficult has been the suggestion that the EU work towards harmonizing tax rates in other areas, notably corporation tax or the setting of minimum withholding tax on savings. Such a suggestion, no matter how limited the scope, is seen by many as the first step towards the development of EU authority over the setting of income tax, a notion that is deeply troubling to many national governments.

- *Technical barriers.* The single market was handicapped by different technical regulations and standards, most based on different safety, health, environmental, and consumer protection standards. The Community tried to remove technical barriers by developing EU-wide standards, but this was time-consuming and tedious, and did little to discourage the common image of interfering Eurocrats. Three breakthroughs helped clear many bureaucratic and political hurdles: a 1979 decision by the Court of Justice established the principle of mutual recognition (if a product met local standards in one country, it could not be barred from another); a 1983 mutual information directive requiring member states to tell the Commission and the other member states if they planned to develop new domestic technical regulations; and a 'new approach' to technical regulation introduced by the Cockfield report, whereby instead of the Commission working out agreements on every rule and regulation, the Council of Ministers would agree laws with general objectives, and detailed specifications could then be drawn up by existing private standards institutes, such as the European Standardization Committee (CEN) and the European Confederation of Posts and Telecommunications Administrations (ETSI).

A critical step in the final removal of border controls came in June 1985 when France, West Germany, and the Benelux countries signed the Schengen Agreement. Named for the town in Luxembourg near which it was signed, the Agreement set off a series of meetings among the five countries aimed at agreeing and implementing the measures needed to end internal border controls. The process was delayed by problems setting up the computerized Schengen Information System (SIS, a database of undesirables whose entry to the Schengen area local officials wanted to control), and although a trial application began in early 1995, the Agreement was to remain informal until the Treaty of Amsterdam brought it under the umbrella of the Union in 1997. All but two western EU member states – along with Iceland and Norway – joined Schengen, the exceptions being Britain, which has cited concerns about security and its special problems and needs as an island state, and Ireland, which has a customs agreement with Britain. Extension of the agreement to Eastern Europe had been slowed by concerns about weaknesses in the management of the EU's external borders in the east. But with investment in the training of border police, the improvement of border controls, and the integration of the new member states into SIS, ten of the 12 countries (along with Switzerland) joined in December 2007/2008, leaving only Cyprus, Bulgaria, and Romania outside the fold, but not for much longer.

Effects of the single market

The Single European Act was, in its time, the most radical of all the steps taken in the process of European integration since the signing of the treaties of Paris and Rome. It not only accelerated the process of economic integration, but it also changed the lives of every European, making economic integration more real to millions of people. The effects have been felt across a wide spectrum of activities, and have moved the EU into generally predictable but sometimes surprising new areas of activity.

Freedom of movement

Europeans have felt the impact of falling borders most obviously in their personal freedom of movement: almost any legal resident of an EU member state can now live and work in any other EU member state, open a bank account, take out a mortgage, transfer unlimited amounts of capital, and even vote (in some countries) in local and European elections. More specifically, anyone who is a citizen of an EU member state can freely enter any other member state and stay for up to three months, and the most that they will be asked to do is to present a valid identity card or passport. For stays of more than six months, they must either have a job to go to, or must have sufficient resources and health insurance to ensure that they do not become a burden on local social services, or be a student engaged in a formal course of education, or be a family member of someone who meets one of these three criteria. No visas or residence permits are required, although new arrivals may be required to register with local authorities. After five years of legal residence, citizens of other EU member states can apply for permanent residence in the new country. Rights of entry and residence can only be limited or denied on the grounds of public policy, public security, or public health, and not for economic reasons. As noted earlier, there are greater restrictions on residents of Eastern Europe, because of concerns about migration, but these will ease with time.

Migration historically has been driven by economic and political factors – people looking for better jobs, or escaping persecution and instability. In the case of the EU, however, the pressures for migration are now much broader and based more on freedom of choice. Thus people may be looking to move to a new culture, seeking a different climate, or retiring to a different part of the continent; in other words, they are making a free choice to move. With the removal of most of the physical and legal barriers to free movement, the remaining barriers are increasingly psychological, and there will be little that the EU can do to take care of these. Language barriers are a potent disincentive, but cultural barriers must also be taken into consideration: the reluctance that some Europeans will have to move to another country where the history, popular culture, and the simple everyday functions of living are often quite different from what they know at home.

Trans-European networks

A key element in the successful operation of markets is integrated infrastructure. Realizing this, the EU has been actively involved in the development of trans-European networks (TENs) aimed at integrating the different transport, energy supply, and telecommunications systems of the member states. Until 1987, harmonization of the transport sector was one of the great failures of the single market: little of substance had been done to deal with problems such as an airline industry split along national lines, time-consuming cross-border checks on trucks, national systems of motorways that did not connect with each other, air traffic control systems using 20 different operating systems and 70 computer programming languages, and telephone lines incapable of carrying advanced electronic communications. Two developments have since made a difference.

First, there has been a dramatic increase in tourism. Europe is the biggest tourist destination in the world, capturing about 60 per cent of the world tourist trade; in 2004, France and Spain were the two biggest tourist destinations in the world, and Italy, Britain, and Germany were all ranked in the top ten (World Tourism Organization website, 2007). In spite of concerns about terrorism and about the overcrowding of the most popular attractions, Europeans are travelling in ever greater numbers to each other's countries, which has helped break down prejudices, made Europeans more familiar with each other, and encouraged greater cooperation on transportation by increasing the demand for cheap and easy access. Tourism now employs 21.5 million Europeans (about 13 per cent of the workforce in the EU), and generated revenues in 2004 of about $1.42 trillion, or just under 12 per cent of the GDP of the EU (World Travel and Tourism Council website, 2007).

Second, rail transport has been revitalized as a cost-efficient and environmentally friendly alternative to road and air transport. The EU has plans to develop a 35,000 km high-speed train (HST) network connecting Europe's major cities, the way being led by France with its high-speed TGV, which needs special new track, and Germany with its ICE network, which can use existing track. With trains travelling at 200–300 kph (some of them with coaches finished to luxurious standards), the HST system has cut travel times considerably. Investments have been made along the way in building the tunnels and bridges needed to ensure uninterrupted travel: the completion in

1994 of the $15 billion Eurotunnel under the channel between Britain and France and in 1998 of road/rail bridges linking Denmark and Sweden were important pieces in the jigsaw.

The development of TENs is now one of the priorities of the EU, and the European Commission has a programme aimed at improving transport links within the EU; a projected €330 billion will be spent in the period 2007–13 alone, involving the building of 70,000 km of railway track (including 22,000 km of new and upgraded track for HSTs), and 15,000 km of new roads, mainly on the outer edges of the EU. Among the priority projects are high-speed rail links between Berlin and Palermo, between Paris and London, and across southwest and eastern Europe; transport links between Portugal/Spain and the rest of Europe; a Nordic triangle rail–road axis; rail and motorway projects in Eastern Europe; new motorways for Greece; and a 1,400 km Ireland–UK–Benelux road link. Plans are also afoot to encourage the shifting of freight from Europe's increasingly congested roads and highways to rail and water transport, and to integrate road, rail, water and air transport networks.

The EU also has aspirations to develop independence of the US-operated Global Positioning System (GPS) by developing an alternative European Navigation Satellite System known as Galileo. GPS was developed by the United States mainly for military purposes, and because the US reserves the right to limit its signal strength, or to close public GPS access completely during times of conflict, there are clear incentives for the EU to develop an alternative. Galileo is designed for civilian use and is intended to be compatible with GPS, while being capable of operating autonomously. Several non-EU countries have joined the project, including China and India, and there has been talk of several others joining in the future, including Australia, Brazil, Canada, Japan, Mexico and Russia. Hopes of having it operational by 2010 proved overly optimistic, however: delays have arisen out of a failure to agree a public–private funding partnership, only one test satellite was in orbit by 2007 and only four of the projected 30 satellites needed had been ordered. There were doubts about whether a new target of full operations by 2013 was realistic.

Liberalization of air travel

One of the most notable changes brought about by the single market programme has been the loosening of regulations on air transport (see Armstrong and Bulmer, 1998, Chapter 7). Because most European states are too small to support a significant domestic industry, the majority of air traffic in Europe is international. Until the 1980s, most European countries had state-owned national carriers – such as Air France, Lufthansa, and Alitalia – which played an influential role in making national air transport policy, with the result that air transport was highly regulated and expensive to consumers; it was sometimes cheaper to fly from one European city to another via the United States, rather than direct. Changes began in the mid-1980s when the Thatcher government privatized British Airways and negotiated bilateral agreements with several other EU member states. Meanwhile, the European Civil Aviation Conference recommended liberalization, as did a number of national and European interest groups, and the idea was incorporated into the Cockfield report. Three packages of laws and regulations worked their way through the EU institutions in 1987–92, substantially opening up and restructuring the air transport market.

In recent years there has been an increase in the number of international airline alliances (resulting in reduced costs, combined ticketing, and route consolidation), new pressure for airlines to merge (leading, for example, to the merger in 2003 between Dutch KLM and Air France to create Europe's biggest airline, and to rumours of takeovers or mergers involving British Airways and Iberia, Lufthansa and Swiss, and Aer Lingus and Ryanair), and a growth in the number of cut-price operators such as easyJet, Ryanair, WizzAir, Germania Express, Blue Air and Thomson Fly. These changes have resulted in greater choice for consumers, who can now fly more cheaply than before. The more open markets, though, have not immunized European airlines against the economic downturn that has hit airline travel in recent years.

A new dimension was added in 2007 with an 'open skies' agreement between the EU and the United States aimed at liberalizing air travel across the Atlantic. The agreement allows any EU- or US-based airline to fly from any city within the United States to any city within the EU and vice versa, rather than being limited to the usual major hubs, such as London, Frankfurt, Paris, New York, Chicago, and Los Angeles. The European Commission has championed the agreement, and most European airlines and governments are in favour, the notable exceptions being Britain and British Airways, which have the most to lose: because the agreement involves ending the control that national airlines have traditionally had on their major domestic airports, more competition would be posed to London's Heathrow airport, the busiest international airport in the world. The agreement was nonetheless due to come into effect in 2008, raising speculation of a new round of airline mergers.

Mergers and acquisitions

After the Second World War, European companies lost markets at home and abroad to competition, first from the United States and then from Japan. US and Japanese corporations were more dynamic, invested more in research and development, and had access to large home markets. Meanwhile, European business was handicapped in its attempts to move across borders into neighbouring states, facing merger and capital gains taxes, double taxation on company profits, different legal systems, differences in regulations and

Box 7.2 Europe and the aerospace industry

Few areas of multinational business have seen quite such dramatic change in recent years as the aerospace industry, where rationalization, competition, and other economic pressures have cut the number of large civilian aircraft producers in the world from dozens to just two. Famous names of Western European aviation – from Vickers to Hawker Siddeley, Supermarine, Dornier, Messerschmitt and Sud Aviation – have all gone. In Britain, alone, the 19 aircraft producers of the 1940s had been whittled down by the mid-1980s to just one, BAE Systems. Similar pressures have led to similar changes in the United States, where Lockheed now focuses on military aircraft and McDonnell-Douglas was taken over in 1997 by Boeing, now the only remaining American manufacturer of large civilian aircraft.

Much of the responsibility for the changes on both sides of the Atlantic lies with the success of Airbus, a European consortium founded in 1970, and whose share of the new civil aircraft market has grown since 1975 from 10 per cent to more than 50 per cent. The Airbus consortium is owned by the European Aeronautic Defence and Space company (EADS), created in 2000 by a merger between Aérospatiale Matra of France, DaimlerChrysler Aerospace of Germany, and Construcciones Aeronauticas (CASA) of Spain (BAE had a 20 per cent share until 2006, when it decided to sell out and focus on the US defence market). Airbus produces a line of 12 different airliners, the newest being the controversial super-jumbo double-decker A380, the world's largest passenger aircraft, capable of carrying 500–800 passengers, depending upon the seating configuration. After some delays related to production problems, the A380 took its first commercial flight in October 2007.

The creation of both Airbus and EADS was prompted by the argument that economies of scale were giving American manufacturers an advantage over their European competitors, whose national markets were too small to sustain them. Similar arguments have encouraged transnational cooperation in Western Europe on military aircraft and missiles. Individual member states still make competitive products, such as France's Mirage jet fighters, and Britain's Harrier jump jets, but are finding that it makes better commercial sense to pool resources. Successful collaborations include production of the Tornado fighter-bomber and the Eurofighter Typhoon, both made by British-German-Italian consortiums. In April 2001, BAE, EADS, and Finmeccanica of Italy joined forces to create MBDA, the world's second largest producer of missiles after Raytheon of the United States.

standards, and limits on the movement of goods and services. Hence the majority of merger and takeover activity was either within individual countries or between European and non-European companies.

With competitiveness pushed to the top of the European agenda by the single market programme, the Commission by the late 1980s had become actively involved in trying to overcome market fragmentation and the emphasis placed by national governments on promoting the interests of often state-owned 'national champions'. The Community also launched new programmes aimed at encouraging research in information technology, advanced communications, industrial technologies, and weapons manufacture (Tsoukalis, 1997, pp. 49–51). The single market was helping remove many of the barriers that national corporations once faced, increasing the number of consumers they could reach. The euro also made it easier for companies in search of acquisitions to borrow money and buy other companies, which combined with privatization programmes in many countries and the general trend towards globalization to greatly increase the number of acquisition opportunities, joint ventures, and corporate mergers, both within the EU and between European and non-European corporations.

Notable joint ventures have included those between Thompson of France and Philips of the Netherlands on high-definition television, Pirelli of Italy and Dunlop of Britain on tyres, BMW and Rolls-Royce on aeroengines, and among the members of the European Space Agency (ESA). Set up in 1973 in an attempt to promote European cooperation in space research, the ESA now has 17 members: Switzerland, Norway, and all the EU-15 members. Europe has also offered competition to the Americans in the field of satellite launching, with ten European countries working together in the development of Arianespace, a space-launch consortium owned by governments and state-owned companies (France has a stake of just over 60 per cent). Since the launch of the first in its series of Ariane rockets in 1979 from Kourou in French Guiana, Arianespace has taken over more than half the global market for commercial satellite launches, eating into a business long dominated by the United States.

The growth of new pan-European businesses seeking to profit from the opportunities offered by the single market, and looking to create 'world-size' companies to compete more effectively with the United States and Japan, has led to a surge in merger and acquisition activities, notably in the chemicals, pharmaceuticals, and telecommunications industries. In 1989–90 the number of intra-EC mergers overtook the number of national mergers for the first time (Owen and Dynes, 1992, p. 222), since when the European mergers and acquisitions market has grown to be bigger than that of the United States. Notable recent examples include:

- The mergers among a number of British, Canadian and American pharmaceuticals companies to create GlaxoSmithKline.
- A string of takeovers by the French insurance company AXA, now ranked among the 20 biggest corporations in the world.
- A series of takeovers by the Royal Bank of Scotland, now the world's fifth largest bank.
- The mergers and acquisitions which in the space of two years transformed Britain's Vodaphone into one of the world's biggest mobile phone businesses. In 2000 it took over the much larger German company Mannesmann,

which had earlier taken over Orange, Britain's third biggest mobile phone company.

- The 2004 merger between Securicor of Britain and Group 4 Falck of Denmark to create the world's second largest security company.
- Two large mergers in 2006 in the energy market, when E.ON of Germany bought Endesa of Spain, and Suez of France bought Gaz de France.
- The 2007 purchase by the Dutch company Akzo Nobel of Britain's ICI.

The new opportunities offered at home have been accompanied by remarkable growth in the flows of foreign direct investment both into the EU, and from the EU into other countries. In the period 1994–2003, more than $3 trillion was invested in the EU-15, or more than twice the amount that was invested over the same period in the United States. Belgium, Luxembourg, Britain and France were the main targets, drawing in more than half the EU total among them. In terms of outflows, the EU in that period invested nearly $3.9 trillion, or nearly three times the amount invested by the United States, and nearly 15 times the amount invested by Japan. In 2006, the biggest EU spenders – in order – were France, Spain, Luxembourg, Britain, Germany, and Belgium (which together spent nearly $510 billion, or twice as much as the United States), and the biggest EU recipients were Britain, Luxembourg, France, and Belgium (which together received nearly $390 billion, or more than twice as much as the United States) (OECD website, 2007). The more notable examples of European companies reaching outside the EU to create large new corporations include:

- The 1998 takeover by British Petroleum of Amoco in the United States, and the subsequent merger between BP Amoco and Atlantic Richfield.
- The 1999 takeover by Germany's Daimler of the US automobile manufacturer Chrysler (which came to an unhappy end in 2007).
- The 2000 takeover by Germany's Deutsche Telekom of Voicestream in the United States.
- The 2003 merger between Britain's P&O Princess and Carnival of the United States to create the world's largest cruise vacation group.
- As an indication of the changing nature of the international marketplace, discussions were held in 2007 to investigate the possibilities of a merger between two trade unions: Amicus of Britain and the United Steel Workers of the United States. The underlying argument was that unions increasingly had to work together to deal with new global companies.

Competition policy

Bigger is not necessarily better in the corporate world, because takeovers can reduce competition and consumer choice, and they run the danger of creating industries that dominate or monopolize a particular sector of the economy. The success of the single market ultimately relies on an effective competition policy, ensuring that companies do not become too big in concentrated markets, that supplies are not limited by segmented markets, and that national governments do not give domestic companies unfair advantages through subsidies and tax breaks (Baimbridge *et al.*, 2004, p. 36). Competition policy was built in to the Treaty of Rome (Article 3 notes that Community activities would include 'the establishment of a system ensuring that competition shall not be distorted in the Common Market'), and this has turned out to be an area in which the EU has clearly intervened in the economic life of member states, and even of non-member countries where mergers and acquisitions are seen to pose a threat to competition. EU competition policy has four key objectives:

• Discouraging the development of monopolies and cartels. The Commission watches for attempts by companies to build and abuse dominant market positions, and promotes greater transparency in pricing in order to ensure that the same goods and services cost the same from one member state to another (allowing for some differences in local tax systems). It also watches for domestic laws that interfere with competition; thus in 2003–04 it ordered Germany to cancel a law adopted in the 1960s that prevented the vehicle manufacturer Volkswagen from being taken over by another company.
• Merger control. The Commission monitors plans for corporate mergers and acquisitions in order to prevent the development of companies with too great a share of their particular markets, which would allow them to squeeze out smaller competitors. So, for example, it changed the terms of a 2006 merger between French oil companies TotalFina and Elf Aquitaine, and blocked the proposed takeover in 2007 by low-cost carrier Ryanair of the Irish national airline Aer Lingus.
• State aids. The Commission monitors the provision of subsidies, loans, grants and tax breaks to companies so as to ensure that they are not given an unfair advantage over competitors (Allen, 1996). Temporary aid is permissible in times of real need, as is aid for research and development and for regional development, but state aid must generally be in the interest of the EU as a whole.
• Promoting the competitiveness of European companies by protecting intellectual and industrial property, reducing the bureaucratic burden, providing help with research and development, and providing aid to small and medium enterprises.

One notable concern of competition policy has been the car market, where manufacturers have sometimes priced the same vehicles differently in different markets, and have even occasionally refused to sell vehicles to buyers from foreign markets seeking a better deal (see Baimbridge *et el.*, 2004, p. 43). They have, for example, set prices higher in the UK, and lower in countries where the costs of running a vehicle (such as taxes) have been higher. This has led to the curious sight of organized coach trips by British consumers to countries such as the Netherlands, where car prices have been lower, and dealers have stocked right-hand drive cars specifically for the British market. Part of the explanation for the relative ease of this exploitation arises from the fact that about 75 per cent of the EU vehicle market is dominated by six major manufacturers (including Fiat, Renault, Volkswagen and BMW).

Reflecting the new economic influence of the EU at the global level, recent targets of Commission investigations into mergers have even included American corporations. Thus it blocked a proposed merger in 2000 between telecom companies MCI/WorldCom and Sprint out of concern that the two American companies would dominate internet operations in the EU. It also stopped a planned takeover in 2001 of Honeywell by General Electric, which would have been the biggest corporate merger in history and would, argued the Commission, have created dominant positions in the markets for the supply of avionics and non-avionics equipment, particularly jet engines. It then made world headlines in March 2004 by imposing a record fine of €479 million (then $622 million) on the software-maker Microsoft, whose Windows operating system can be found on 90 per cent of the world's personal computers. The Commission accused Microsoft of abusing its dominant market position by bundling in its media player with its Windows operating system, thereby discouraging consumers from buying media players made by other companies. The Commission ordered Microsoft to begin offering within 90 days a version of Windows without the media player installed, and to reveal its Windows software codes so that rival companies could more easily design compatible products. Microsoft appealed the decision and lost, and finally began complying with the ruling in 2007.

Considerable progress has been made since 1987 in moving towards the completion of the single market, but work still remains to be done. In June 1997, the Commission launched a Single Market Action Plan aimed at generating a political commitment to the completion of the single market by January 1999. This divided remaining actions into three groups: those that could be implemented quickly because they did not need new EU legislation, those that had already been proposed but still needed approval from Parliament and the Council of Ministers, and those that were more complex, such as a reworking of the VAT system. Much progress has been made on implementation of the nearly 1,340 existing single-market-related directives, but the implications of the single market are still not fully understood by Europeans or their leaders, and much still relies less on deliberate political decisions than on the pressures of the marketplace to reduce or remove remaining barriers.

Two areas in which there has been a notable lack of progress have been integration of the European energy market, and integration of the financial services market. In the former case, the main problem is the high level of state intervention found in member states such as France. EU goals include improving the competitiveness of the gas and electricity sectors, reinforcing security of supply, and protecting the environment, but the energy market in the EU remains fragmented, and coordination is not what it should be. Recent EU regulations have been aimed at separating production and supply from transmission, encouraging cross-border energy trade, strengthening the independence of national regulators, and encouraging greater price transparency. In the case of the financial services market (banking, insurance and investment services), integration offers the benefits of stimulating competition, promoting convergence, and encouraging EU-wide pricing (Gillingham, 2003, p. 462), but handicaps continue to exist in the form of different tax systems, bureaucratic hurdles, and a lack of price transparency. The introduction of the euro has helped by removing the barriers created by different currencies, but it has not yet proved the catalyst for change that many hoped it would be.

A new set of challenges to the internal market was introduced with eastern enlargement. It brought greater social and economic diversity to the EU, but it also widened the gap between wealth and poverty (see Chapter 8 for details). The rural populations of Eastern European member states are typically bigger than those of the EU-15, unemployment rates are higher, there has been less investment in infrastructure and communications, and the labour force is less educated. In the years leading up to accession, eastern states made so many changes to their trade and investment policies that – it has been argued – they had already felt most of the economic effects of enlargement before joining, they were already competing in the single market, and there was already free movement of money, goods, and services (but not labour) (Grabbe, 2004). However, improvements in competitiveness are still needed, as well as investments in infrastructure and worker education. Eastern Europe provides many market opportunities, but there are also many challenges ahead.

Meanwhile, there has been the bigger question of the place of the EU in the global marketplace. As a result of calls in the late 1990s for a new focus on modernizing the European economy, the European Council meeting in Lisbon in March 2000 set the goal of making the changes needed to finally complete the single market and to create 'the most competitive and dynamic knowledge-based economy on the planet within ten years', bringing the EU up to the levels of competitiveness and dynamism that are features of the US economy. The Lisbon Strategy called on EU governments to make a wide range of changes, including integration and liberalization of the telecommunications market, liberalization of the gas and electricity markets, rationalized road tax and air traffic control systems, lower unemployment, movement towards harmonization of EU corporate tax, and more progress towards making the EU a digital, knowledge-based economy (Wallace, 2004).

An interim report prepared in 2004 by a committee chaired by former Dutch prime minister Wim Kok argued that the Lisbon Strategy was not working because too few EU governments had been prepared to make the necessary reforms: there was still too much regulation, too much protection for workers against dismissal, and not enough market liberalization or entrepreneurial freedom. The EU had also fallen behind in research and development, with expenditure as a percentage of GNP stagnating since the mid-1990s, contrasting with the much higher levels in the United States (much of it generated by the vast US defence industry), and with the high growth in Japan, China and South Korea. There is a tension between the continental European (or Rhenish) model of economic management, which favours more state control, and the so-called Anglo-Saxon model, which favours greater freedom for the marketplace. One of the first moves made by incoming French president Nicolas Sarkozy in 2007 was to have a reference to 'free and undistorted competition' removed from the draft Lisbon treaty. But supporters of the free market ask how the goals of the Lisbon Strategy can be met as long as the interventionist philosophy prevails.

Inside the euro zone

In March 2002, after years of controversy and often difficult economic adjustment, 12 EU member states took one of the most far-reaching steps so far in the history of integration: they abolished their separate national currencies and replaced them with the new European currency, the euro. It was a move that was a long time coming, meeting considerable political resistance along the way and causing economic problems for several member states, and yet it was driven by the understanding that few barriers to the completion of the single market were as fundamental as the existence of multiple different currencies with fluctuating exchange rates. At the same time, the surrender of national currencies raised many questions about sovereignty and independence: by giving up their national currencies, the governments of the countries in the euro zone were agreeing to give up control over important domestic economic policy choices, such as the ability to adjust interest rates. Critics also saw the adoption of the euro as another step towards the creation of a unified system of European government.

It was understood as early as the 1950s that stable exchange rates would be an important part of the effective functioning of a single market. That stability was provided by the postwar system of fixed exchange rates, but then the system began to crumble in the late 1960s, and finally collapsed with the US decision in 1971 to end the link between gold and the US dollar. A committee headed by Luxembourg prime minister Pierre Werner met in 1969–70 to discuss monetary union, and concluded that the Community should work towards adopting a single currency in stages by 1980. But international currency turbulence in the wake of the energy crises of the 1970s undermined their efforts, and by 1977 only five of the 12 Community member states were still in the scheme.

A second attempt was made in March 1979 with the launch of the European Monetary System (EMS). An artificial currency called the European Currency Unit (ecu) was created, whose value was based on a basket of European currencies, each weighted roughly according to the size of the economies of the different member states (the Deutschmark made up about 30 per cent of the ecu, the British pound about 11–15 per cent, the Italian lira about 9 per cent, and so on). Exchange rates between member states were set in ecus, and countries in the EMS undertook to make sure that those rates fluctuated by no more than 2.25 per cent either way, using a regulatory scheme known as the Exchange Rate Mechanism (ERM). Although several member states found it difficult to keep their currencies stable relative to the ecu, the EMS contributed to exchange rate stability in the 1980s, and helped accustom Europeans to the idea of a single currency.

In 1989 a plan developed under the leadership of Commission president Jacques Delors proposed another staged move towards a single currency: all member states would join the ERM, the band of exchange rate fluctuations would be narrowed and then fixed irrevocably, and the ecu would become the new single currency. Despite the near-collapse of the ERM in 1992–93 – when Britain and Italy pulled out, several other countries had to devalue their currencies, and the bands of exchange rate fluctuation had to be widened – the Maastricht treaty affirmed the basic principles behind the Delors plan. EU member states wanting to adopt the single currency had to meet several convergence criteria that were considered essential prerequisites:

• A national budget deficit of less than 3 per cent of GDP.
• A public debt of less than 60 per cent of GDP.
• A consumer inflation rate within 1.5 per cent of the average in the three countries with the lowest rates.
• A long-term interest rate within 2 per cent of the average in the three countries with the lowest rates.
• A record of keeping exchange rates within ERM fluctuation margins for two years.

At the Madrid European Council in December 1995, EU leaders decided to call the new currency the euro, and agreed to introduce it in three stages. The first stage came in May 1998 when it was determined which countries were ready: all member states had met the budget deficit goal, but only seven member states had met the debt target, Germany and Ireland had not met the inflation reduction target, and Greece had not been able to reduce its interest rates sufficiently. Maastricht, however, included a fudge clause that allowed

Box 7.3   The European Central Bank

Although it has – until recently – been one of the least known of the EU institutions, the European Central Bank (ECB) is now playing an important role in the lives of Europeans with the euro having replaced most national currencies. As it has become increasingly involved in the direction of European monetary policy, however, questions have been raised about its powers, and about the lack of effective checks on those powers.

First proposed in 1988, the framework of the Bank was described in the Maastricht treaty. It was founded in 1994 as the European Monetary Institute (EMI), and it was finally established in June 1998 as the European Central Bank. Based in Frankfurt, its main job is to ensure monetary stability by setting interest rates in the euro zone. It has a governing body consisting of the central bank governors from each participating state, and a six-member full-time executive board. Directors serve non-renewable terms of eight years and can only be removed by their peers or by an order from the European Court of Justice. The Bank also has links to non-participating countries through a general council composed of the central bank governors of all EU member states. A new exchange rate mechanism (ERM II) links the euro with the national currencies of non-participating countries, and the ECB is allowed to take action to support non-participating countries so long as this does not conflict with its primary task of maintaining monetary stability among participating countries.

Concerned about the need to convince the sceptical German public that the new European currency would be as strong as the Deutschmark (Daltrop, 1987, pp. 175–6), Helmut Kohl insisted that the ECB should be an almost direct copy of the famously independent German Bundesbank. In fact, it makes the Bundesbank seem quite restricted by comparison, and was by 1998 already being described as 'the most powerful single monetary authority in the world' (*European Voice*, April 1998). But Howarth and Loedel (2005, p. xi) may be going too far when they describe it as a 'leviathan', and as 'the most important institutional creation in Europe since the institutionalization of the nation state in the seventeenth century'. Neither national nor EU leaders are allowed to try to influence the Bank, its board, or its constituent national central banks, and the only body that can play any kind of watchdog role over the Bank is the monetary subcommittee of the European Parliament, but it so far lacks the resources to be able to hold the Bank or its president – Jean-Claude Trichet of France since 2003 – particularly accountable. This makes it quite different from the United States Federal Reserve, whose chair is regularly brought to account for its policies before the banking committee of the US Senate.

countries to qualify if their debt-to-GDP ratio was 'sufficiently diminishing and approaching the reference value at a satisfactory pace'. In the event, despite the fact that the national debt in Belgium and Italy was nearly twice the target, all but Britain, Denmark (both of which had met all the criteria), Greece and Sweden announced their intention to adopt the euro.

Map 7.1   *The euro zone*

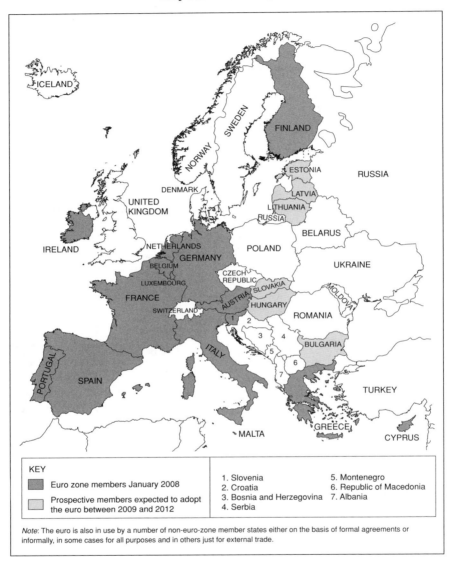

KEY

■ Euro zone members January 2008

□ Prospective members expected to adopt the euro between 2009 and 2012

1. Slovenia
2. Croatia
3. Bosnia and Herzegovina
4. Serbia
5. Montenegro
6. Republic of Macedonia
7. Albania

Note: The euro is also in use by a number of non-euro-zone member states either on the basis of formal agreements or informally, in some cases for all purposes and in others just for external trade.

The second stage came on 1 January 1999 when the euro was officially launched, participating countries fixed their exchange rates, and the new European Central Bank began overseeing the single monetary policy. All its dealings with commercial banks and all its foreign exchange activities were subsequently transacted in euros, and the euro was quoted against the yen and the dollar. Pause for thought was provided in September 2000 when, in a national referendum, Danes voted against adopting the euro. Polls also showed that a majority of Swedes were against adoption (they finally voted against the euro in a September 2003 referendum), and in Britain found opposition running at three to one. Concerns also arose when the value of the euro against other currencies fell steadily: its value against the US dollar fell from $1.17 to as low as 85 cents (it was back up to $1.40 by mid-2007). Nonetheless, plans for the transition proceeded, with the printing of 14.5 billion euro-banknotes and the minting of 56 billion coins. In January 2001 Greece became the twelfth member state to join the euro zone, having met the targets for reduced inflation and budget deficits.

The final stage began on 1 January 2002, when euro coins and notes became available. The original plan had been for the euro and national currencies to be in concurrent circulation for six months, but it was subsequently decided that Europeans were to be given just two months to make the final transition from national currencies to the euro, and national currencies ceased to be legal tender in the euro zone on 1 March 2002. After centuries of fiscal independence, the 12 members of the euro zone made the final irrevocable step to abolish their national currencies, and Deutschmarks, drachmas, escudos, francs, guilders, liras, marks, pesetas, punts, and schillings faded into history. In January 2007 Slovenia became the first Eastern European member state to adopt the euro, and it was followed in January 2008 by Cyprus and Malta. The remaining Eastern European member states are committed to adopting the euro, but must first show that they can participate fully in the single market, show progress towards achieving the conditions needed for adoption, and meet the convergence criteria.

Opinions have been mixed on the benefits and costs of the euro, and it is probably safe to say that no one chapter in the history of European integration was approached with so much trepidation. Its introduction raised questions about the long-term economic effects for the EU, few of which are fully understood, even by economists. Among the benefits:

1. The euro provides monetary stability. The devaluations and revaluations of national currencies that were so much a feature of national monetary policy in euro zone countries in the 1970s and 1980s have been replaced with greater stability, removing the planning problems that once came with changes in the value of currencies.

2. There is greater convenience for travellers. Instead of having to change currencies when they cross borders, and paying for goods and services with unfamiliar banknotes and coins, travellers now use the same currency wherever they go in the euro zone. This has the added psychological benefit of making them more aware of being part of the common enterprise of integration. It also makes foreign visitors more aware of the EU; they may not always understand the latter, but they cannot ignore the effect of the euro in their pocket.

3. There is greater price transparency, because instead of costs being expressed in different currencies from one country to another, they are all expressed in euros, and consumers can make comparisons more easily. This also promotes competition as businesses try to make their goods and services available at similar prices throughout the euro zone.

4. There are fewer bureaucratic barriers to the transfer of large sums of money across borders, and businesses no longer have to spend time and money changing currency, thus saving everyone transaction costs.

5. The stock and bond markets in the euro zone will likely continue their tendency to unify, and investors, instead of focusing on their home markets alone, will become used to the idea of a European stock market.

6. The euro is now a world class currency in the same league as the US dollar and the Japanese yen, providing the euro zone with a tool that allows it to have greater influence over global economic policy, rather than having to react to developments in the United States and Japan. A growing number of analysts see it as a substantial threat to the global dominance of the US dollar.

At the same time, the adoption of the euro has been a gamble. Never before has a group of sovereign states with a long history of independence tried combining their currencies into one on a similar scale, and the risks were significantly greater than those involved in completing the single market. Furthermore, all the key preparatory decisions about the euro were taken by European national leaders with little or no regard to public opinion, which was often hostile to the idea, and uncertain about the implications. The potential costs of the euro include the following:

1. Different countries have different economic cycles, and separate currencies allow them to devalue, borrow, adjust interest rates, and take other measures in response to changed economic circumstances. Such flexibility is no longer available in the euro zone, because the European Central Bank cannot follow different fiscal policies for different parts of the EU. The members of the euro zone must rise or fall together.

2. Some economists were concerned about the underlying weaknesses in EU economies in 1997–98, and raised questions about the extent to which figures relating to the convergence criteria were being fudged to allow countries that had not met those criteria to take part. Some feared that these weaknesses could result in a high-credibility Deutschmark being replaced with a low-credibility euro, undermining economic health throughout the EU. The most sceptical even doubted that all the euro zone countries would be able to keep within the ERM.

3. Unless Europeans learn each other's languages and are able to move freely in search of jobs, the euro could perpetuate the pockets of poverty and wealth that already exist across the EU, thereby interfering with the development

of the single market. Having a common currency in a country as big as the United States works mainly because people can move freely; this is not true of the EU, where there are still psychological, fiscal, technical and social barriers to movement.

Some of the problems inherent in the euro became clear even before it was finally adopted, with the signature in 1997 – at the insistence of Germany – of a stability and growth pact. Generated by concerns that governments in the euro zone might try to get around ECB monetary policies by increasing spending and running large budget deficits, the pact – which was signed by all 15 EU member states – required that they keep their budget deficits to less than 3 per cent of their gross domestic product, and placed a 60 per cent limit on government borrowing. Any country that was in breach of the pact could be fined by the European Commission. Unfortunately, recession came to most industrialized countries in 2002–03, and France, Germany, Italy and Portugal quickly found themselves either in breach of the deficit limit or running the danger of crossing the 3 per cent barrier; they were later joined by Greece and the Netherlands. While there was general agreement on the principle of the pact, there was criticism that it was too inflexible (in that it made no distinctions among countries with different economic bases) and that its focus on curbing inflation left it poorly equipped to deal with slow economic growth. Commission president Romano Prodi even went so far in October 2002 as to describe attempts to enforce the pact without taking heed of changing circumstances as 'stupid'.

By the second half of 2003 the European Central Bank was warning that most euro zone countries were in danger of failing to meet the target on budget deficits, thereby damaging the prospects for economic growth. In November 2003, the two biggest euro zone economies – France and Germany – both broke the limits and prevented other EU finance ministers from imposing large fines on the two countries (a decision that was annulled by the European Court of Justice in July 2004). Its ministers, along with their British counterpart, argued that the rules of the pact were too rigid and needed to be applied more flexibly if they were to work. By December the pact had all but collapsed and new rules were being explored to promote fiscal stability in the euro zone, including the granting of permission to selected countries in difficulties to temporarily carry larger deficits.

Conclusions

Although the work of the European Union has been driven most obviously by economic factors – and particularly by the goal of free trade in a single market – European leaders have found, through neofunctionalist logic, that economic integration has had a spillover effect on many other policy areas. Most notably, they have found that completion of the single market was a more complex notion than originally expected. The primary objective of the single market was the removal of tariffs and non-tariff barriers to trade; while tariff barriers were relatively easy to identify, the seeming innocuousness of the term 'non-tariff barriers' hid a multitude of problems, handicaps, and obstacles.

Among other things, economic integration has meant removing cross-border checks on people and goods, controlling the movement of drugs and terrorists, agreeing standard levels of indirect taxation, harmonizing technical standards on thousands of goods and services, agreeing regulations in the interests of consumer safety, reaching agreement on professional qualifications, allowing Europeans to take capital and pensions with them when they move to another country, opening up the European market for joint ventures and corporate mergers, developing trans-European transport and energy supply networks, providing the means by which Europeans can communicate with each other electronically, developing common approaches to working conditions, establishing common European environmental standards, promoting the development of poorer rural and urban areas in order to avoid trade distortions, and creating an equitable and efficient agricultural sector.

In a sense, however, everything that was agreed during the 1960s, the 1970s, and the 1980s – the thousands of decisions taken by prime ministers, chancellors, presidents, ministers, and European bureaucrats, and the thousands of directives, regulations, and decisions developed and agreed by the different EU institutions – was simply a prelude to the biggest project of all, the conversion to a single currency. In March 2002, 12 of the 15 member states abolished their national currencies and adopted the euro, while three – Britain, Denmark, and Sweden – opted to remain out, at least temporarily. Many questions remained about the wisdom of the positions taken both by the champions and the opponents. Have the former been too hasty in their decision to press on, regardless of their domestic economic problems? Are Britain and Denmark being wisely cautious or typically Eurosceptic in their decisions to wait and see? Will the adoption of the euro prove to be a disruptive step too far, or one of the most far-sighted and creative decisions ever taken by Europe's leaders? What impact will it have, directly or indirectly, on economic development in Eastern Europe?

Whatever happens over the next few years, the single market has had widespread and irreversible implications for everyone living in the European Union, and for all the EU's trading partners. It has helped create new wealth and opportunity, has brought down many of the economic barriers that have for decades divided Europeans, and has paved the way for the creation of trans-European economic ties that have reduced national differences and promoted the idea of Europe as a powerful new actor on the world stage.

Chapter 8

Improving the Quality of Life

For most of its early life, the European Economic Community focused on quantitative issues: rebuilding the economies of Western Europe, agreeing a customs union and building a single market in order to promote economic development, and seeking ways to make the European marketplace more open, efficient, competitive, and profitable. True, one of the core motives behind the Treaty of Rome was to improve the living and working conditions of Europeans, but this was a general goal rather than the basis for a series of specific policies.

It quickly became clear that wealth and efficiency would not be evenly distributed in the Community as long as there were differences in opportunity, economic and social standards, personal income, education, and the overall quality of life both within and among member states. There would be no level playing field on which Europeans could compete, some would be handicapped by local problems while others had easier access to jobs and wealth, and differences in regulatory standards, access to natural resources, access to funds for investment, and environmental quality would all stand as barriers to the completion or at least the effective operation of the single market.

Thus the Community began to pay more attention during the 1960s and 1970s to qualitative issues, and to setting up the mechanisms needed to transfer resources to those parts of the Community suffering the most difficulties and the greatest handicaps. The result was the development of common policies in three major areas:

- *Agricultural policy*, which was factored in to the Treaty of Rome, and was designed to ensure that Community farmers had a market for their produce. The Common Agricultural Policy (CAP) eventually became the most expensive and controversial of all the policies pursued jointly by the member states, although efforts to reform CAP have reduced its costs and improved its efficiency.
- *Cohesion policy*, which aims to even out regional economic differences within and among the member states by investing in rural development and focusing on issues relating to employment, including job creation, the free movement of labour, improved living and working conditions, and the rights and benefits of workers.

- *Environmental policy*, concerns for which were all but unknown in the 1950s, but which grew in the 1960s as the air and water pollution created by economic growth promoted a reaction from increasingly affluent Europeans. Differences in environmental standards and regulations also posed a barrier to the single market, so that by the 1980s there was new political support for addressing the problem.

Improving the quality of life for Europeans is today one of the core priorities of the EU, and the member states have worked together to reinforce national efforts to reduce economic and social differences. The results have been mixed, with notable achievements in improving the lives of farmers, investing in poorer parts of the EU, and in raising environmental standards, but with a puzzling failure to deal with the persistence of high unemployment and poverty in many parts of the EU.

Levelling the playing field

As with all societies, the European Union contains many economic and social divisions. It is home to some of the wealthiest communities in the world, particularly in its major cities, but the rich do not have to look far to find decaying industrial areas, underdeveloped rural areas, pockets of poverty and high unemployment, social dysfunction, and regions heavily dependent on low-profit agriculture or fisheries. This has been especially true since the 2004–07 enlargement, when 15 countries with a per capita gross domestic product (GDP) mainly in the range of $20,000–30,000 were joined by 12 countries with a per capita GDP mainly in the range of $2,000–5,000.

The statistics clearly illustrate the economic and social disparities with which the EU is struggling:

- Economic productivity varies significantly. Expressing the average per capita GDP for the EU as 100, levels ranged in 2004 from a high in Luxembourg of 251 to lows in Lithuania, Poland, Latvia, Romania and Bulgaria of between half and one-third the EU average (see Figure 8.1).
- Although unemployment rates in Eastern Europe have fallen in recent years, there was still a notable variation in 2007, with a low of 4–5 per cent in the Netherlands, Denmark, Cyprus, Austria and Britain, a medium range of 7–8 per cent in Sweden, Romania, Finland, and Portugal, and a high of 13–14 per cent in Poland and Slovakia (nearly twice the EU average).
- While about 70–72 per cent of the economic wealth of the wealthier western member states is generated by services and just 1–3 per cent by agriculture, services account for 61–62 per cent of GDP in Slovenia and Lithuania, 57 per cent in the Czech Republic, and 54 per cent in Ireland. In both Greece and Lithuania, farming accounts for about 7 per cent of GDP.

Figure 8.1 *Per capita GDP in the European Union*

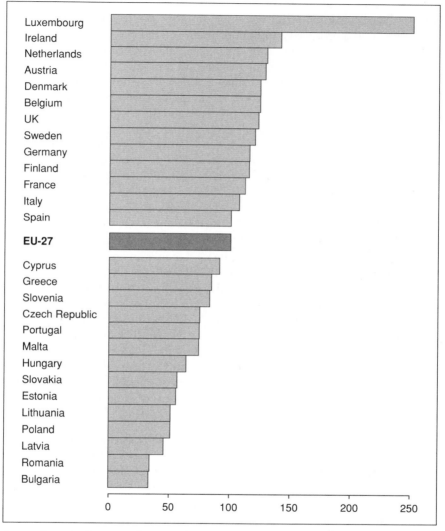

Source: Eurostat figures on Europa website, 2007, http://www.europa.eu.int. Figures are for 2004, and indicate per capita GDP relative to the average for the EU-27, which is expressed as 100.

The wealthiest parts of the EU are in the north–central regions, particularly in the quadrilateral area between London, Paris, Milan and Hamburg. The poorest parts are on the eastern, southern, and western margins: Eastern Europe, eastern Germany, Greece, southern Italy, Spain, Portugal, western Ireland, and western Scotland. The relative poverty of these regions has several different sources: some are depressed agricultural areas with little industry and high unemployment, some are declining industrial areas with outdated factories and machinery, some (notably islands) are geographically isolated from the prosperity and opportunity offered by bigger markets, and most suffer relatively low levels of education and health care and have under-developed infrastructure, especially roads and utilities.

The preamble to the Treaty of Rome included the sentiment that economic unity and 'harmonious development' required that the member states should work to reduce 'the differences existing between the various regions and the backwardness of the less favoured [regions]'. As well as the obvious moral need to address poverty and economic handicaps wherever they existed, there was a clear strategic need as well: variations in the economic wealth of the member states would interfere with the smooth functioning of the single market by creating barriers to trade and opportunity. As a result, jobs would move to the poorer parts where cheaper labour was available, inequality would interfere with the development of a skilled labour force, Europe would lack the well-educated and affluent consumers needed for a vibrant marketplace, and poorer regions would not attract the kind of investment and infrastructure needed to help the EU compete at the global level.

Recognizing these problems, the EU has given priority to cohesion, meaning a reduction in economic disparities in the interests of promoting economic and social progress. In order to do this, the EU has increased efforts to help bring the poorer member states closer to the level of their wealthier partners. While free marketeers have always hoped that the single market would have a 'trickle-down' effect by directing more investment towards the poorer parts of Europe, the EU has taken a more proactive approach by setting up several structural funds, aimed at spending in the interests of cohesion. They include the following:

- The European Regional Development Fund (ERDF), which is spent mainly on underdeveloped areas (particularly those affected by the decline of traditional industries such as coal, steel, and textiles) and inner cities. Its goal is to encourage sustainable integrated economic development, particularly in the areas of transport, energy, health and social infrastructure, the environment, and tourism.
- The European Social Fund (ESF), which was mentioned in the Treaty of Rome and is designed to promote employment and worker mobility, combat long-term unemployment and help workers adapt to technological change; particular attention is paid to the needs of migrant workers, women, and the disabled.
- The Cohesion Fund, which compensates poorer states (mainly Cyprus, Malta and the ten Eastern European member states) for the costs incurred by the tightening of environmental regulations, and provides financial assistance for transport projects.

- The Guidance Section of the European Agricultural Guidance and Guarantee Fund (EAGGF), which is part of the Common Agricultural Policy (see below) and is aimed at the reform of farm structures and the development of rural areas.

Additional structural funds have been set up in recent years with more focused goals: the Solidarity Fund (created in 2002 in response to serious floods in several countries) is designed to help the EU respond more quickly to natural disasters, and the Globalization Adjustment Fund is designed to help address some of the effects of globalization by helping affected businesses restructure and rebuild their competitiveness. Among them, the funds now account for about one-third of EU spending, and they have played a major role in spreading wealth and opportunity to poorer parts of the western EU, and helping level the playing field of the single market. The prospects of repeating this record in Eastern Europe are of a greater order, and the free market is likely to play a greater role, with investment flows from the west exploiting new opportunities, consumers, and pools of labour in the east. But the principle of harmonious development still applies.

Agricultural policy

Agriculture is not usually a headline issue in most industrialized countries, because it accounts for only a small fraction of economic activity. But in the hallways of the EU institutions it has long been a bone of contention: it employs barely 7 per cent of European workers, and accounts for just 3 per cent of the combined GDP of the EU, but it was for decades the most expensive, the most complex, and sometimes the most politically charged of the policy areas in which the EU was involved. The EU has more powers over agriculture, has passed more legislation on agriculture, and has seen more political activity on agriculture than on probably any other policy area. Only the foreign ministers meet more often than the agriculture ministers, and until recently agricultural subsidies swallowed up the biggest piece of the EU budget.

Agricultural policy has also been structurally different from other EU policy areas in two important respects. First, while barriers have been removed and markets opened up in almost every area of EU economic activity, agriculture remains heavily interventionist. The EU has taken a hands-on approach to keeping agricultural prices high, drawing criticism not only from within the EU but from the EU's major trading partners. Second, unlike most other EU policy areas, agricultural policy was built into the Treaty of Rome, where the commitment to inaugurate a common agricultural policy was listed in Article 3, although the details were only agreed in the 1960s. Why has agriculture been so prominent?

First, at the time the Treaties of Rome were being negotiated, farming was important to European economies, societies, and cultures. It accounted for about 12 per cent of the gross national product (GNP) of the Six, and for about 20 per cent of the workforce. The Second World War had also made Europeans aware of how much they depended on imported food, and of just how prone those imports were to disruption. Many farms in the Six were small and vulnerable, and several national governments operated agricultural support and protection programmes that, for political reasons, could not be ended. At the same time, separate national systems might have interfered with the common market; hence the suggestion for a Community support system.

Second, it was a key element in the tradeoff between France and Germany when the terms of the EEC were under negotiation (Grant, 1997, pp. 63–8). France was concerned that the common market would benefit German industry while providing the French economy with relatively few benefits. In the mid-1950s France had a large and efficient agricultural sector, which contributed significantly to employment and economic activity. Concerns that the common market would hurt its farmers encouraged the French government to insist on a protectionist system. Even though this was to prove expensive, talk of changing the system can even today bring protesting French farmers out in their thousands.

Third, agricultural prices are more subject to fluctuation than prices on most other goods, and since Europeans spend about a quarter of their incomes on food, those fluctuations can have knock-on effects throughout the economy. Price increases can contribute to inflation, while price decreases can force farmers to go deeper into debt, perhaps leading to bankruptcies and unemployment. The problem of maintaining minimum incomes has been exacerbated by mechanization, which has led to fewer people working in farming. European governments felt that subsidies could help prevent or offset some of these problems, encouraging people to stay in the rural areas and discouraging them from moving to towns and cities and perhaps adding to unemployment problems.

Finally, farmers in the richer EU states have traditionally had strong unions working for them. As well as national unions, more than 150 EU-wide agricultural organizations have been formed, many of which directly lobby the EU. Among these is the Committee of Professional Agricultural Organizations (COPA), which has member organizations from all 27 EU member states and represents farmers on a wide range of issues. Not only are farmers an influential lobby in the EU, but there are many other people who live in rural areas, and many rurally based services. The residents of small towns and villages add up to a sizeable proportion of the population, and of the vote. No political party can afford to ignore that vote, especially as there is little organized resistance to the agricultural or rural lobbies, either at the national or at the EU level.

At the core of EU activities is CAP, which has three underlying principles: the promotion of a single market in agricultural produce, a system of protectionism aimed at giving advantages to EU produce over imported produce, and joint financing (that is, the costs of CAP must be shared equitably across all the member states). What this has meant in practical policy terms is that EU farmers have until recently been guaranteed the same minimum price for their produce, irrespective of how much they produce, of world prices, or of prevailing levels of supply and demand. Meanwhile, the EU's internal market is protected from imports by tariffs, and the member states share the financial burden for making this possible.

The costs of CAP come out of the EAGGF, which was the single biggest item on the EU budget from 1962 until 2005. The bulk of funds are spent in the Guarantee Section, which is used to buy and store surplus produce, and to encourage agricultural exports. Most of that money goes to the producers of dairy products, cereals, oils and fats, beef, veal, and sugar. Meanwhile, the Guidance Section is one of the elements that makes up the EU's structural funds, and is used to improve agriculture by investing in new equipment and technology, and helping those working in agriculture with pensions, illness benefits, and other supports.

In terms of its original goals – increasing productivity, ensuring a fair standard of living for farming communities, stabilizing markets, securing supplies, and protecting European farmers from the fluctuations in world prices – CAP has been an outstanding success. Western European farmers have never been wealthier, and their livelihoods have become more predictable and stable. The EU has become by far the world's biggest agricultural exporter, accounting for 43 per cent of the world total, or more than four times as much as the United States (World Trade Organization website, 2007). Encouraged by guaranteed prices, Western European farmers have squeezed more and more from their land, so that production has gone up in virtually every area, and the EU is now self-sufficient in almost every product it can grow or produce in its climate (including wheat, barley, wine, meat, vegetables, and dairy products), and produces far more butter, cereals, beef and sugar than it needs. CAP alone cannot be credited with all the successes, because farmers have also been helped by intensification, mechanization, and the increased use of agrochemicals, but it has certainly been at the core of agricultural change in the EU.

Unfortunately, CAP has also created many problems:

- EU-15 farmers have produced more than the market can bear, creating stockpiles of surplus produce, including cereal, powdered milk, beef, olive oil, raisins, figs, and even manure.
- CAP funding has been blighted by fraud. Differences between EU prices and world prices have meant high refunds that have provided an irresistible temptation for less honest farmers and – in Italy – for organized crime (Grant, 1997, pp. 99–101).

- CAP has created economic dependency (sustaining farmers who would have gone out of business), has pushed up the price of agricultural land, and has failed to close the income gap between rich and poor farmers. While mechanization and intensification have brought new profits to farmers in states with efficient agricultural sectors, such as Denmark, France, and the Netherlands, those in less efficient states, such as Greece, Italy, and Portugal, remain relatively poor. The gap has grown with eastern enlargement.
- CAP has encouraged the increased use of chemical fertilizers and herbicides, and encouraged farmers to cut down hedges and trees and to 'reclaim' wetlands in the interests of making their farms bigger and more efficient.
- CAP has made food more expensive for consumers, despite the surpluses.
- Because so much of the EU budget has been swallowed up by agriculture, and because there is a cap on the size of the budget, there is less available for spending in other areas.
- CAP has distorted world agricultural prices, soured EU relations with its major trading partners, and perpetuated the idea of a protectionist European Union.

With growing political and public pressure for change, numerous attempts have been made over the years to reform EU agricultural policy, but they have only recently begun to pay dividends. The first came at the end of the 1960s when rising concerns about the cost of price supports prompted the suggestion by the Commission that small farmers should be encouraged to leave the land, and that farms should be amalgamated into bigger and more efficient units. This was vehemently opposed by small farmers in France and Germany. In the early 1990s, agreement was reached to replace guaranteed prices with a system of direct payments if prices fell below a certain level, to reduce subsidies on grain, beef, and butter, and to encourage farmers to take land out of production (the 'set-aside' system) (Lewis, 1993, p. 337). Food surpluses fell and farm incomes rose as a result, and growing world cereal prices helped negate the effects for farmers of CAP price cuts.

Further reforms agreed in 2003 led to breaking the link between subsidies to farmers and the amount they produce, with farmers instead receiving a single payment (although individual member states are allowed a limited reversion to the old system if there is a danger of significant job losses). Guaranteed prices on milk powder, butter, and other products have all been reduced and direct payments for bigger farms cut. At the same time, member states such as Britain that want to move ahead with more radical reforms have been allowed to do so. The Commission argued that the reforms would make CAP less trade-distorting and more market-oriented, that they would offer more opportunities for farmers to diversify, and that they would give the EU a stronger hand in negotiations within the World Trade Organization. Opponents demurred, arguing that it would be several years before the long-term effects became clear.

Box 8.1   The Common Fisheries Policy

The fishing industry employs barely 300,000 people in the EU, or less than 0.2 per cent of the workforce, but the state of the industry has important implications for coastal communities all around the EU. Disputes over fishing grounds in European waters have also led to sometimes bitter confrontation between EU partners and their neighbours. There were, for example, the infamous 'cod wars' of the 1960s between Britain and Iceland over access to fisheries in the north Atlantic. Similarly, in 1984 French patrol boats fired on Spanish trawlers operating inside the Community's 320 km limit, and more than two dozen Spanish trawlers were intercepted off the coast of Ireland. Spain's fishing fleet was bigger than the entire EC fleet at the time, and fishing rights were a major issue in Spain's negotiations to join the EC. In the 1990s, Spanish fishing boats became an issue in domestic British politics when Eurosceptics in the Major government quoted their presence in traditional British waters as one of their many complaints about the effects of British membership of the EU.

For all these reasons, fishing has been an unusually prominent issue in policy developments in the EU, which since 1983 has pursued a Common Fisheries Policy (CFP). The main goal of this is to resolve conflicts over territorial fishing rights and to prevent overfishing by setting catch quotas. The goals of the policy are pursued in four main ways. First, all the waters within the EU's 320 km limit have been opened up to all EU fishing boats, although member states have the right to restrict access to fishing grounds within 19 km of their shores. Second, the CFP prevents overfishing by imposing national quotas (or Total Allowable Catches) on the take of Atlantic and North Sea fish, and by regulating fishing areas and equipment, for example by setting standards on the mesh size of fishing nets. Third, it set up a market organization to oversee prices, quality, marketing, and external trade. Finally, it guides negotiations with other countries on access to waters and the conservation of fisheries. Problems with the enforcement of the CFP led to the creation in 2005 of the Fisheries Control Agency, set up to pool EU and national fisheries control systems and resources.

Eastward enlargement has added a new dimension to the issue of agriculture, because of the small size of most Eastern European farms and the relatively low productivity of farmers. Investment in agriculture also has greater political, economic and social significance, given the relatively large farming populations in the east (see Figure 8.2). Opening CAP immediately to the new member states would likely have bankrupted the EU, but special efforts also needed to be made to make sure that Eastern European farmers were not made to feel like second-class citizens. The compromise agreed was to allow them a small but growing proportion of agricultural payments. At the same time, €22 billion ($26 billion) was budgeted to be spent in the period 2000–06 under a programme called SAPARD (designed to help applicant countries prepare for CAP), a rural development package worth €5.1 billion ($6.1 billion) was made available for 2004–06, and it was agreed that direct aids would be

Figure 8.2   *Population engaged in agriculture*

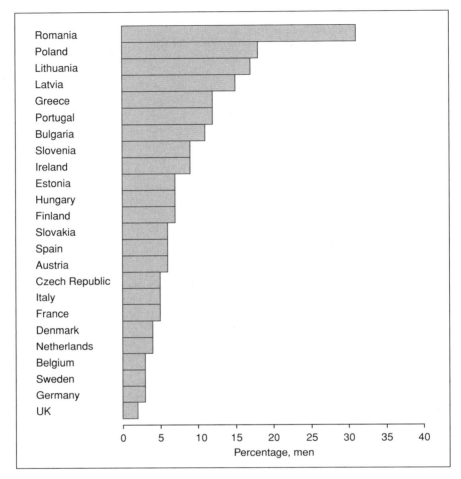

Source: World Bank website, http://www.worldbank.org/data, 2007. Figures are for 2000–05, except 2001 for Ireland. No figures available for Cyprus, Luxembourg or Malta.

phased in over ten years, starting at 25 per cent in 2004 and moving up in annual increments of 5 per cent.

Cohesion policy

The EU's cohesion policy is aimed at reducing differences in the levels of wealth, income and opportunity in the interests of promoting balanced economic and social development. The free market unavoidably contains inequalities, many of which have defied – and will continue to defy – attempts to address them, but there is strong political and public support in the EU for public programmes aimed at redistributing wealth and providing social safety nets. The wealthier EU member states have long had their own domestic programmes of economic and social development, aimed at encouraging new investment in poorer areas, at offsetting the effects of rural decline, and at trying to revive old industrial areas and the centres of large cities. But while these programmes may help offset disparities *within* member states, there is a limit to how much they can deal with such disparities *among* member states. And as long as those differences exist, attempts to build a level playing field for economic activity and social progress throughout the European single market will be undermined. Little surprise, then, that the EU has given priority to development in the poorer parts of the member states.

Armstrong (1993) suggests that there are several benefits to a joint EU approach: it ensures that spending is concentrated in the areas of greatest need, it ensures coordination of the spending of the different member states, and it encourages the member states to work together on one of the most critical barriers to integration. A common cohesion policy also means that the member states have a vested interest in the welfare of their EU partners, helps member states deal with some of the potentially damaging effects of integration (such as loss of jobs and greater economic competition), and introduces an important psychological element: citizens of poorer regions receiving EU assistance are made more aware of the benefits of EU membership, while citizens of the wealthier states that are net contributors have a vested interest in ensuring that such spending is effective.

There are two parts to cohesion policy. First, regional policy focuses on the reduction of disparities in regional wealth and income through investments in decaying industrial areas and poorer rural areas, promoting employment and equal opportunities, and improving living and working conditions. Its goal is to strengthen the European marketplace by reducing economic differences, promoting balanced economic development, addressing the handicaps posed by geographic remoteness or underdeveloped links between urban and rural areas, and dealing with the causes of social deprivation and poor education. Second, social policy addresses problems relating to employment, including job creation, the free movement of labour, improved living and working conditions, and protecting the rights and benefits of workers. At its heart are the European Employment Strategy, aimed at addressing the worryingly high and curiously persistent unemployment rates in parts of the EU (although they have improved of late in the euro zone), and the Social Agenda, aimed at providing jobs, fighting poverty, reforming pensions and health care, and addressing inequality and discrimination.

European regional policy dates back to the 1950s when provision was made by the European Coal and Steel Community for grants to depressed areas for industrial conversion and retraining. Funds were later provided under CAP for the upgrading of farms and farming equipment, the improvements of farming methods, and the provision of benefits to farmers. In 1969, the Commission proposed a common regional policy, including the creation of a regional development fund, but found little support among the governments of the member states. The climate changed after the first round of enlargement in the early 1970s, when a complex pattern of political and economic interests came together to make the idea of a regional policy more palatable. Most importantly, the 'rich man's club' of the 1950s (Italy excepted) had been joined by Britain and Ireland, whose regional problems not only widened the economic disparities within the EEC, but also strengthened Italy's demands for a regional policy. The Commission-sponsored Thomson report argued in 1973 that regional imbalances were acting as a barrier to one of the goals of the Treaty of Rome ('a continuous and balanced expansion' in economic activity), threatened to undermine plans for economic and monetary union, and could even pose a threat to the common market (Commission of the European Communities, 1973). Agreement was reached to create a European Regional Development Fund (ERDF) in 1975.

The Single European Act brought new attention to regional policy, introducing a new Title V on Economic and Social Cohesion, and arguing the need to 'clarify and rationalize' the use of the structural funds. Reforms agreed in 1988, based on Britain's insistence on reduced CAP spending and increased spending under the structural funds, helped improve the efficiency of regional policy by setting up Community Support Frameworks under which the Commission, the member states and the regions would work more closely together on agreeing the means to achieve regional development planning goals. More changes to regional policy came with Maastricht, under which a Committee of the Regions (COR) was created to give regional authorities a greater say in European policy, and the Cohesion Fund was created. The latter grew out of concern that economic and monetary union might worsen regional disparities, particularly given that poorer countries were going to be handicapped by the requirement (as a prelude to the single currency) for member states to limit their budget deficits to 3 per cent of GDP.

Regional policy is now one of the most important policy concerns of the European Union. In 1975 structural fund spending accounted for less than 5 per cent of the EEC budget, but now it amounts to more than one-third of all EU spending (more than €45 billion in 2007) and more than half of all EU citizens now benefit from projects paid for by the structural funds. A total of €308 billion is budgeted to be spent on regional policy between 2007 and 2013, with the following goals in mind:

- Help for Objective 1 regions, or those with a per capita GDP of 75 per cent or less of the EU average, suffering from low levels of investment, higher than average unemployment rates, a lack of services for businesses

Box 8.2 Europe's standard of living

Assessed by almost any objective measure of the quality of life, Western Europeans are among the most privileged people in the world. They have access to an advanced system of education and health care, an extensive and generous welfare system, a vibrant consumer society, and a sophisticated transport and communications system. An African infant is 21 times more likely to die at birth than a European infant, and the average European can expect to live 24 years longer than the average African and 18 years longer than the average Indian. Europeans enjoy almost universal literacy, employed Europeans enjoy more paid holiday leave and leisure time than almost anyone else, and the provision of shelter and nutrition is more than adequate. Eastern Europe still has to work to catch up, but the opportunities offered by European integration are helping it with investments in education, health care, and infrastructure, and its citizens are seeing significant change. One author even argues that the quality of life of Europeans as a whole is eclipsing that of Americans, long thought of as living in the world's most socially privileged country (Rifkin, 2004).

Much can be attributed to the philosophy adopted by most Western European governments after the Second World War that the state should provide a wide range of basic social services, creating a safety net through which even the poorest and the most underprivileged would not be allowed to slip. Hence every EU member state has some form of state education and national health care, and the provision of care for children and the aged has increased as the number of lone-parent families and retirees has grown. Most wealthier European states even do well in comparison with the United States, which has the most technologically advanced health care in the world but lacks a national health service, and is one of the richest economies in the world yet still has 15 per cent of its people living in poverty.

Not all of Europe's welfare policies have succeeded, and it is one of the great ironies of life in modern industrialized democracies that considerable want continues to exist in the midst of plenty. Poverty has not gone away and in several places has worsened, creating considerable differences across Europe. This is particularly true of the number of children living in poverty, which stands at less than 10 per cent in Germany, the Netherlands, and Sweden, but is almost twice as high in Britain and Italy. On these and other indicators, the Eastern European states still lag behind, but the benefits of EU membership will likely help them in much the same way as it has helped Greece, Ireland, Portugal, and Spain, all of which have seen dramatic improvements in quality of life.

and individuals, and poor basic infrastructure. They once included areas on the margin of the EU, such as Greece, southern Italy, Spain, Portugal, Ireland, and northern Finland, but with eastern enlargement they have now moved east; almost the entire area of the ten Eastern European member states qualifies for Objective 1 assistance.

- Help for Objective 2 areas, defined as those suffering from high unemployment, job losses and industrial decline. These are mainly older industrial regions undergoing economic change, rural areas facing a decline in traditional activities, and coastal areas with falling income from fisheries, and are found mainly in southern France, northern Spain and Italy, northern England, and Sweden and Finland.

- The promotion of Objective 3 programmes aimed at developing human resources. The whole of the EU is eligible, and these programmes are aimed at promoting education, training and employment policies in areas not eligible for Objective 1 aid. Germany, Britain, France, Italy, and Spain (in that order) are the biggest recipients.
- There are also a host of specialized 'Community Initiatives' with specific objectives, some of which overlap with social policy. These include Interreg, which promotes cross-border, transnational and inter-regional cooperation with a view to helping the balanced development of multi-regional areas; Urban, which focuses on regenerating cities and declining urban areas; Leader+, which promotes sustainable rural development; and Equal, which addresses inequalities and discrimination in the labour market.

The jury is still out on the effectiveness of EU regional policy. An independent report commissioned by the European Commission and published in 2004 concluded that there was little hard evidence that the structural funds had either made a significant difference to closing regional disparities, or that they had not (Sapir *et al.*, 2004), but the Commission itself disagreed. There is still a substantial gap in per capita GDP between the richest and poorest member states, but it has been closing, and the case of Ireland stands as an example of what is possible. Once one of the poorest parts of the EU, it saw double-digit economic growth during much of the 1990s and falling unemployment. EU structural support cannot be given sole credit, but in combination with sensible domestic economic policies – including cuts in corporate and capital gains tax – and a general upturn in the economic fortunes of most capitalist economies, it certainly helped.

The focus of regional policy in the period 2007–14 will be on three objectives: the convergence objective (which will take up more than four-fifths of funding) will focus on the poorest member states, helping them develop infrastructure and exploiting their economic and human potential; the regional competitiveness and employment objective will focus on research, sustainable development, and job training, and all member states will be eligible to apply for support; and the European Territorial Cooperation programme will focus on cross-border and inter-regional projects.

Meanwhile, EU social policy is aimed at reducing social differences among Europeans. Without equal pay, equal working conditions, comparable standards on workers' rights and women's rights, and an expansion of the skilled workforce, the foundations of a workable single market will be undermined. Poorer European states will suffer the effects of competition from their wealthier partners in the EU, while those with less progressive employment laws will lose jobs to those that offer better working conditions. These concerns combined with the long history of welfare promotion in individual Western European states have helped make social policy an important part of the EU agenda.

Social policy deals mainly with questions related to employment, or the rights, opportunities, and benefits provided to potential, actual, or former workers. These activities have proved controversial, because social policy treads on sensitive ideological and cultural toes. Conservatives and liberals will never agree on the best way of building a level social playing field, and programmes that may be seen as progressive by one member state may be seen as a threat to economic progress or even cultural identity by another. Generally speaking, national labour unions have been in favour of EU social policy, as have the Commission and Parliament (dominated as it was until the 1999 elections by social democratic parties), while business interests and conservative political parties have been opposed, arguing that social policy could make European companies less competitive in the global market (Geyer and Springer, 1998, p. 208).

Relatively little attention was paid to social issues in the early days of the EEC: concern about the competitive implications of different levels of social security payments and labour costs encouraged the EEC Six to avoid addressing social questions head-on during the negotiations leading up to the Treaty of Rome. The treaty ended up being based on the naive assumption that the benefits of the single market would improve life for all European workers. This proved true to the extent that it helped increase wages, but market forces failed to deal with gender and age discrimination, wage disparities, different levels of unemployment, and safety and health needs in the workplace.

The Treaty of Rome made it the Community's business to deal with such matters as the free movement of workers, equal pay for equal work, working conditions, and social security for migrant workers. However, social issues were pushed down the EEC agenda while governments concentrated on completing the single market and resolving battles over agricultural policy, and the movement of workers was heavily restricted. Restrictions began to be eased so that labour shortages in the larger northern economies could be overcome. This led to an influx of immigrants from southern Europe, mostly from non-EC states such as Greece, Portugal, Spain, and Turkey, and what was then Yugoslavia. Enlargement in 1973 brought an increase in the disparities in levels of economic wealth within the Community, so social policy was pushed up the political agenda. The European Social Fund was set up in 1974, and the first in a series of four-year Social Action Programmes (SAPs) was launched, aimed at developing a plan of action to achieve full employment, improved living and working conditions, and gender equality. However, a combination of recession and ideological resistance from several European leaders ensured that many of the words failed to be translated into practical change on the ground.

Because a core goal of the Single European Act (SEA) was the freedom of Europeans to live and work wherever they liked in the EC, social policy came to the fore again as questions were raised about the mobility of workers and about 'social dumping': money, services, and businesses moving to those parts of the Community with the lowest wages and social security costs. The Commission tried to focus the attention of national governments on the 'social dimension' of the single market, but economic recession made sure that the SEA initially lacked such a dimension. This encouraged the then Commission president Jacques Delors – a moderate socialist – to launch an attempt in 1988 to draw more attention to the social consequences of the single market.

The Belgian government had raised the idea of a charter of basic social rights during its presidency of the Council of Ministers in 1987, modelled on its own new national charter. The idea was taken up by Delors, and was given a helping hand by the determination of the socialist government of François Mitterrand to promote social policy during the French presidency of the EC. Other countries with socialist governments – such as Spain and Greece – were in favour, as was the moderately conservative government of Helmut Kohl in Germany. The only opposition came from the conservative government in Britain. Margaret Thatcher considered it 'quite inappropriate' for laws on working regulations and welfare benefits to be set at the Community level, and dismissed the Social Charter as 'a socialist charter – devised by socialists in the Commission and favoured predominantly by socialist member states' (Thatcher, 1993, p. 750).

When the Charter of Fundamental Social Rights of Workers (or the Social Charter) was adopted at the 1989 Strasbourg summit, Britain refused to go along. Plans to incorporate the Social Charter into Maastricht were undermined by the refusal of Thatcher's successor John Major to agree to its content, and it was only when Britain changed its position following the 1997 election of Tony Blair that the charter was incorporated by the Treaty of Amsterdam. Among other things, it notes the right to freedom of movement, to fair remuneration for employment, to social protection (including a minimum income for those unable to find employment), to freedom of association and collective bargaining, to equal treatment, to health, safety, and protection in the workplace, and to a retirement income that allows a reasonable standard of living.

Despite all the rhetoric about social issues, most attention since the 1990s has focused on just one problem: the failure of the EU to ease unemployment, the persistence of which was once described as equivalent to the persistence of poverty in the United States (Dahrendorf, 1988, p. 149). The single market has not been able to generate enough jobs for Europeans, and although unemployment rates in the EU-15 fell during the 1990s, they still do not compare well with the United States and Japan (see Figure 8.3). The causes are unclear, but at least part of the problem has been the relative weakness of trade unions and the relative ease with which workers can be laid off. Another factor is the size of the informal labour market in Europe, which accounts for as much as one-fifth of GDP in some states and is all but institutionalized in southern Italy, where it overlaps with organized crime. The EU has launched a host of retraining programmes, and is shifting resources to the poorer parts of the EU through various regional and social programmes, but with mixed results. Geyer and Springer (1998, p. 210) argue that EU employment policy has had 'high visibility but little focus', and that the search for solutions is hampered by a lack of support in the member states, which have been responsible for employment policy. They also note that the EU has the problem of trying to create jobs through increased competitiveness while preserving the traditional rights of employees.

One of the changes that came with the Amsterdam treaty was the introduction of an employment chapter that called on member states to 'work towards developing a coordinated strategy for employment'. However, it only requires the Commission and the member states to report to each other, and most of the responsibility for employment policy still remains with the member states. Unemployment has been high on the agendas of several recent European Council summits, which have agreed common guidelines on employment policy, including a fresh start for the young and the long-term unemployed, and simplified rules for small and medium-sized enterprises. Although millions of new jobs have been created in the EU since the 1990s, nearly half are temporary or part-time jobs, many of them are in the service sector, and because most are being filled by men and women new to the job market, they have done little to help ease long-term unemployment.

Another issue on the social agenda has been an improvement in the status of women. The position of women in politics and the workforce in the EU is not that different from their relative position in other liberal democracies, but the situation varies significantly from one member state to another, giving added importance to EU social policy and the goal of building economic and social cohesion. In general, women are in a better position in progressive northern European states such as Denmark, Finland, and Sweden, and relatively worse off in poorer states such as Portugal, Spain, Greece, and Eastern Europe.

About one in three European workers are women, but career options are still limited, proportionately more women than men are employed in part-time jobs, and women are more likely to work in traditionally feminized jobs – such as nursing and teaching – than in management, and in the less well-paid and more labour-intensive sectors of industry (Springer, 1992, p. 66). Unemployment figures are higher for women than for men in most EU states, and women are also paid less than men for comparable work – about 80 per cent of the wages earned by a man. On the other hand, about 75 per cent of

Figure 8.3   *Unemployment in the European Union*

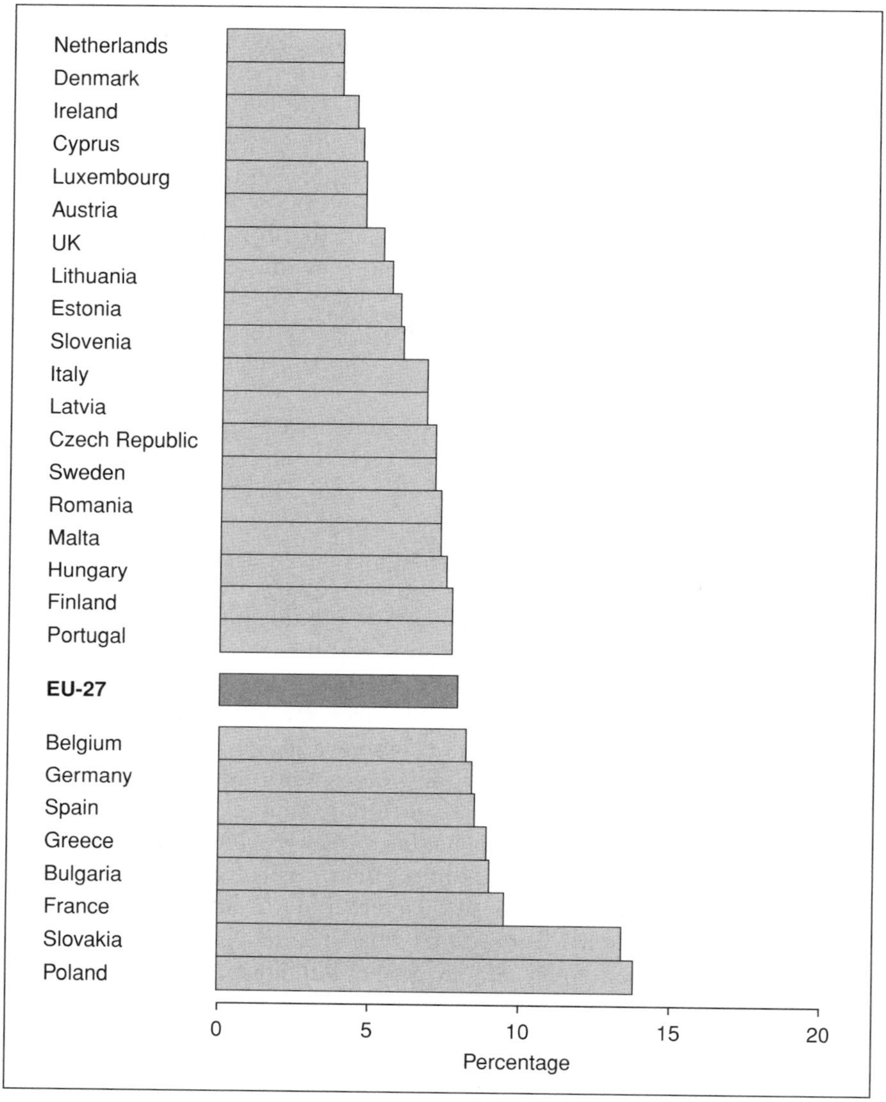

Netherlands	
Denmark	
Ireland	
Cyprus	
Luxembourg	
Austria	
UK	
Lithuania	
Estonia	
Slovenia	
Italy	
Latvia	
Czech Republic	
Sweden	
Romania	
Malta	
Hungary	
Finland	
Portugal	
EU-27	
Belgium	
Germany	
Spain	
Greece	
Bulgaria	
France	
Slovakia	
Poland	

Percentage (0, 5, 10, 15, 20)

Source: Eurostat website, http://epp.eurostat.ec.europa.eu, 2007. Figures are for 2006.

working women are employed in the expanding service sector, all EU member states are legally obliged to provide maternity leave, several member states offer parental leave, and the public provision of child care is improving.

Although the rights of working women were mentioned in the Treaty of Rome (which, for example, establishes the principle of equal pay for men and women), it was not until the EEC began to look more actively at social policy in the 1970s that women's issues began to be addressed. The 1974 SAP included the goal of achieving gender equality in access to employment and vocational training, and equal rights at work were promoted by new laws such as the 1975 equal pay directive and the 1976 equal treatment directive. Even though direct and indirect gender discrimination is illegal under EU law, however, women still face invisible barriers and glass ceilings.

Elitism and gender bias in the EU are exemplified by imbalances in the staffing of the major EU institutions, although things are improving. The first woman ever appointed to the College of Commissioners was Vasso Papandreou of Greece in 1991. There were five women in the 1999–2004 College, and thanks to a specific request to governments from president José Manuel Barroso to nominate more women, eight of the 27 commissioners in 2004–09 were women. Female membership of the European Parliament has also improved, with about one third of MEPs being women in the 2004–09 Parliament. Meanwhile, however, there are many more men than women in the more senior bureaucratic positions in the Commission and Council of Ministers, and many more women than men in secretarial and clerical positions, only three of the 27 judges on the Court of Justice in 2007 were women, and only three women – Margaret Thatcher, Angela Merkel and former French prime minister Edith Cresson – have ever taken part in meetings of the European Council.

Environmental policy

When the Treaty of Rome was drafted and signed, environmental concerns barely registered on the radars of European governments. It would not be until the 1960s that broader public and political awareness of the need to manage natural resources and to limit the damaging effects of human activity began to emerge, but even then the response of most governments was to create new institutions rather than develop substantive policies to pass new laws; the environmental implications of economic development were little appreciated or understood. The few pieces of 'environmental' law that were agreed by the Community in the 1960s were prompted less by concern about environmental quality than by worries over the extent to which different national environmental standards were distorting competition and complicating progress on the common market.

By the early 1970s thinking had begun to change. There was a public reaction against what was seen as uncaring affluence, generated by a combination of improved scientific understanding, worsening air and water quality, several headline-making environmental disasters, and new affluence among the western middle classes (see McCormick, 1995, Chapter 3, for more details).

Just as the governments of the member states could not avoid being caught up in the growing demand for a response, so the improvement of environmental quality had to be pushed up the agenda of European integration. The first step was taken with the publication in 1973 of the first Environmental Action Programme. More programmes followed, emphasizing the importance of environmental protection as an essential part of 'harmonious and balanced' economic growth. In 1986 the Single European Act gave the environment legal status as a Community policy concern, while later institutional changes gave the European Parliament a greater role in environmental policy making, and introduced qualified majority voting on most issues related to environmental law and policy.

A multinational response to environmental problems makes sense at several levels:

- Many problems – such as air and water pollution – are not limited by national frontiers, and are best addressed by several governments working together. Thus the air pollution created in Britain and Germany and blown by the winds to Scandinavia can only effectively be addressed by producers and recipients working together, and the management of rivers that run through several countries – such as the Rhine and the Danube – can only work if designed and implemented by all these countries.

- Individual countries working alone may not want to take action for fear of saddling themselves with costs that would undermine their economic competitiveness; they have fewer such fears when several countries are working towards the same goals at the same time. As states become more dependent on trade and foreign investment, and the barriers to trade come down, so parochial worries about loss of comparative economic advantage become less important.

- The economic benefits of removing barriers to free trade (including different environmental standards) help offset some of the costs of taking action.

- Rich countries can help poor countries address environmental problems through funding assistance and a sharing of technical knowledge, and over the long term will see fewer factories closing and being moved to countries with lower environmental standards.

Community policy was initially based on taking preventive action and working to make sure that divergent national policies did not act as barriers to free trade, a problem noted by the Court of Justice in 1980 when it argued that competition could be 'appreciably distorted' in the absence of common environmental regulations. States with weak pollution laws, for example, had less of a financial or regulatory burden than those with stricter ones, and might attract corporations that wanted to build new factories with a minimum of built-in environmental safeguards.

By the early 1980s the Community had switched to a focus on environmental management as the basis of economic and social development. Environmental factors were consciously considered in other policy areas, notably agriculture, industry, energy and transport, and were no longer taking second place to the goal of building a single market. The logic of this idea was taken a step further in the 1990s when the EU adopted the principle of sustainable development, agreeing that no economic development should take place without careful consideration of its potential impact on the environment.

There has since been strong public support for EU activities on the environment. Eurobarometer polls have found that most Europeans rank environmental protection above finance, defence, or employment as an issue of EU concern, that most feel pollution is an 'urgent and immediate problem', and that most agree that environmental protection is a policy area better addressed jointly by EU states than by member states alone. Underpinning these opinions has been the growth in support for Green political parties. In the 1989 EP elections, 30 Green members were returned from seven member states, and by the late 1990s Greens were also sitting in the national legislatures of most EU-15 member states, and were members of coalition governments in Belgium, Finland, Germany, and Italy. In 2004 there were members from about a dozen (mainly western) member states.

A substantial body of environmental law has been agreed by the EU, covering everything from environmental impact assessment to controls on lead in fuel, sulphur dioxide and suspended particulates, lead in air, pollutants from industrial plants and large combustion plants, nitrogen dioxide, and vehicle exhaust emissions. Six action programmes have been published (the sixth covers the period 2000–10), a plethora of Green and White Papers has generated discussion on a wide range of issues, and the goals of EU policy have been given new definition since 1995 by the work of the European Environment Agency (EEA), a data-gathering agency that provides information to the other EU institutions. The EEA has been involved in the publication since 1995 of a series of triennial regional assessments of the state of the European environment.

Environmental management is now one of the most important areas of policy activity for the EU, ranking only behind foreign policy cooperation, economic issues and agriculture in terms of the level of political activity involved. Environmental policy in the EU is now made more as a result of joint European initiatives than as a result of activities at the level of the member states. In the cases of countries such as Portugal and Spain, and of most Eastern European states, which had taken little action on the environment before joining the EU, their national laws are now almost entirely driven by the requirements of EU law.

Box 8.3   Principles of European environmental policy

The goals of EU environmental policy are outlined in the treaties and in the six Environmental Action Programmes, but they are broad and generalized. They include the improvement of the quality of the environment, the protection of human health, the prudent use of natural resources, increased environmental efficiency (meaning improvements in the efficiency with which resources are used so that consumption is reduced), and the promotion of measures at the international level to deal with regional or global environmental problems.

Whatever the goals say, EU policy has so far focused on problems that are better dealt with jointly than nationally, such as the control of chemicals in the environment, the reduction of air and water pollution, the management of waste, fisheries conservation, and the control of pesticides. The EU has also been active in areas not normally defined as 'environmental' at the national level, including noise pollution and the control of genetically modified organisms. It has been less involved in the protection of ecosystems, natural habitats, and wildlife, the management of natural resources such as forests and soil, and the promotion of energy conservation and alternative sources of energy. Among the underlying principles of EU policy are the following:

- *Sustainable development*: renewable natural resources such as air, water, and forests should be used in such a way as to ensure their continued availability for future generations.
- *Integration*: environmental protection must be a component of all EU policies that might have an environmental impact. This principle applies in only three other EU policy areas: consumer protection, culture, and human health.
- *Prevention*: the EU emphasizes action to prevent the emergence of environmental problems, rather than just responding to problems as they arise.
- *Subsidiarity*: the EU restricts itself to issues that are best dealt with jointly, leaving the rest to be addressed by the member states.
- *Derogation*: member states unable to bear the economic burden of environmental protection are given longer deadlines, lower targets, or financial assistance.

Although there has been progress on environmental policy making, the record on implementation is not so good, and experience in this field says something more broadly about the difficulties that policy making faces at the level of the EU. The record on the environment is explained by several factors:

- A lack of financial and technical resources.
- Organizational problems within EU institutions.
- The fact that most EU law has focused on developing policies rather than the means of implementing and enforcing them.
- The failure of all the parties involved in making policy to recognize the difficulty of meeting the goals they have set.
- The limited ability of the Commission to ensure that member states implement EU law.
- The long-term lack of a legal basis to EU environmental policy.

It is also explained by differences between the regulatory programmes and systems of the member states. Where Greece and Spain have had a poor record on implementation because their local government is relatively poorly organized and under-equipped, Germany and the Netherlands have a bad record because they have sophisticated systems of domestic environmental law, and lack the motivation to fully adapt their own measures to EU requirements. Meanwhile Denmark has a good record on implementation, helped by a high degree of public and official environmental awareness, effective monitoring systems, and the involvement of the Danish parliament in negotiating new environmental law (Collins and Earnshaw, 1993).

It has been argued that the Commission – through the European Environment Agency – should be given the power to carry out inspections and ensure compliance by member states, but this would raise worries about loss of sovereignty and the 'interference' of the Commission in the domestic affairs of member states. Besides, effective inspections would need huge resources: even the United States Environmental Protection Agency – with a staff of 18,000 and a multibillion dollar budget – is hard-pressed to keep up with everything it is expected to do. For the foreseeable future the Commission will have to continue to rely – as it has done for many years – on whistle-blowing by environmental interest groups, and on cases being brought before national courts and the European Court of Justice.

Regional cooperation among countries promises a quicker and more effective resolution of transnational environmental problems than any other approach, at least among countries with similar political systems and similar levels of economic development. The 2004–06 enlargement muddied the waters because of the significantly different environmental standards inherited by Eastern Europe from the Soviet era. But free market forces of the kind brought by the European Union are likely to have a more efficient and effective result than the imposition of regulations that give developing industries little incentive to think about environmental planning. Given the extent to which the causes and effects of environmental problems do not respect national frontiers, and the extent to which shared responses are more effective than unilateral responses, the EU model may provide the only adequate response to such problems, mainly because it encourages different states to cooperate rather than to adopt potentially conflicting objectives.

Conclusions

The EU approaches to agricultural, cohesion and environmental policy provide illustrations of the kinds of forces that are at work in the process of European integration, aimed at levelling the playing field and at both creating new opportunities and removing barriers to free trade.

The case of agricultural policy has been something of an aberration, the result of a political pact between two of the founding member states. In practice it is interventionist, but in principle it began as an attempt to offer equal opportunities to farmers across the EU, and to invest in rural economies that might otherwise have been left behind. It has been almost too successful, offering a blank cheque that has invited European farmers to produce as much as the land would sustain, rather than being driven by what the market would bear. But this is now changing.

Regional development has meant an attempt to help the poorer regions catch up with their richer neighbours, with the utopian goal of encouraging an equitable distribution of the benefits of integration. The EU has tended to equate development with growth, but whether quantity and quality go hand in hand has long been debatable. It is also debatable whether the free market can ever entirely eliminate inequalities of opportunity, which is why regional policy has been based on a kind of grand welfare system that sees the redistribution of wealth as a means of encouraging equal opportunity. It remains to be seen how long it will take to bring the different parts of the EU to the same economic level, assuming this is even possible.

Social policy has been aimed at reducing differences in income, working conditions, and worker skills with a view to creating an even playing field in the labour market. The attempt to build a common approach has stepped on ideological toes, but has ultimately brought all the member states around to a standard set of objectives. The biggest failure has been the inability to reduce unemployment across the EU, a problem which promises to compromise some of the achievements of the single market unless it can be relatively quickly turned around.

In the case of the environment, there is little question that international cooperation is desirable and even inevitable. Problems such as air and water pollution ignore national boundaries, and there are repeated examples from around the world of one state being a producer and downwind or downstream states being recipients. As the global economy expands, the barriers posed to trade by different environmental standards add a new dimension. There will always be strong ideological disagreement about the extent to which the state should manage natural resources and regulate industry, but there is a strong internal logic to international cooperation on environmental management. There is an emerging consensus that the EU has been a positive force in environmental protection, and that European environmental problems are better dealt with at the EU level than at the national or local level.

Chapter 9

The EU and the World

The EU presents a confusing image to the outside world. Should the 27 member states still be thought of and dealt with separately, should the European Union be considered a single large bloc, or is the best approach something in between? The answer really depends on the issue at stake. On defence and security policy the states still mainly go their own way, and so they can still be considered in isolation. But when trade negotiations are on the agenda, third parties must deal with the EU as a whole, because the member states allow the Commission to represent their collective interests. And on fiscal policy, there are two groups of states: those that have adopted the euro and those that have not.

The lack of focus and consistency, the long-time absence of policy leadership, and the confusion felt by other countries was neatly summed up in a (sadly, apocryphal) question credited to former US Secretary of State Henry Kissinger: 'When I want to speak to Europe, whom do I call?' The problem was eased in 1999 when four external relations portfolios in the Commission were replaced with one, and a High Representative was appointed to be the first point of contact on foreign and security policy matters. Another step proposed under the draft constitution, and due to be carried over into the Lisbon treaty, is to appoint a European minister responsible for 'conducting' foreign and security policy. Meanwhile, that policy has been given more definition in recent years as the leaders of the EU member states have reached agreement on a broader set of issues, allowing them to take common positions in their dealings with third parties.

But the deliberations and the decisions of those leaders may ultimately prove to have been just a prelude to the new global role thrust on the EU by a series of unconnected developments: the 2001 terrorist attacks on the United States, the 2002 launch of the euro, the 2003 US-led invasion of Iraq, and the 2004–07 eastern enlargement of the EU. Until the 2001 attacks the dominating global role of the United States was undisputed. But its failure (or at least that of the administration of George W. Bush) to provide leadership in the response to international terrorism, and the launching of a war in Iraq that was without strategic merit, have combined with the new economic and political power of Europe to help the EU to crystallize what it represents, to make Europeans conscious of how they differ on goals and values with the United States, and to provide a new source of international leadership.

While the steps taken by the EU to build a common foreign and security policy have been halting, there are no longer any doubts about its status as an economic superpower. It is the world's biggest and richest marketplace, accounting for 30 per cent of global GDP, 39 per cent of merchandise trade, and 42 per cent of trade in commercial services. It is the dominating actor in global trade negotiations, the biggest market in the world for mergers and acquisitions, and the biggest source of foreign direct investment. Its influence over the global economy continues to grow as the euro is adopted by more countries and strengthens its credentials, posing formidable competition to the US dollar and the Japanese yen. Much more is now expected of the EU as a global actor, both by its own members and by other countries. The result has been new momentum on the development of common foreign and security policies, and a reassertion of the European perspective in international affairs. The implications of this are not yet fully recognized or understood.

Building a European foreign policy

In their attempts to build a common European foreign policy, EU leaders have found themselves being pulled in two directions. On the one hand it has been clear that the EU will have more power and influence in the world if its member states act as a group rather than independently. On the other hand there has been the fear that coordination will interfere with the freedom of member states to address matters of national rather than of European interest, and will lead inexorably to the surrender of national sovereignty and the creation of a European federation. There has also been a difference of opinion regarding European relations with the United States and NATO, some leaders opting for strong continued relations, and others opting for more independence. But Europeans themselves are more certain about where the EU is headed; polls find that 75 per cent of Europeans support a common defence and security policy, 68 per cent support a common foreign policy, and 49 per cent believe that decisions on defence policy should be taken by the EU (compared to 21 per cent by national governments and 17 per cent by NATO). They also feel (by large margins) that the EU can play a more positive role than the United States in promoting international peace, encouraging environmental protection, pursuing the war on terrorism, and fighting poverty (Eurobarometer 66, December 2006).

The Treaties of Rome make no mention of foreign policy, and the EEC long focused on domestic economic policy, although the logic of spillover implied that the development of the single market would make it difficult to avoid the agreement of common external policies. There were several abortive moves in that direction in the early years of integration, including the European Defence Community (EDC) and the European Political Community, and Charles de Gaulle's plans for regular meetings among the leaders of the Six to coordinate foreign policy. The EDC was proposed in 1950, was pursued most actively by the French, and was to have been built on the foundations of a common European army and a European minister of defence. However, Britain was opposed to the idea, preferring to pursue the goals of the Treaty of Brussels (see below) and to bring Italy and West Germany into the fold. All prospects of an EDC finally died in 1954 when the French National Assembly turned it down (Urwin, 1995, pp. 60–8).

Community leaders subsequently focused on building the single market, and it was only at their summit in The Hague in 1969 that they decided to look again at foreign policy. The following year they agreed to promote European Political Cooperation (EPC), a process by which the six foreign ministers would meet to discuss and coordinate foreign policy positions. EPC was not incorporated into the founding treaties, it remained a loose and voluntary arrangement outside the Community, no laws were adopted on foreign policy, each of the member states could still act independently, and most of the key decisions on foreign policy had to be unanimous. Nonetheless, consultation became habit-forming, and the European Council was launched in 1974 in part to bring leaders of the member states together to coordinate policies.

EPC was strictly intergovernmental, and was overseen by the foreign ministers meeting as the Council of Ministers, with overall leadership coming from the European Council. Regular meetings of senior officials from all the foreign ministries provided continuity, and a small secretariat was set up in Brussels to help the country holding the presidency of the Council of Ministers, which provided most of the momentum. Larger or more active states such as Britain and France had few problems providing leadership, but policy coordination put a strain on smaller and/or neutral countries such as Ireland and Luxembourg. The shifting of responsibilities every six months gave each member state its turn at the helm, but complicated life for non-Community states, which had to switch their attention from one member state to another, and to establish contacts with ministers and bureaucrats in six, then nine, then 12 capital cities.

EPC was given formal recognition with the Single European Act, which confirmed that the member states would 'endeavour jointly to formulate and implement a European foreign policy'. But then came the Gulf War of 1990–91, which found the Community both divided and unprepared. When Iraq invaded Kuwait in August 1990, the United States orchestrated a multinational campaign involving 13 countries in defence of Saudi Arabia, followed by a six-week air war against Iraq and a four-day ground war in February 1991. The Community was quick to ban Iraqi oil imports, suspend trade agreements, freeze Iraqi assets, and give emergency aid to frontline states (Ginsberg, 2001, p. 193), but in terms of hard military action, Community member states took quite different positions: Britain and France made major commitments of troops, warplanes and naval vessels; Germany was limited by a strong postwar tradition of pacifism and constitutional limits on the deployment of German

Box 9.1   The EU on the world stage

What is the legal basis of the EU's role in international affairs? It can adopt laws that are binding on its member states, but can it also negotiate with third parties on behalf of the member states, and enter into binding agreements with those parties? The answer depends on where one looks.

The Treaty of Rome included a Common Commercial Policy, which gave the Commission authority to negotiate with third parties, and to make recommendations to the Council of Ministers on agreements with third parties. It also allowed the Council to authorize the Commission to open and conduct the necessary negotiations. But there were questions about the policy areas to which this applied, and it took a 1971 case before the Court of Justice (*Commission* v. *Council* (*AETR*)) to clarify matters. The immediate issue was a dispute between the Commission and the Council over an international agreement on road transport. The Commission claimed that it had competence, because the power to develop a common transport policy included the right to reach agreements with third parties. The Council disagreed, arguing that the Treaty of Rome only allowed the Commission to reach such agreements in areas specifically listed in the treaty.

The Court sided with the Commission, arguing that there were implied powers for the Commission to conclude treaties with third parties in areas which flowed from 'other provisions of the Treaty and from measures adopted ... by the Community institutions'. In other words, the Court concluded that whenever the Community adopted common rules in a particular area, the member states no longer had the right – individually or collectively – to enter into agreements with third parties that affected those rules: 'as and when those rules come into being, the Community alone is in a position to assume and carry out contractual obligations with third countries affecting the whole sphere of application of the Community legal system'.

The result was that in policy areas within which the EU has competence (authority), the Commission can sign an international agreement without the member states also signing. These areas include the Common Agricultural Policy, the Common Commercial Policy, competition, and common policies on fisheries and air transport. In such cases, the EU has only one vote. Conversely, in policy areas where the EU has little or no competence – including criminal justice, education, and taxation – the member states alone have the power to sign, in which case they have 27 independent votes. However, because there are political and practical difficulties in defining the boundaries between domestic and external policy, and between economic and non-economic policy, authority is sometimes shared, and the result is what are called 'mixed agreements': they are signed both by the EU and the member states (Smith, 1997).

troops; Belgium, Portugal and Spain made minimal military contributions; and Ireland remained neutral (van Eekelen, 1990; Anderson, 1992). The overall response, charged Luxembourg foreign minister Jacques Poos, underlined 'the political insignificance of Europe'. For Belgian foreign minister Mark Eyskens, it showed that the EC was 'an economic giant, a political dwarf, and a military worm' (*New York Times*, 25 January 1991).

The divisions over the war – coupled with the dramatic changes then taking place in Eastern Europe and the former USSR – emphasized the need for Europe to address its foreign policy more forcefully, and political pressure grew for a review of EPC. The result was its replacement under Maastricht by the Common Foreign and Security Policy (CFSP). Despite the new label, however, the goals of the CFSP were only loosely defined, with vague talk about the need to safeguard 'common values' and 'fundamental interests', 'to preserve peace and strengthen international security', and to 'promote international cooperation'.

CFSP brought about a steady convergence of positions among the member states on key international issues. Their UN ambassadors met frequently to coordinate policy, the EU agreed several 'common strategies', such as those on Russia and the Ukraine, 'joint actions', such as transporting humanitarian aid to Bosnia and sending observers to elections in Russia and South Africa, and 'common positions' on EU relations with other countries, including the Balkans, the Middle East, Myanmar, and Zimbabwe. The EU also coordinated western aid to Eastern Europe, Russia and the former Soviet republics during the 1990s, and has become the major supplier of aid to developing countries (see later in this chapter). The significance of the EU as an actor on the global stage is also reflected in the fact that almost every country in the world now has diplomatic representation in Brussels (both for Belgium and for the EU), and that the Commission has opened more than 130 overseas delegations. In his study of the EU's international political influence, Ginsberg (2001) concludes that it has had more impact, and on a wider range of issues, than is generally recognized.

But there have also been many examples of weakness and division, perhaps nowhere more so than in the Balkans in the 1990s (see Peterson, 2003). When the ethnic, religious and nationalist tensions that had long been kept in check by the Tito regime (1944–80) broke into the open, and Croatia and Slovenia seceded from Yugoslavia in June 1991, the Yugoslav federal army responded with force. The EU brokered a peace conference, but then lost its credibility when it recognized Croatia and Slovenia in January 1992, and it was left to the United States to broker the Dayton peace accords in 1995. The EU also failed to act on a 1996 dispute between Greece and Turkey over an uninhabited Aegean island, prompting Richard Holbrooke, the US Assistant Secretary of State for European affairs, to accuse the EU of 'literally sleeping through the night'. Then there was the EU's feeble response to the 1998 crisis in the Yugoslav province of Kosovo. When ethnic Albanians in Kosovo began agitating for independence from Serb-dominated Yugoslavia, the government of Slobodan Milosevic responded with force, leading to a massive refugee problem and reports of massacres of both Kosovars and Muslims. When the military response eventually came, in March 1999, it was led not by the EU but by the United States under the auspices of NATO.

Some of the structural weaknesses in the CFSP were addressed by the Treaty of Amsterdam: as well as opening up the possibility of limited majority voting on foreign policy issues, the rotation of countries holding the presidency of the EU was changed so that large member states alternated with small ones, more effectively balancing leadership. A Policy Planning and Early Warning Unit was also created in Brussels to help the EU anticipate foreign crises, and the old habit of having four different regional external affairs portfolios in the European Commission ended with the creation of a single foreign policy post and the appointment of a High Representative on foreign policy; the first office-holder was Javier Solana, former secretary-general of NATO. Under the terms of the Lisbon treaty, the High Representative and the external relations commissioner will be rolled into a European foreign minister, who will be appointed by the European Council and will both chair the General Affairs and External Relations Council and be a member of the Commission. If the formula works, then Henry Kissinger's question might finally be answered.

Towards a European defence policy

Dealing with the 'foreign' element of the CFSP – while not easy – has been less politically troubling than dealing with the 'security' element. Together the EU member states have formidable military power at their disposal, with nuclear weapons, nearly 1.9 million active personnel, nearly 3,500 combat aircraft, and more non-nuclear submarines and surface naval combat vessels than the United States (aircraft carriers excepted) (see International Institute for Strategic Studies, 2007). Were it to agree a common defence policy and shared command structures, it could transform itself into a military superpower. But European governments have independent opinions and priorities when it comes to committing their forces, there is still only limited coordination on policy, and progress on setting up a European defence force has been slow. There has also been an ongoing division of opinion within the EU about how to relate to NATO and the United States (see Box 9.2).

Maastricht stated that one of the goals of the EU should be 'to assert its identity on the international scene, in particular through the implementation of a common foreign and security policy including the eventual framing of a common defence policy'. But while the CFSP moved defence more squarely onto the EU agenda, Maastricht provided a loophole by committing member states to a common policy that would 'include all questions related to the security of the Union, including the *eventual* framing of a common defence policy, *which might in time* lead to a common defence' (emphasis added).

In June 1992, EU foreign and defence ministers meeting at Petersberg, near Bonn, issued a declaration in which they agreed that military units from member states could be used to promote the 'Petersberg tasks': humanitarian, rescue,

Box 9.2   A European or an Atlantic defence?

One of the core issues in the debate about European foreign policy is the question of how the EU should relate to the North Atlantic Treaty Organization (NATO) and the United States. Among governments, there are two main schools of thought:

- Atlanticists such as Britain, the Netherlands, Portugal, and several Eastern European states emphasize the importance of the security relationship with the United States, and are loath to do anything that could be interpreted as undermining or replacing the transatlantic security relationship.
- Europeanists such as France, Italy, Spain, and sometimes Germany look more towards European independence, and believe that the EU should reduce its reliance on the American defensive shield.

During the cold war (1945–91), Atlanticists had the upper hand because the main defence issue was security against a Soviet attack, something that fell squarely under the remit of a US-dominated NATO. Furthermore, member states had different policy positions and different defence capacities: the British and the French had special interests in their colonies and former colonies, the Germans and the Dutch saw their armed forces as part of the broader NATO system, and several countries – notably Ireland – were neutral. Europeans became used to coordinating their defence policies within the NATO framework, guided by US leadership.

With the end of the cold war, Europeanists appeared to gain ground, in part thanks to changes in US policy. President Kennedy had spoken during his inauguration in 1960 of the willingness of the United States to 'bear any burden' and 'meet any hardship ... to assure the survival and success of liberty'. By the mid-1990s, though, American public opinion had turned against such an idea, and the term 'burden sharing' became more common in transatlantic discussions, with demands for the EU to take on greater responsibility for addressing its own security threats. Meanwhile, the ability of the EU to respond to security threats was clearly inadequate, a problem that became more critical during the 1990s as US defence spending fell (Barber, 1998). Then came the divisions over how to conduct the war on terrorism, and the transatlantic fallout over the 2003 US-led attack on Iraq, the latter in particular showing that European public opinion was taking an increasingly independent view. According to a Eurobarometer poll taken in 2003 (in the EU-15 only), 75–77 per cent of Europeans favoured foreign policy independence from the United States.

peacekeeping, and other crisis management jobs (including peacemaking). Early indications of how this might work came when EU personnel worked with NATO in monitoring the UN embargo on Serbia and Montenegro, helped set up a unified Croat-Muslim police force to support the administration of the city of Mostar in Bosnia in 1994–96, and helped restructure and train the Albanian police force in 1997. Also in 1997, the Treaty of Amsterdam resulted in the incorporation of the Petersberg tasks into the EU treaties, and newly-minted British prime minister Tony Blair signalled his willingness to see Britain play a more central role in EU defence matters. He and French president Jacques Chirac explored the potential of the Anglo-French axis in European security matters, and – after a December 1998 meeting in St. Malo, France – the two leaders declared that the EU should be in a position to play a full role in international affairs, 'must have the capacity for autonomous action, backed up by credible military forces, the means to decide to use them, and the readiness to do so', and suggested the creation of a European rapid reaction force. This was later endorsed by German chancellor Gerhard Schröder (for more details, see Collester, 2000).

An attempt had already been made to build a common European military outside EU and NATO structures with the founding in May 1992 of Eurocorps, set up by France and Germany to replace an experimental Franco-German brigade set up in 1990. Headquartered in Strasbourg, the 60,000-member Eurocorps became operational in November 1995, has been joined by contingents from Belgium, Luxembourg, and Spain, and has sent missions to Bosnia (1998), Kosovo (2000), and Afghanistan (2004). But this was now side-tracked by a bigger initiative: the launch in 1999 of the European Security and Defence Policy (ESDP) (see Howorth, 2003). An integral part of the CFSP, this was to consist of two key components: the Petersberg tasks, and a 60,000-member Rapid Reaction Force (RRF) that could be deployed at 60 days' notice and sustained for at least one year, and could carry out these tasks. The Force – championed mainly by Britain and France – was not intended to be a standing army, was designed to complement rather than compete with NATO, and could only act when NATO had decided not to be involved in a crisis. The plan was to have it ready by the end of 2003, but it proved more of a challenge than expected, and by 2004 the EU was talking of the more modest goal of creating 'battle groups' that could be deployed more quickly and for shorter periods than the RRF. The groups would consist of 1,500 troops each that could be committed within 15 days, and could be sustainable for between 30 and 120 days.

The terrorist attacks on the World Trade Center in New York and on the Pentagon in Washington DC in September 2001 brought new issues into the equation. The meaning of 'war' and 'defence' had already changed with the end of the cold war, but the attacks – and the response to the attacks – forced a review of defence policy priorities on both sides of the Atlantic: terrorism (especially when it involved suicide attacks) could not be met with conventional military responses. Many European leaders hoped for a new era in transatlantic relations, with a new US emphasis on multilateralism and diplomacy. But although there was general political unity on the US-led invasion of Afghanistan in 2002, there was a dramatic parting of the ways over the problem with Iraq. The Bush administration charged Iraqi leader Saddam Hussein with possessing weapons of mass destruction (notably chemical and biological agents), aspiring to build nuclear weapons, and being a threat to neighbouring states and to American interests, and tried to win passage of a UN resolution condemning Iraq and authorizing military action. When this failed, an attack on Iraq was launched in March 2003.

The crisis saw European governments split into three camps: supporters of US policy included Britain, Denmark, Italy, the Netherlands, Spain, and many in Eastern Europe; opponents included Austria, Belgium, France, Germany, and Greece; those that took no position included Finland, Ireland, Portugal, and Sweden. US Defense Secretary Donald Rumsfeld caused much bafflement when, in January 2003, he dismissed France and Germany as 'Old Europe' and as 'problems' in the crisis over Iraq, contrasting them with the Eastern European governments that supported US policy. A new element was added to the debate when, in April 2003, Belgium, France, Germany, and Luxembourg announced plans to establish an independent European military headquarters that could plan operations undertaken by EU member states, and to launch a European Security and Defence Union.

Whatever the divisions of opinion among European leaders, far more significant was the remarkable uniformity of public opposition to the war in the EU. Opinion polls found that 70–90 per cent were opposed in every EU member state, including Britain, Denmark, France, Germany, and in several 'Old' Eastern European countries such as the Czech Republic and Hungary. Several pro-war governments – notably those in Britain and Spain – found themselves in trouble with their electorates, and massive public demonstrations were held in most major European capitals, including Berlin, London, and Rome. A June 2003 survey found reduced faith in American global leadership, with less than half of those questioned wanting to see a strong global US presence. In Germany, long a staunch US ally, 81 per cent of respondents felt that the EU was more important than the United States to their vital interests, up from 55 per cent in 2002 (German Marshall Fund survey, September 2003). Most remarkably, another survey found that 53 per cent of Europeans viewed the United States as a threat to world peace on a par with North Korea and Iran (Eurobarometer poll, October 2003).

In December 2003, the European Council adopted the European Security Strategy, the first ever declaration by EU member states of their strategic goals. The Strategy declared that the EU was 'inevitably a global player', and 'should be ready to share in the responsibility for global security'. It listed the key threats facing the EU as terrorism, weapons of mass destruction, regional conflicts, failing states, and organized crime. Against the background of a rapidly changing transatlantic relationship, the draft EU constitution included the stipulation that the EU should take a more active role in its own defence, talking of the 'progressive framing of a common Union defence policy' leading to a common defence 'when the European Council, acting unanimously, so decides'. But even if they are to be limited to the Petersberg tasks, the question still remains as to how European defence forces should be organized. Europeanists such as France continue to want to develop an independent EU capability. The United States is content to see the Europeans taking responsibility for those tasks from which NATO should best keep its distance, but insists that there should be no overlap or rivalry in the event of the creation of a separate European institution. Meanwhile, Atlanticists such as Britain continue to feel nervous about undermining the US commitment to Europe.

While there is no questioning the American superiority in the field of military power (the United States currently spends more on defence every year than the rest of the world combined), an issue often overlooked in the debate about the global role of the EU is the question of 'soft power'. This is defined by Joseph Nye as 'the ability to get what you want through attraction rather than coercion' (Nye, 2004, p. x), and is centred on culture, political ideals, and policies rather than on the threat of violence. Critics of US foreign policy argue that it relies too heavily on hard power rather than soft power, and that this has been one of the causes of the decline in the credibility of US foreign policy. By contrast, the EU – lacking the resources or the joint command structures to launch an effective independent military operation of any substance, and dominated by US influence in the hallways of NATO – has become adept at using soft power in its dealings with other countries. In a world in which violence is increasingly rejected as a tool of statecraft (at least among wealthy liberal democracies), the use of diplomacy, political influence, and the pressures of economic competition may be giving the EU a strategic advantage that reduces the need to develop a significant common military capacity.

But this is not to suggest that the EU is either unwilling or unable to use hard power. It is important to note that in spite of all the political disagreements, the EU has achieved far more on security cooperation than most people think, driven by a desire to decrease its reliance on the US (Jones, 2007). It is also both willing and able to use hard power when needed (Giegerich and Wallace, 2004). In 2003, it deployed peacekeeping troops in Macedonia (Operation Concordia) and in the Democratic Republic of Congo (Operation Artemis), and in December 2004 launched its biggest peacekeeping mission when 7,000 troops (many coming from outside the EU, it is true) took over from NATO in Bosnia. By 2006, the EU was contributing 50 per cent of the peacekeeping forces in Bosnia (where the office of High Representative in charge of implementation of the Dayton peace accords has always been held by an EU national), 60 per cent of the forces in Afghanistan, 70 per cent of the forces in Kosovo, and 72 per cent of the forces in Lebanon, while 12 EU states had 19,000 troops in Iraq. National military interventions have also continued, including Britain's operation in Sierra Leone in 2001 (establishing order after a UN force had failed) and France's operation in Côte d'Ivoire in 2002.

The European economic superpower

While opinion is divided on the prospects of the EU becoming a military superpower, there are no doubts at all about its new status as an economic superpower. The common external tariff is in place, the single market is all but complete, the euro has been adopted by 15 member states (with more ready to join in the next few years), the Commission has powers to represent the governments of all the member states in negotiations on global trade, and it is now well understood by everyone that the EU is the most powerful actor in those negotiations. There has also been rapid economic growth in most of the EU over the last 20 years, with even some of the poorer regions catching up as a result of the opportunities offered by the single market and investments made under the structural funds.

The figures paint a clear and incontestable picture of European power:

- With just under 8 per cent of the world's population, the European Union accounts for 30 per cent of the world's GDP (more even than the United States). It also accounts for nearly 40 per cent of global merchandise trade (more than twice as much as the United States) (see Figure 9.1).
- With enlargement in 2004–07, the population of the EU grew from 375 million to 489 million, giving the EU 63 per cent more consumers than the United States. More importantly, the personal wealth of Western Europeans – combined with the largely open internal market that now exists in the EU – means that the EU is the largest capitalist market in the world. Just as multinational corporations have found it essential since the Second World War to sell to the US market in order to maximize their profits, so they now seek a foothold in the European market, which is more accessible thanks to the completion of the single market and adoption of the euro.
- Fifteen of the 27 member states (which among them account for 74 per cent of the GDP and 64 per cent of the population of the EU) have a common currency that competes with the US dollar and the Japanese yen in terms of credibility and influence. The euro is increasingly regarded as a challenger to the status of the US dollar in global trade and finance, and suggestions have been made that it might eventually replace the dollar as the primary international reserve currency (Chinn and Frankel, 2005). Governments and corporations are increasingly borrowing in euros, nearly 40 per cent of foreign exchange transactions are now carried out in euros, central banks are holding more of their reserves in euros, and euros are increasingly used by consumers outside the euro zone, notably in Eastern Europe. Meanwhile, faith in the US dollar has declined thanks in large part to concerns about the snowballing US national debt, and to questions about American political leadership in the world.
- One-third of the corporations in the Fortune 100 list of the world's largest industrial corporations are European – mainly German, French, British,

Figure 9.1 *The EU in the global economy*

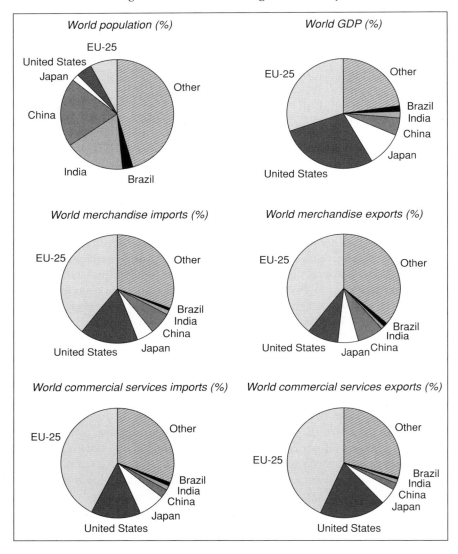

Sources: Population and GDP figures from World Development Indicators Database, World Bank website, 2007, http://www.worldbank.com. Trade figures from World Trade Organization home page, 2007, http://www.wto.org. All figures are for 2005.

Italian and Dutch. They include Royal Dutch/Shell, BP, Allianz, Total Fina Elf, Volkswagen, Siemens, AXA, Vivendi Universal, Fiat, and Peugeot.
• As noted in Chapter 7, the EU has become the biggest mergers and acquisitions market in the world, thanks to the unprecedented surge of corporate

takeovers and mergers that has occurred in the EU since the completion of the single market, notably in the chemicals, pharmaceuticals, and electronics industries. European multinationals have also become increasingly aggressive in pursuing targets outside the EU, such that the EU is now the source of two-thirds of all investment coming from OECD member states, and more than three times as much as the United States (OECD website, 2007).

- The EU has become the engine of economic growth for Eastern Europe and the former USSR, which have a combined population of more than 260 million, enormous productive potential, and a wealth of largely untapped natural resources.

The international economic presence of the EU has been built on the foundations of the removal of trade restrictions and the lowering of customs barriers that were championed by the Treaty of Rome. This outlined a Common Commercial Policy, stating that the Community would contribute 'to the harmonious development of world trade, the progressive abolition of restrictions on international trade, and the lowering of customs barriers'. To this end the EU has built a complex network of multilateral and bilateral trading networks and agreements, some based on proximity (agreements with Eastern Europe and Mediterranean states), some on former colonial ties (see the section on development cooperation below) and some on expediency (agreements with the United States and Japan).

The growth of European trade power has also been helped by an institutional structure that – unlike the structure set up for security policy – promotes common positions among the member states. The Council of Ministers is responsible for making the final decisions, but it uses qualified majority voting, and the Commission plays an active role at every level. The latter generates policy initiatives, is responsible for investigating and taking action against unfair trading practices, and makes suggestions to the Council of Ministers when it thinks that agreements need to be negotiated with other countries or international organizations. Most importantly, once the member states have agreed a position among themselves, they leave it up to the Commission to negotiate almost all external trade agreements on behalf of the EU as a whole. So if Henry Kissinger was to ask to whom he should speak in Europe regarding trade matters, the answer would be clear.

The power of the EU is particularly clear in the role it has played in global trade negotiations. In 1948, the General Agreement on Tariffs and Trade (GATT) was founded to oversee a programme aimed at removing trade restrictions and liberalizing trade; it was replaced in 1995 by the World Trade Organization (WTO). The GATT/WTO negotiations have taken place in successive rounds in which the EU states negotiate as a group, and are typically represented by the European commissioner for trade. The most recent round – which began in 2001 in Doha, Qatar – was designed to open up world markets for agricultural and manufactured goods. By 2006 they had stalled because rich and poor countries could not agree over farm subsidies and import taxes. The poor countries accused the EU in particular of supporting and protecting its farmers through CAP export subsidies (which has made European farmers more competitive and productive), and of 'dumping' their produce cheaply in poor countries, undermining the efforts of local farmers. (The United States was also criticized for its subsidies, particularly to cotton farmers.)

But more telling as a measure of EU trading power has been the frequency with which it has been at odds with the United States, the other giant at the table. If a country adopts a trade policy measure or takes an action that is considered to be a breach of a WTO agreement, the dispute can be taken to the WTO, which investigates and issues a judgment that is binding upon member states. The EU and the United States have brought more cases before the WTO than anyone else, and in many instances the disputes have been between the EU and the US, which have tussled over hormone-treated beef, banana imports, trade with Cuba, tariffs on steel, subsidies to aircraft manufacturers, and even over intellectual property rights, trade in services, and the tax regimes of third countries (Billiet, 2005).

Relations with the United States

The transatlantic relationship has blown hot and cold, which is only to be expected given that the EU and the United States are both major allies and major competitors (see Lundestad, 2003). Relations were strong after the Second World War, the United States having played a critical role in ridding Europe of Nazism, then guaranteeing European reconstruction and integration with the investments it made under the Marshall Plan and the security umbrella it provided for Western Europe during the cold war. US administrations saw integration as a way of helping the region recover from the ravages of war and of improving European (and American) security in the face of the Soviet threat. Relations cooled in the early 1960s with Charles de Gaulle's concerns about American influence in Europe, and continued to cool as the Europeans fell out with the United States over Vietnam, and over West German diplomatic overtures to Eastern Europe.

The 1971 collapse of the Bretton Woods system – precipitated by the decision of the Nixon administration to abandon the gold standard – not only marked the beginning of a steady withdrawal of the US responsibility for global leadership, but also emphasized to many Europeans the unwillingness of the United States always to take heed of European opinion on critical issues. The Community was by then rapidly catching up with the United States in economic wealth, it traded less with the United States and more with Eastern Europe, and the revival of the Western European anti-nuclear movement in the early 1980s placed a further strain on transatlantic relations.

Trade was the focus of early EC–US relations, the United States preferring to deal with security matters either through NATO or bilaterally with allies such as Britain and West Germany. The end of the Soviet hegemony in Eastern Europe in the late 1980s led to a new volatility in Europe that encouraged the first Bush administration to call for stronger transatlantic ties on political matters. The result was the signature in November 1990 of a Transatlantic Declaration committing the United States and the Community to regular high-level meetings. Contacts were taken a step further in 1995 with the adoption of a New Transatlantic Agenda and a Joint EU–US Action Plan under which both sides agreed to move from consultation to joint action aimed at promoting peace and democracy around the world, expanding world trade, and improving transatlantic ties. Biannual meetings have since taken place between the presidents of the United States, the Commission and the European Council, between the US Secretary of State and EU foreign ministers, and between the Commission and members of the US cabinet.

The EU and the United States are each other's major trade partners, and the largest sources and destinations of foreign direct investment. They continue to hold many common views on foreign policy and on the promotion of democracy and capitalism around the world, but divisions of opinion have become more common and more substantial with time. This is hardly surprising, because there has been a reassertion of European economic power since the end of the cold war, a relative decline of US influence, a revision of US economic and security priorities, and a recalculation of international relations in the vacuum left by the collapse of the USSR. An early example of a disagreement was the slowness of the Community to criticize the 1979 Soviet invasion of Afghanistan, and the unwillingness of any EC member state except West Germany to support the resulting US-led boycott of the 1980 Moscow Olympics. Since then, the two sides have disagreed over a wide variety of political, economic, and security issues, and over the trade issues discussed earlier.

Nothing illustrates the many questions that now hover over the transatlantic relationship quite so vividly as the fallout from the US-led invasion of Iraq. It is still too early to fully appreciate its impact, but there is no question that Americans and Europeans now view each other differently. At one level, the dispute could be dismissed as just another of the many that have coloured US-European relations since 1945, and perhaps as more reflective of the short-term goals and values of the Bush administration than of long-term US policy on Europe. But the depth of public opposition to US policy was remarkable, as was the division among the leaders of the EU's four major powers: Germany, Britain, France, and Italy. For some, the dispute has shown that the worldviews of the United States and the European Union are now so different, and the opportunity so clear for an influential actor to emerge that can offer alternative analyses and prescriptions for global problems (see Box 9.3), that the war on terrorism may ultimately be seen as the beginning of

Box 9.3   The European superpower

Since the end of the cold war and the collapse of the Soviet Union, it has become increasingly common to hear the United States described as the world's last remaining superpower. 'We live in a one-superpower world,' argues American political scientist John Ikenberry, 'and there is no serious competitor in sight' (Ikenberry, 2002, p.1). But this idea of a single dominating power – the unipolar analysis – has begun to tire, and there are many who now argue that American power is in decline. Analysts quote historical precedent, noting that the dominance of a single power – a hegemon – has often encouraged the rise of other powers to balance against it (see, for example, Waltz, 1991; Layne, 1993; Huntington, 1999). Charles Kupchan (1998), while noting that the peace and prosperity of the late 1990s rested on American power, argued that America's will to underwrite the international order would not last indefinitely, and that its global influence would decline as other large countries become less enamoured of following the US lead.

Popular opinion holds that China and India are the two most likely new superpowers, but their economies are still small and their military power restricted, and China's political influence is undermined by its poor record on human rights. Instead, the most obvious challenger to US hegemony is the EU. Not only is it now quite clearly an economic superpower, but it no longer so clearly needs the security umbrella provided by the United States during the cold war, and so has been more inclined to assert its policy differences with the United States. As noted in Chapter 2, the two actors agree in general on the promotion of capitalism and democracy, and they are deeply intertwined through trade and investment, but they see the world from different perspectives. Iraq was a case in point, but Americans and Europeans have also been out of step on issues as varied as the Arab-Israeli conflict, climate change, capital punishment, support for the United Nations, how to deal with Iran and North Korea, and participation in the International Criminal Court.

The United States is not just at odds with the EU, but with much of the rest of the world. For US critics, its foreign policy choices are too heavily influenced by unilateralism, by the use of force to achieve its objectives, and by the uniqueness of the American worldview. Furthermore, the credibility of US claims to be the champion of democracy are undermined by flaws in the practice of American democracy, in particular the many questions recently raised about the American electoral process. Under the circumstances, the European Union has the opportunity to exert itself as a new global power. Building on the foundation of a different set of values, it can offer a different set of analyses of international problems, a different set of solutions, and an approach to international relations based more on diplomacy and multilateralism. The EU case suggests that great power need no longer be seen exclusively in military terms (for more detailed arguments, see McCormick, 2007).

a fundamental change not just in the nature of the transatlantic relationship, but in the balance of influence in the post-cold war world. It is certainly difficult to imagine the effects being quickly forgotten.

Relations with Eastern Europe

The dominant presence of the United States in the external relations of the EU has been supplanted to some extent in recent years by the growing importance of Eastern Europe. Not only is the EU the major source of foreign aid for the region, but the EU has now enlarged into Eastern Europe, with important political and economic implications: Eastern enlargement has increased the size of the European marketplace, opened up new investment opportunities, increased the presence of the EU as a global actor, has had critical implications for the spread of democracy and capitalism into Eastern Europe, and has helped redefine the meaning of 'Europe' – the old cold war distinctions between the east and the west are fading away, as are the differences between the boundaries of the EU and those of Europe. All is not well, however: there are concerns about the abilities of some new eastern member states to integrate with the rest of the EU, there are concerns about immigration from east to west, and an 'enlargement fatigue' has set in, raising questions about how long it will be before more countries join the EU.

The Community was quick to take a leading role in responding to the fallout from the end of the cold war, taking responsibility for coordinating western economic aid to the east, and creating in 1990 the European Bank for Reconstruction and Development (EBRD), which has since channelled public money from the EU, the United States, and Japan into development of the private sector in the east. Meanwhile, the EU signed trade and cooperation agreements with almost all Eastern European states, several billion dollars in loans were made available by the European Investment Bank, the EU sent food aid to the east, and several programmes were launched to help east European economic and social reform. More significantly, the end of the cold war generated several requests from Eastern Europe for associate or full membership of the EU, and Europe Agreements – designed to integrate Eastern European economies with those of the EU through the staged removal of barriers to trade in industrial and agricultural goods, and to the movement of workers – were signed with Hungary, Poland, Bulgaria, the Czech Republic, Romania, Slovakia, and the three Baltic states. The Treaty of Amsterdam paved the way for eastward expansion, which was confirmed in 1998 when membership negotiations began with the Czech Republic, Estonia, Hungary, Poland, and Slovenia.

In order to help these countries make the transition and prepare them for EU membership, the EU launched the Agenda 2000 programme in 1997. Essentially a working programme for the EU until 2006, it included a list of all the measures that the Commission believed were needed to bring Eastern European states into the EU without risking institutional paralysis and substantially increased costs for the existing members. The measures included reform of the structural funds to ensure that they were spent in the regions of greatest need, and the EU also agreed 'pre-accession strategies' with all applicant countries, and began publishing reports every year on the progress each country was making towards aligning their national laws and standards with those of the EU.

The enlargements of 2004–07 brought eight Eastern European states into the EU, including three former republics of the Soviet Union: Estonia, Latvia, and Lithuania. The challenge of integrating them into the EU is far from met: their governments and citizens are still struggling with the task of transforming their economies from central planning to the free market, and their political systems from one-party authoritarianism to multiparty democracy. They also face the daunting task of making sure that all domestic laws fit with EU law, which has in turn meant hiring and training staff to strengthen the capacities of domestic government departments. Eastern Europe is also relatively poor. While per capita GNP is in the $15,000–30,000 range in most EU-15 states, it is in the $1,000–5,000 range for most Eastern European states. The 12 countries that joined in 2004–07 increased the population of the EU by 20 per cent, but its wealth by less than 5 per cent.

Theoretically, any European country that meets the 'Copenhagen conditions' outlined in Chapter 3 (democracy, a free market, and the ability to adopt all existing EU laws) can be considered for membership, but more enlargement is unlikely until a clearer picture has emerged about the implications of the last round, and is impractical until the Lisbon treaty adjusts the institutional arrangements of the EU. Croatia, Macedonia and Turkey have been accepted as 'candidate countries', meaning that membership has been agreed in principle and negotiations have begun, but political and public support for further enlargement has cooled. For now, the focus of the EU has switched to improving economic and political ties with its neighbours. In 2004 the European Neighbourhood Policy was launched, encouraging a relationship that the EU describes as 'privileged', with the goal of promoting democracy, human rights, the rule of law, good governance, and market economics. Sixteen countries are targeted: Algeria, Armenia, Azerbaijan, Belarus, Egypt, Georgia, Israel, Jordan, Lebanon, Libya, Moldova, Morocco, the Palestinian Authority, Syria, Tunisia, and Ukraine.

Even if there are still many doubts about the substance and potential for success of the EU foreign and security policies as a whole, few now question the critical and dominating role that EU policy has had in ensuring the spread of democracy and free market ideas to the former Soviet bloc. The EU's leading role in this area has not only helped define EU foreign policy, but has also made the EU a major independent actor in the economic and political future of Eastern Europe. The story with EU-Russian relations, however, is not quite so happy. Links improved during the 1990s, the Russians looking for the respectability and economic opportunities that would come from a good relationship with the EU, while the EU looked for Russian support for eastern enlargement, and needed some of the oil and natural gas that Russia has in abundance. But neither side fully trusts the other, and the EU has to balance staying on good terms with Russia against its criticism of the remnants of Russian authoritarianism.

Development cooperation

European colonialism has left the European Union with a heritage of close economic and political ties to the South: Latin America, south Asia, and Africa. Several of the founding members of the Community – notably France and Belgium – still had large colonies when the Treaty of Rome was signed, and when Britain joined the EU in 1973 it brought several dozen more countries into the equation. As a result, the South has been a significant factor in the external relations of the EU, the core of the relationship being a programme of aid and trade promotion involving several dozen former European colonies in Africa, the Caribbean and the Pacific – the so-called ACP states (see Table 9.1).

EU development aid policies have been based partly on remedying quality of life issues such as poverty and hunger, but there are also less altruistic motives: the South accounts for a significant share of EU exports, and the EU continues to rely on the South as a source of oil and of key raw materials such as rubber, copper, and uranium. The EU aid programme has several different aspects. As well as allowing all Southern states to export industrial products to the EU tariff- and duty-free (subject to some limitations on volume), the EU provides food and emergency aid, and sponsors development projects undertaken by NGOs. The EU has also negotiated a series of cooperative agreements with the ACP countries, mainly non-Asian former colonies of Britain and France. These began with the 1963 and 1969 Yaoundé Conventions (named after the capital of Cameroon, where they were signed), which gave 18 former colonies preferential access to Community markets. The 18 in turn allowed limited duty-free or quota-free access by the EC to their markets. The provision of trade concessions was expanded by the four Lomé Conventions (named after the capital of Togo), which were signed in 1975, 1979, 1984, and 1989.

Lomé IV, which covered the period 1990–2000 and was revised in 1995, had three main elements. First, it provided financial aid to 71 ACP states under the European Development Fund, in the form mainly of grants for development projects and low-interest loans. Second, it provided free access to the EU for products originating in ACP countries, with the exception of agricultural products covered by CAP. About 95 per cent of ACP exports entered the EU duty-free, compared to just 10 per cent of agricultural goods from other countries, and other goods were subject to tariffs in the range of 17–23 per cent. Finally, it offered an insurance fund for ACP exports called Stabex, designed to offset falls in the value of 50 specified ACP agricultural

Table 9.1   *The ACP states*

AFRICA (48)	Mali	Dominica
Angola	Mauritania	Dominican Republic
Benin	Mauritius	Grenada
Botswana	Mozambique	Guyana
Burkina Faso	Namibia	Haiti
Burundi	Niger	Jamaica
Cameroon	Nigeria	St. Kitts and Nevis
Cape Verde	Rwanda	St. Lucia
Central African Republic	São Tomé and Principe	St. Vincent and Grenadines
Chad	Senegal	Suriname
Comoros	Seychelles	Trinidad and Tobago
Congo (Brazzaville)	Sierra Leone	
Congo (Kinshasa)	Somalia	**PACIFIC** (15)
Djibouti	South Africa	Cook Islands
Equatorial Guinea	Sudan	Fiji
Eritrea	Swaziland	Kiribati
Ethiopia	Tanzania	Marshall Islands
Gabon	Togo	Micronesia
Gambia	Uganda	Nauru
Ghana	Zambia	Niue
Guinea	Zimbabwe	Palau
Guinea-Bissau		Papua New Guinea
Côte d'Ivoire	**CARIBBEAN** (16)	Samoa
Kenya	Antigua and Barbuda	Solomon Islands
Lesotho	Bahamas	Timor-Leste
Liberia	Barbados	Tonga
Madagascar	Belize	Tuvalu
Malawi	Cuba	Vanuatu

exports. If prices fell below a certain level, Stabex made up the deficit. If they went above that level, ACP countries invested the profits in the fund for future use.

Opinions were mixed about the effects of the Yaoundé and Lomé conventions. On the one hand, they helped build closer commercial ties between the EU and the ACP states, and there was an overall increase in the volume of ACP exports to Europe from the 1960s to the 1990s. On the other hand, the conventions were widely criticized for promoting economic dependence, and for perpetuating the flow of low-profit raw materials from the ACP to the EU, and the flow of high-profit manufactured goods from the EU to the ACP. Questions were also raised about the extent to which they helped the ACP states invest in their human capital, and helped them develop greater economic independence.

Other problems were structural. Stabex did not help countries that did not produce the specified commodities, payments from the European Development Fund were small by the time the fund had been divided among 71 countries, the ACP programme excluded the larger Southern states that had negotiated separate agreements with the EU (for example, India and China), too little attention was paid to the environmental implications of the focus on cash crops for export, and the programme neither helped deal with the ACP debt crisis nor really changed the relationship between the EU and the ACP states.

The biggest problem was internal to the ACP countries themselves. They mostly failed to diversify their exports, to invest in infrastructure, to build up a more skilled labour force, and to become more competitive in the world market. The EU provided them with a generous set of trade preferences, and yet imports from the ACP as a share of the EU total fell from 6.7 per cent in 1976 to just 3 per cent in 1998. Oil, diamonds, gold, and other industrially related products accounted for about two-thirds of ACP exports to the EU, the balance being made up by agricultural products (30 per cent) and fish (5 per cent). Four countries – Nigeria, Côte d'Ivoire, Cameroon, and Mauritius – between them accounted for more than 40 per cent of EU imports from the ACP countries. At the same time, economic growth in many sub-Saharan African states was sluggish, and there was very little trade taking place among African ACP states.

Negotiations began in 1998 on a new EU-ACP agreement, which was signed in Cotonou, Benin, in 2000. Designed to run for 20 years, with revisions every five years, the Cotonou agreement added seven more countries to the ACP group, including Cuba. It places a stronger requirement on ACP states to improve domestic political, economic, and social conditions, and it emphasizes the importance of human rights and democracy, its objectives including the promotion of the interests of the private sector, gender equality, sustainable environmental management, and the replacement of trade preferences with a progressive and reciprocal removal of trade barriers. Whether this will be enough to address the structural problems of the ACP programme remains to be seen.

Meanwhile, the EU has become the single biggest source of official development assistance in the world, collectively accounting for nearly 57 per cent of the total of $104 billion given in 2006 (compared to 22 per cent from the United States and 19 per cent from Japan) (OECD website, 2007). Most EU aid (15 per cent of which is channelled through the EU) goes to sub-Saharan Africa, but an increasing proportion is going to Latin America. The EU also provides emergency humanitarian aid (nearly €500 million in 2001), much of which has gone in recent years to the victims of conflicts in Afghanistan, Armenia, Azerbaijan and Tajikistan. It has also become the second largest provider of food aid in the world after the United States, supplying food worth about €500 million per year.

Conclusions

The process of European integration was born as a way to help Western Europe rebuild after the Second World War, and to remove the historical causes of conflict in the region. Over time the EC/EU has become increasingly extroverted, and integration now has implications not just for internal European relations, but for Europe's relations with the rest of the world. While the EEC initially focused on bringing down the barriers to internal trade, it quickly became involved in external trade matters, and the EU has turned increased attention to common foreign and security policies. The process had several problems along the way, and the EU has yet to rid itself of a reputation for fumbling and for internal division, and cooperation has acquired consistency and regularity, and the development of common foreign and security policies has become one of the core endeavours of European integration.

With the end of the cold war, the clear security threat posed by the Soviet Union was replaced by economic concerns, by regional security problems such as those in the Balkans and the Middle East, and by less easily defined threats such as nationalist pressures in Russia, the movement of political refugees, the spread of nuclear weapons, the implications of new technology, and environmental problems. Meanwhile globalization proceeded under the auspices of the World Trade Organization, and the wealth and competitiveness of China, India and other newly industrializing countries continued to grow, altering the balance of global economic power. Thanks to all these changes, it seemed that the European Union would have difficulty defining its global role.

Then came the September 2001 terrorist attacks in the United States, followed by the US-led invasion of Iraq in March 2003. Coincidentally, the EU was launching its new single currency, expanding its membership deep into Eastern Europe, and upgrading the CFSP to the ESDP. Its role in the world was dramatically redefined. The new economic power of the EU has combined with new levels of alarm at US foreign policy and growing criticism of US global leadership to suggest that a new role is being imposed on the Europeans. They are clearly out of step with the United States not just on the immediate problem of international terrorism and the most effective response, but on a wide variety of longer-term issues relating to trade, security, the environment, and more.

The changes of the last few years have made it clear that the EU must work to give its international identity clearer definition, to assert itself on the global stage, and to build the kind of political influence that it needs as a superpower.

Europe may never achieve the qualities of a military superpower that are so overtly on show in the United States, and increasingly in China, and it may be that Europe instead becomes more adept at using soft power, and at building on its political, economic, and diplomatic advantages as an alternative to the increasingly discredited policies of the United States. Even though the EU may still present a rather confused and confusing image to the outside world, the outline of that image is slowly becoming sharper.

Conclusions

Two contradictory forces have been at work in Europe in the last 60 years. On the one hand, there has been the remarkable effort to put the continent's troubled history behind it, and to create the conditions under which internal conflict and competition might be replaced by perpetual peace and cooperation. Europe has, in that time, enjoyed the longest spell of generalized peace in its recorded history, and has witnessed dramatic growth in economic prosperity, and the rapid expansion of cooperation into almost every significant field of public policy. There are multiple explanations for the changes, including a new climate of international cooperation, the role of the United States in providing security guarantees and investment opportunities in Western Europe, and the effects of globalization, of which the Europeans have taken advantage. But at the core of the changes has been the impact of European integration; without the opportunities for political, economic and social change offered by the EEC/EU, the history of postwar Europe would have been quite different.

At the same time, the process of integration has been accompanied by an often widespread climate of cynicism, resistance and even outright hostility. Doubters and critics have seized every opportunity to claim that Europe is in crisis, that the idea of European unity is dead, that European leaders are fatally divided, and that Europe has shown its weaknesses rather than its strengths. Europe, it seems, has become typecast as a failure, the sceptics all too ready and willing to play up the bad news in everything from disagreements on new treaties to failed foreign policy initiatives, worries about the democratic deficit, sluggish economic growth, declining birth-rates and aging populations, negative votes in national referendums, and even the implications of delivery problems with the Airbus A380 super-jumbo. There are many competing explanations for the pall of doubt that has hung over the European experiment: fears for the loss of national sovereignty and identity, worries about the creation of a new level of government lacking the obvious and typical lines of accountability to the citizens, concerns about the effects that integration might have on the power and influence of the big EU states (particularly Germany and France), the difficulty that many have with understanding the European Union, fear of the unknown, and a failure by many to stand back from immediate and short-term problems, and to look instead at long-term trends. And then of course there are the cynics who *want* Europe to fail.

In spite of all the doubts, this book argues that the rise of the European Union has been one of the most important developments in global politics

212

and economics since 1945, while also one of the least understood. For many years, regional integration was little more than a gleam in the eye of a few pan-Europeanists and a huddle of technocrats in Brussels, and it presented a rather dull and uninspiring face to the world. But it has taken on a new personality and significance since the end of the cold war, and particularly since the landmark event of the March 2003 US-led invasion of Iraq. This had the dual effect of stirring up once again the many lingering doubts in Europe about the wisdom and motives of American global leadership, and of encouraging the most open and forthright criticism of US foreign policy by European leaders in decades. It is still too early to be sure of the long-term effects of the disagreement, but there is every possibility that history will eventually show it to have represented a seismic shift in the structure of the international system, and of the place of Europe in that system. This is especially likely if the invasion is seen in the context of several broader developments that have given new meaning to Europe.

Consider, first, the impact of the single market programme. The most obvious effect of bringing down borders has been to help create the biggest capitalist marketplace in the world, with nearly 500 million consumers. It is not yet complete, to be sure, but long gone are the days when 'Europe' revolved around squabbles over farm subsidies. The barriers to the free movement of people, money, goods, and services have all but gone, giving corporations an expanded market in which to sell their goods and services, affording consumers access to a wider array of products, and allowing Europeans increased freedom to move around their region, and no longer just for economic need – as was once the case – but out of personal choice. The freedoms of the new Europe have been underpinned – at least in 15 of the member states – by the adoption of the euro, which has not only made it easier for goods and services to cross national boundaries, but has given the EU a world-class currency that poses the most serious threat ever to the postwar global dominance of the US dollar, in turn giving the EU a new level of influence over international economic and monetary policies.

Consider, second, the impact of the eastward expansion of the EU. For many years, the EU was an exercise in cooperation among the capitalist economies of Western Europe. Eastern Europe still suffered the effects of nearly 50 years of Soviet domination, with a tradition of single-party politics and central planning. But when countries like Poland, Hungary, the Czech Republic, and, most notably, three former Soviet republics (Estonia, Latvia, and Lithuania) joined the EU in 2004, it not only brought a final emphatic end to cold war attitudes, but meant that for the first time in several generations it was possible to talk about 'Europe' as a whole, rather than always qualifying the label with 'Western' and 'Eastern'. Enlargement increased the size of the European marketplace and opened Eastern Europe to investment from the west, helping free eastern economies and underpinning the process of democratization. Doubters charge that enlargement came too soon and threatened to overextend the EU, perhaps even undermining its new global economic role. They also continue to point to the problems of adjustment that Eastern European member states must inevitably face, but we should not forget what integration contributed to political and economic reform in Ireland, Greece, Portugal, and Spain.

Consider, third, the impact of common policies on the member states of the European Union. The development of common European laws has not always been met with enthusiasm by Europeans, but it has been much easier for sceptics to point at the costs of the trivial – common sets of weights and measures, uniform shapes and sizes for fruits and vegetables, and so on – than to consider the longer-term benefits of removing technical barriers to the single market, and of allowing states with progressive laws (for example, on environmental protection) to change procedures in states that have lagged behind. Common agricultural, social, and regional policies have helped European farmers become more productive, and have helped the EU to direct new investment to those parts of the continent in greatest need, to build transport networks that have underpinned the single market, and to remove some of the bumps and hollows in the economic playing field.

Consider, finally, the impact of the changing global role of the European Union, and – in particular – its new relationship with the United States post-Iraq. Throughout the cold war, Western Europe mainly followed the lead of the United States in the struggle against the Soviet Union; it was understood that the United States was the dominating partner in the alliance in both security and economic terms, and while the two sides often disagreed on policy, the Europeans were rarely in a position to provide much more than symbolic opposition. The relationship began to change with the end of the cold war, when it became clear that the US protective shield in Western Europe was no longer essential, and that the resurgent European economy was offering real competition to the Americans. The Europeans embarrassed themselves in the Gulf and in the Balkans, but as much as anything these underlined the need for more effective European foreign policies. Transatlantic differences were brought home most clearly by Iraq in 2003, which showed that the wisdom of US policy could not be assumed and that it was sometimes right and proper for allies to disagree in public. Europeans finally realized that they could and should offer alternatives to US analyses and policies. They no longer felt obliged to follow the American lead, and they also saw with new clarity the need to back up their uncontested economic power by building on their fundamentally different approach to the use of power.

The combined effect of these changes has been to show that Europe has finally come of age, and has come closer to fulfilling the promise that its founders and champions have so long predicted. It still has many problems to address, there is still a deep and abiding scepticism about its value and achievements, it is still widely misunderstood, and neither Europeans themselves nor the rest of the world have yet become used to the idea of thinking of Europe as a single actor, in addition to – or even instead of – the 27 separate national actors of which it consists. But we have gone far beyond thinking about integration as the tool for keeping peace among Europeans, or as a means of encouraging the French and the Germans to live with each other, or as the channel for opening up Europe's internal borders. All of that has been achieved. Today the most important questions relate to what the new Europe will do with its achievements, and what European integration means for the rest of the world.

Appendix:
A Chronology of European
Integration, 1944–2008

1944	July	Bretton Woods conference
1945	May	Germany surrenders; European war ends
	October	Creation of United Nations
1947	June	Announcement of Marshall Plan
1948	January	Creation of Benelux customs union
	April	Organization for European Economic Cooperation founded
1949	April	North Atlantic Treaty signed
	May	Council of Europe founded
1950	May	Publication of Schuman Declaration
1951	April	Treaty of Paris signed, creating the European Coal and Steel Community
1952	March	Nordic Council founded
	May	Signature of draft treaty creating the European Defence Community (EDC)
	July	Treaty of Paris comes into force
1953	March	Plans announced for European Political Community (EPC)
1954	August	Plans for EDC and EPC collapse
	October	Creation of Western European Union
1956	June	Negotiations open on creation of European Economic Community (EEC) and Euratom
	October–December	Suez crisis
1957	March	Treaties of Rome signed, creating Euratom and the EEC
1958	January	Treaties of Rome come into force
	February	Benelux Economic Union founded
1960	May	European Free Trade Association (EFTA) begins operations
1961	February	First summit of EEC heads of government
	July–August	Britain, Ireland and Denmark apply to join EEC
1962	April	Norway applies for EEC membership
1963	January	De Gaulle vetoes British membership of the EEC; France and Germany sign Treaty of Friendship and Cooperation
1965	April	Merger treaty signed
	July	Start of empty-chair crisis (resolved January 1966)

1966	May	Britain, Ireland and Denmark apply for the second time to join EEC (Norway follows in July)
1967	November	De Gaulle again vetoes British membership of the Community
1968	July	Agreement of a common external tariff completes the creation of an EEC customs union
1970	June	Membership negotiations open with Britain, Denmark, Ireland and Norway; concluded in January 1972
1971	August	US leaves gold standard; end of the Bretton Woods system of fixed exchange rates
1972	September	Referendum in Norway rejects EEC membership
1973	January	Britain, Denmark and Ireland join the Community, bringing membership to nine
1975	March	First meeting of European Council in Dublin; creation of the European Regional Development Fund
	June	Greece applies to join Community
1977	March	Portugal applies to join Community
	July	Spain applies to join Community
1978	December	European Council establishes European Monetary System (EMS)
1979	March	EMS comes into operation; death of Jean Monnet
	June	First direct elections to the European Parliament
1981	January	Greece joins the Community, bringing membership to ten
1984	January	Free trade area established between EFTA and the EEC
1985	June	Schengen Agreement signed by France, Germany and Benelux states
	December	European Council agrees to drawing up of Single European Act (SEA)
1986	January	Portugal and Spain join Community, bringing membership to 12
	February	SEA signed in Luxembourg
1987	April	Turkey applies to join Community
	July	SEA comes into force
1989	April	Delors report on economic and monetary union
	July	Austria applies to join Community
	December	Adoption of Social Charter by 11 EC member states
1990	July	Cyprus and Malta apply to join Community
	August	Iraqi invasion of Kuwait
	October	German reunification brings former East Germany into the Community
1991	June	Outbreak of war in Yugoslavia
	July	Sweden applies to join Community
1992	February	Treaty on European Union (Maastricht treaty) signed
	March	Finland applies to join Community
	May	Switzerland applies to join Community

	June	Danish referendum rejects terms of Maastricht
	November	Norway applies again for Community membership
1993	May	Second Danish referendum accepts terms of Maastricht
	November	Treaty on European Union comes into force. European Community becomes a pillar of the new European Union
1994	January	Creation of the European Economic Area
	March	Hungary applies to join EU
	April	Poland applies to join EU
	May	Opening of Channel Tunnel, linking Britain and France
	June–November	Referendums in Austria, Finland and Sweden accept EU membership, but Norwegians again say no
1995	January	Austria, Finland and Sweden join the European Union, bringing membership to 15
	March	Schengen Agreement comes into force
	July	Europol Convention signed
	October–December	Bulgaria, Estonia, Latvia and Lithuania apply to join EU
	December	Dayton peace accords end war in Yugoslavia
1996	January	Czech Republic applies to join EU
	June	Slovenia applies to join EU
1997	October	Treaty of Amsterdam signed
1998	June	Establishment of European Central Bank
1999	January	Launch of the euro in 11 member states
	May	Treaty of Amsterdam comes into force
2000	September	Danish referendum rejects adoption of euro
2001	February	Treaty of Nice signed
	March	Swiss referendum rejects EU membership
	June	Irish referendum rejects terms of Nice
2002	January	Euro coins and notes begin circulating in 12 member states
	February	Opening of Convention on the Future of Europe
	October	Second Irish referendum accepts terms of Nice
2003	February	Treaty of Nice comes into force
	March	US-led invasion of Iraq sparks the most serious fallout in postwar transatlantic relations
	July	Publication of draft treaty establishing a constitution for Europe
	September	Swedish referendum rejects adoption of euro
2004	May	Cyprus, Czech Republic, Estonia, Hungary, Latvia, Lithuania, Malta, Poland, Slovenia, Slovakia join the EU, bringing membership to 25
	June	European Council accepts terms of draft constitutional treaty
	October	European leaders sign the treaty on the European constitution

	November	Lithuania becomes the first EU member to ratify the constitution
2005	May	French referendum rejects constitution
	June	Dutch referendum rejects constitution
2007	January	Bulgaria and Romania join the EU, bringing membership to 27; Slovenia becomes 13th country to adopt the euro
	December	Treaty of Lisbon signed
2008	January	Cyprus and Malta adopt the euro

Sources of Further Information

Publishing on the European Union has grown exponentially in the last few years, with the number of new books, journal articles and websites increasing to match the pace of change in the EU itself, and of expanding interest in EU affairs. The following list of sources offers a flavour of what is currently available. For new titles, monitor acquisitions at your nearest library, watch the catalogues of the publishers with the best lists on the European Union (including Lynne Rienner, Oxford University Press, Palgrave Macmillan, Routledge, and Rowman & Littlefield), and search online book dealers such as Amazon.

Books

For general introductions to the EU, see McCormick (2008), Ginsberg (2007), Cini (2007), Bache and George (2006), Nugent (2006), Wood and Yesilada (2006), Bomberg and Stubb (2006), Dinan (2005), and Van Oudenaren (2004). Edited collections on recent developments in the EU include Jabko and Parsons (2005), Cowles and Dinan (2004), Börzel and Cichowski (2003), and Cowles and Smith (2001).

The best summary of integration theory is Rosamond (2000). An assessment of the key debates about the political identity of the EU is offered by Magnette (2005), and an illuminating set of discussions about the comparative character of European federalism can be found in Menon and Schain (2006). Discussions about the meaning of Europe can be found in Dunkerley et al. (2002), Pagden (2002), Heffernan (2000) and Unwin (1998).

For histories of the EU, see Eichengreen (2007), Dinan (2004), Gilbert (2003), Gillingham (2003), Stirk and Weigall (1999), and Urwin (1995). For general histories of postwar Europe, see Judt (2005) and Hitchcock (2004), and for the best history of postwar transatlantic relations see Lundestad (2003).

For general surveys of EU institutions and decision making, see Peterson and Shackleton (2006), Hix (2005), and Warleigh (2001). Regarding specific institutions:

- The Commission is covered by Spence (2006), Smith (2004), Nugent (2001, 2000), and Cini (1996).
- The Council of Ministers is assessed by Hayes-Renshaw and Wallace (2006), Westlake and Galloway (2004), and Sherrington (2000). For the role of the presidency of the Council of Ministers, see Elgström (2003).
- Parliament is the subject of studies by Corbett et al. (2005), Judge and Earnshaw (2003), Corbett and Hansch (2002), and Lodge (2001), and political parties are the focus of a book by Hix and Lord (1997).
- Most studies of the European Council are now quite dated, and include Johnston (1994) and Werts (1992).
- For general surveys of the European Court of Justice, see Lasok et al. (2001), Brown and Kennedy (2000), and Dehousse (1998). For more political analysis see Sweet

(2004) and Conant (2002). For an explanation of the EU legal system, see Shaw (2000).

- The work of the European Central Bank has been reviewed by Kaltenthaler (2006) and Howarth and Loedel (2005), and of Europol by Occhipinti (2003).

For edited collections dealing with a variety of EU policy areas, see Richardson (2006) and Wallace *et al.* (2005). Neal (2007), de Grauwe (2007), and McDonald and Dearden (2005) offer assessments of EU economic policy and the single market, while Hosli (2005) and Padoa-Schioppa (2004) have written about the euro. Publication on specific areas of EU policy has been on the rise in recent years, with studies of agriculture (Ackrill, 2000; Grant, 1997), cohesion (Molle, 2007), competition (Cini and McGowan, 1998), energy (Matláry, 1997), enlargement (Nugent, 2004), the environment (Jordan, 2005; McCormick, 2001), social policy (Roberts and Springer, 2001; Hantrais, 2000), and technology (Peterson and Sharp, 1998).

In spite of all the debates about the problems related to EU foreign and security policy, it has been the subject of a burgeoning literature. For example, see Bretherton and Vogler (2006), Adamski *et al.* (2006), Hill and Smith (2005), and March and Mackenstein (2004). For a discussion of the new international role of the EU, see McCormick (2007). One particular area of recent growth has been assessments of the transatlantic relationship and the fallout over the 2003 Iraqi invasion: for example, see Gordon and Shapiro (2004), Shawcross (2004), Peterson and Pollack (2003), and Kagan (2003).

Periodicals and EU publications

The Economist. A weekly news magazine that has stories and statistics on world politics, including a section on Europe (and occasional special supplements on the EU). Selected headline stories can be found on *The Economist* website:

http://www.economist.com

The Economist also publishes two series of quarterly reports that are treasure-houses of information, but they are expensive, and not every library carries them: *Economist Intelligence Unit Country Reports* (these cover almost every country in the world, and include a series on the European Union), and *European Policy Analyst*. Both provide detailed political and economic news and information.

The Economist also publishes *European Voice*, a weekly newspaper published in Brussels that is packed with all the latest news and information on the EU. Selected headline stories can be found on its website:

http://www.european-voice.com

Journal of Common Market Studies. This quarterly academic journal is devoted to the EU and contains scholarly articles and book reviews. Many other academic journals include articles on the EU, of which the most consistently useful are *Common Market Law Review, Comparative European Politics, European Foreign Affairs Review, European Journal of International Relations, European Journal of Political Research, European Union Politics, Foreign Affairs, International Organization, Journal of European Integration, Journal of European Public Policy, Journal of*

European Social Policy, Journal of Transatlantic Studies, Parliamentary Affairs, and *West European Politics.*

There are several official sources of EU information, all of which are available on the internet through the Europa website:

http://europa.eu.int

Official Journal of the European Communities. Published daily, this is the authoritative source on all EU legislation, proposals by the Commission for new legislation, decisions and resolutions by the Council of Ministers, debates in the European Parliament, new actions brought before the Court of Justice, opinions of the Economic and Social Committee, the annual report of the Court of Auditors, and the EU budget.

General Report on the Activities of the European Union. This is the major annual report of the EU, with a record of developments in all EU policy areas, and key statistical information.

Bulletin of the European Union. Published ten times per year, this is the official record of events in (and policies of) all the EU institutions. It contains reports on the activities of the Commission and other EU institutions, along with special feature articles. Supplements contain copies of key Commission documents, including proposed legislation.

Directorate-General Documentation. Every DG in the Commission publishes its own periodicals, reports and surveys dealing with its specific areas of interest. One of the most useful of the regular publications is the series of biannual Eurobarometer opinion polls. These have been carried out in the EU since 1973, mainly to provide EU institutions and the media with statistics on public attitudes towards European integration.

Eurostat. An acronym for the Statistical Office of the European Communities, Eurostat collects and collates statistical information of many different kinds from the EU member states. Much of this is available on the internet; all of it is published in the form of yearbooks, surveys, studies, and reports.

EUR-Lex. This is the definitive source on EU legislation, containing all the directives, regulations, and other legal instruments adopted by the EU, as well as internal and external agreements.

Websites

The variety of useful websites changes often, as do their URLs, so instead of listing useful sites here, I have set up a short series of links on my home page. The URL is:

http://mypage.iu.edu/~jmccormi

Palgrave Macmillan also has a website for books in the European Union series which provides information on key developments and links to other internet sources. The URL is:

http://www.palgrave.com/politics/eu/euontheweb.asp

Bibliography

Ackrill, Robert (2000) *The Common Agricultural Policy* (London: Continuum).

Adamski, Janet, Mary Troy Johnson and Christina M. Schweiss (eds) (2006) *Old Europe, New Security: Evolution for a Complex World* (Aldershot: Ashgate).

Albert, Michel (1993) *Capitalism v. Capitalism: How America's Obsession with Individual Achievement and Short-Term Profit Has Led to the Brink of Collapse* (New York: Four Walls Eight Windows).

Allen, David (1996) 'Competition Policy: Policing the Single Market', in Helen Wallace and William Wallace (eds), *Policy-Making in the European Union*, 3rd edn (Oxford: Oxford University Press).

Andersen, Svein and Kjell A. Eliassen (eds) (1995) *The European Union: How Democratic Is It?* (London: Sage).

Anderson, Scott (1992) 'Western Europe and the Gulf War', in Reinhardt Rummel (ed.), *Toward Political Union: Planning a Common Foreign and Security Policy in the European Community* (Boulder, CO: Westview).

Archer, Clive (2000) *The European Union: Structure and Process*, 3rd edn (New York: Continuum).

Armstrong, Harvey (1993) 'Community Regional Policy', in Juliet Lodge (ed.), *The European Community and the Challenge of the Future* (London: Continuum and New York: Palgrave Macmillan).

Armstrong, Kenneth and Simon Bulmer (1998) *The Governance of the Single European Market* (Manchester: Manchester University Press).

Aspinwall, Mark and Justin Greenwood (1998) 'Conceptualising Collective Action in the European Union: An Introduction', in Mark Aspinwall and Justin Greenwood (eds), *Collective Action in the European Union: Interests and the New Politics of Associability* (London: Routledge).

Bache, Ian and Matthew Flinders (2004) *Multi-Level Governance* (Oxford: Oxford University Press).

Bache, Ian and Stephen George (2006) *Politics in the European Union*, 2nd edn (Oxford: Oxford University Press).

Baimbridge, Mark, Jeffrey Harrop and George Philippidis (2004) *Current Economic Issues in EU Integration* (Basingstoke: Palgrave Macmillan).

Bainbridge, Timothy and Anthony Teasdale (1995) *The Penguin Companion to European Union* (London: Penguin).

Barber, Lionel (1998) 'Sharing Common Risks: The EU View', *Europe*, no. 374, pp. 8–9.

Bardi, Luciano (2002) 'Transnational Trends: The Evolution of the European Party System', in Bernard Steunenberg and Jacques Thomassen (eds), *The European Parliament: Moving Toward Democracy in the EU* (Lanham, MD: Rowman and Littlefield).

Barnes, Ian and Pamela M. Barnes (1995) *The Enlarged European Union* (London: Longman).

Billiet, Stijn (2005) 'The EC and WTO Dispute Settlement: The Initiation of Trade Disputes by the EC', in *European Foreign Affairs Review*, vol. 10, no. 2, Summer, pp. 197–214.

Bomberg, Elizabeth and Alexander Stubb (2006) *The European Union: How Does it Work?* 2nd edn (Oxford: Oxford University Press).

Booker, Christopher and Richard North (2005) *The Great Deception: Can the European Union Survive?* Rev. edn (London: Continuum).

Börzel, Tanja and Rachel Cichowski (eds) (2003) *The State of the European Union, Vol. 6: Law, Politics and Society* (Oxford and New York: Oxford University Press).

Bretherton, Charlotte and John Vogler (2006) *The European Union as a Global Actor*, 2nd edn (London: Routledge).

Brown, L. Neville and Tom Kennedy (2000) *The Court of Justice of the European Communities*, 5th edn (London: Sweet & Maxwell).

Bugge, Peter (1995) 'The Nation Supreme: The Idea of Europe 1914–1945', in Kevin Wilson and Jan van der Dussen (eds), *The History of the Idea of Europe* (London: Routledge).

Carr, William (1987) *A History of Germany, 1815–1985*, 3rd edn (London: Edward Arnold).

Chryssochoou, Dimitris I. (2000) *Democracy in the European Union* (London: I. B. Tauris).

Chinn, Menzie and Jeffery Frankel (2005) 'Will the Euro Eventually Surpass the Dollar as the Leading International Reserve Currency?', Washington DC, National Bureau of Economic Research Working Paper 11510, July.

Cini, Michelle (1996) *The European Commission: Leadership, Organization and Culture in the EU Administration* (Manchester: Manchester University Press).

Cini, Michelle (ed.) (2007) *European Union Politics*, 2nd edn (Oxford: Oxford University Press).

Cini, Michelle and Lee McGowan (1998) *Competition Policy in the European Union* (Basingstoke and New York: Palgrave Macmillan).

Collester, J. Bryan (2000) 'How Defense "Spilled Over" into the CFSP: Western European Union (WEU) and the European Security and Defense Identity (ESDI)', in Maria Green Cowles and Michael Smith (eds), *The State of the European Union: Risks, Reform, Resistance and Revival* (Oxford: Oxford University Press).

Collins, Ken and David Earnshaw (1993) 'The Implementation and Enforcement of European Community Environment Legislation', in David Judge (ed.), *A Green Dimension for the European Community: Political Issues and Processes* (London: Frank Cass).

Commission of the European Communities (1973) *Report on the Regional Problems of the Enlarged Community* (The Thomson Report), COM(73)550 (Brussels: Commission of the European Communities).

Commission of the European Communities (1985) *Completing the Internal Market* (The Cockfield Report), COM(85)310 (Brussels: Commission of the European Communities).

Commission of the European Communities (1998) Fifteenth Annual Report on Monitoring the Application of Community Law – 1997, in *Official Journal of the European Communities*, C250, vol. 41, 10 August 1998.

Commission of the European Communities (2001a) *European Governance: A White Paper*, COM (2001) 428 (Brussels: Commission of the European Communities).

Commission of the European Communities (2001b) 'Interim Report from the Commission to the Stockholm European Council: Improving and Simplifying the Regulatory Environment', COM (2001) 130 Final (Brussels: Commission of the European Communities).

Commission of the European Communities, *Annual Report on Monitoring the Application of Community Law*, various years.

Conant, Lisa (2002) *Justice Contained: Law and Politics in the European Union* (Ithaca, NY: Cornell University Press).

Corbett, Richard (2001) 'The European Parliament's Progress, 1994–99', in Juliet Lodge (ed.), *The 1999 Elections to the European Parliament* (Basingstoke and New York: Palgrave Macmillan).

Corbett, Richard and Klaus Hansch (2002) *The European Parliament's Role in Closer EU Integration* (Basingstoke: Palgrave Macmillan).

Corbett, Richard, Francis Jacobs and Michael Shackleton (2005) *The European Parliament*, 6th edn (London: John Harper).

Cornell, Tim and John Matthews (1982) *Atlas of the Roman World* (Oxford: Phaidon).

Cowles, Maria Green and Desmond Dinan (eds) (2004) *Developments in the European Union 2* (Basingstoke and New York: Palgrave Macmillan).

Cowles, Maria Green and Michael Smith (eds) (2001) *The State of the European Union: Risks, Reform, Resistance, and Revival* (Oxford: Oxford University Press).

Dahrendorf, Ralf (1988) *The Modern Social Conflict* (London: Weidenfeld & Nicolson).

Daltrop, Anne (1987) *Politics and the European Community* (London: Longman).

de Grauwe, Paul (2007) *Economics of Monetary Union* (Oxford: Oxford University Press).

Dehousse, Renaud (1998) *The European Court of Justice* (Basingstoke and New York: Palgrave Macmillan).

Delanty, Gerard (1995) *Inventing Europe: Idea, Identity, Reality* (Basingstoke and New York: Palgrave Macmillan).

den Boer, Pim (1995) 'Europe to 1914: The Making of an Idea', in Kevin Wilson and Jan van der Dussen (eds), *The History of the Idea of Europe* (London: Routledge).

de Rougemont, Denis (1966) *The Idea of Europe* (London: Macmillan).

Dinan, Desmond (2004) *Europe Recast: A History of European Union* (Boulder, CO: Lynne Rienner, and Basingstoke: Palgrave Macmillan).

Dinan, Desmond (2005) *Ever Closer Union? An Introduction to European Integration*, 3rd edn (Boulder, CO: Lynne Rienner, and Basingstoke: Palgrave Macmillan).

Dunkerley, David, Lesley Hodgson, Stanislaw Konopacki, Tony Spybey and Andrew Thompson (2002) *Changing Europe: Identities, Nations and Citizens* (London: Routledge).

Dye, Thomas (2002) *Understanding Public Policy*, 10th edn (Upper Saddle River, NJ: Prentice Hall).

Dye, Thomas and Harmon Zeigler (2000) *The Irony of Democracy* (Fort Worth, TX: Harcourt Brace).

Edwards, Geoffrey and David Spence (eds) (2006) *The European Commission*, 3rd edn (London: John Harper).

Eichengreen, Barry (2007) *The European Economy Since 1945: Coordinated Capitalism and Beyond* (Princeton: Princeton University Press).

Elgström, Ole (ed.) (2003) *European Council Presidencies: A Comparative Perspective* (London: Routledge).

Eurobarometer polls can be found on the Europa website at http://europa.eu.int/comm/public_opinion/index_en.htm

Eurostat (2007) *Europe in Figures: Eurostat Yearbook 2006–07* (Brussels: European Commission).

Fernández-Armesto, Felipe (ed.) (1997) *The Times Guide to the Peoples of Europe* (London: Times Books).

Forsyth, Murray (1981) *Unions of States: The Theory and Practice of Confederation* (Leicester: Leicester University Press).

Franklin, Mark (1996) 'European Elections and the European Voter', in Jeremy Richardson (ed.), *European Union: Power and Policy-Making* (London: Routledge).

George, Stephen (1996) *Politics and Policy in the European Community*, 3rd edn (Oxford: Oxford University Press).

Geyer, Robert and Beverly Springer (1998) 'EU Social Policy After Maastricht: The Works Council Directive and the British Opt-Out', in Pierre-Henri Laurent and Marc Maresceau (eds), *The State of the European Union*, vol. 4 (Boulder, CO: Lynne Rienner).

Giegerich, Bastian and William Wallace (2004) 'Not Such a Soft Power: The External Deployment of European Forces', *Survival*, vol. 46, no. 2, June, pp. 163–82.

Gilbert, Mark (2003) *Surpassing Realism: The Politics of European Integration Since 1945* (Lanham, MD: Rowman & Littlefield).

Gill, Graeme (2003) *The Nature and Development of the Modern State* (Basingstoke: Palgrave Macmillan).

Gillingham, John (1991; reissued 2002) *Coal, Steel, and the Rebirth of Europe, 1945–1955* (Cambridge: Cambridge University Press).

Gillingham, John (2003) *European Integration, 1950–2003: Superstate or New Market Economy?* (Cambridge and New York: Cambridge University Press).

Ginsberg, Roy H. (2001) *The European Union in International Politics: Baptism by Fire* (Lanham, MD: Rowman & Littlefield).

Ginsberg, Roy H. (2007) *Demystifying the European Union: The Enduring Logic of Regional Integration* (Lanham, MD: Rowman & Littlefield).

Gordon, Philip H. and Jeremy Shapiro (2004) *Allies at War: America, Europe, and the Crisis over Iraq* (New York: McGraw-Hill).

Grabbe, Heather (2004) 'What the New Member States Bring into the European Union', in Neill Nugent (ed.), *European Union Enlargement* (Basingstoke and New York: Palgrave Macmillan).

Grant, Wyn (1997) *The Common Agricultural Policy* (Basingstoke and New York: Palgrave Macmillan).

Graziano, Paolo and Maarten P. Vink (eds) (2007), *Europeanization: New Research Agendas* (Basingstoke: Palgrave Macmillan).

Greenwood, Justin (2003) *Interest Representation in the European Union* (Basingstoke and New York: Palgrave Macmillan).

Guiraudon, Virginie (2004) 'Immigration and Asylum: A High Politics Agenda', in Maria Green Cowles and Desmond Dinan (eds), *Developments in the European Union 2* (Basingstoke: Palgrave Macmillan).

Haas, Ernst B. (1968) *The Uniting of Europe: Political, Social, and Economic Forces, 1950–57* (Stanford, CA: Stanford University Press).

Habermas, Jürgen and Jacques Derrida (2003 [2005]) 'February 15, or What Binds Europe Together: Plea for a Common Foreign Policy, Beginning in Core Europe', in *Frankfurter Allgemeine Zeitung*, 31 May 2003. Reproduced in Daniel Levy, Max Pensky and John Torpey (eds), *Old Europe, New Europe, Core Europe* (London: Verso, 2005).

Hantrais, Linda (2000) *Social Policy in the European Union* (Basingstoke and New York: Palgrave Macmillan).

Hay, David (1957) *Europe: The Emergence of an Idea* (Edinburgh: Edinburgh University Press).

Hayes-Renshaw, Fiona and Helen Wallace (2006) *The Council of Ministers*, 2nd edn (Basingstoke: Palgrave Macmillan).

Heater, Derek (1992) *The Idea of European Unity* (London: Continuum and New York: Palgrave Macmillan).

Heffernan, Michael (2000) *The Meaning of Europe: Geography and Geopolitics* (London: Edward Arnold).

Heisler, Martin O., with Robert B. Kvavik (1973) 'Patterns of European Politics: The European Polity Model', in Martin O. Heisler (ed.), *Politics in Europe: Structures and Processes in Some Postindustrial Democracies* (New York: David McKay).

Hill, Christopher and Michael Smith (eds) (2005) *International Relations and the European Union* (Oxford: Oxford University Press).

Hitchcock, William I. (2004) *The Struggle for Europe: The Turbulent History of a Divided Continent* (New York: Anchor Books).

Hix, Simon (1994) 'The Study of the European Community: The Challenge to Comparative Politics', *West European Politics*, vol. 17, no. 1, pp. 1–30.

Hix, Simon (2005) *The Political System of the European Union*, 2nd edn (Basingstoke and New York: Palgrave Macmillan).

Hix, Simon and Christopher Lord (1997) *Political Parties in the European Union* (Basingstoke and New York: Palgrave Macmillan).

Hobsbawm, Eric (1991) *The Age of Empire 1848–1875* (London: Cardinal).

Hoffman, Stanley (1964) 'The European Process at Atlantic Crosspurposes', *Journal of Common Market Studies*, vol. 3, pp. 85–101.

Hogan, Michael J. (1987) *The Marshall Plan: America, Britain, and the Reconstruction of Western Europe, 1947–52* (New York: Cambridge University Press).

Hooghe, Lisbet and Gary Marks (2001) *Multi-Level Governance and European Integration* (Lanham, MD: Rowman & Littlefield).

Hosli, Madeleine O. (2005) *The Euro: A Concise Introduction to European Monetary Integration* (Boulder, CO: Lynne Rienner).

Howarth, David and Peter Loedel (2005) *The European Central Bank: The New European Leviathan?* 2nd edn (Basingstoke: Palgrave Macmillan).

Howorth, Jolyon (2003) 'Foreign and Defence Policy Cooperation', in John Peterson and Mark A. Pollack (eds), *Europe, America, Bush: Transatlantic Relations in the Twenty-First Century* (London: Routledge).

Huntington, Samuel (1999) 'The Lonely Superpower', *Foreign Affairs*, vol. 78, no. 2.

Hutton, Will (2003) *The World We're In* (London: Abacus).

Ikenberry, G. John (2002) 'Introduction', in G. John Ikenberry (ed.), *America Unrivaled: The Future of the Balance of Power* (Ithaca, NY: Cornell University Press), p. 1.

Ionescu, Ghita (1975) *Centripetal Politics: Government and the New Centres of Power* (London: Hart-Davis McGibbon).

International Institute for Strategic Studies (2007) *The Military Balance 2007* (London: Routledge).

Jabko, Nicolas and Craig Parsons (eds) (2005) *The State of the European Union, Vol. 7: With US or Against US? European Trends in American Perspective* (Oxford and New York: Oxford University Press).

Johnston, Mary Troy (1994) *The European Council: Gatekeeper of the European Community* (Boulder, CO: Westview Press).

Jolly, Mette Elise (2007) *The European Union and the People* (Oxford: Oxford University Press).

Jones, Seth G. (2007) *The Rise of European Security Cooperation* (Cambridge: Cambridge University Press).

Jordan, Andrew (2005) *Environmental Policy in the European Union: Actors, Institutions and Processes* (London: Earthscan).

Judge, David and David Earnshaw (2003) *The European Parliament* (Basingstoke and New York: Palgrave Macmillan).

Judt, Tony (2005) *Postwar: A History of Europe since 1945* (New York: Penguin).

Kagan, Robert (2003) *Of Paradise and Power: America and Europe in the New World Order* (New York: Alfred A. Knopf).

Kaltenthaler, Karl (2006) *Policy-making in the European Central Bank: The Masters of Europe's Money* (Lanham, MD: Rowman and Littlefield).

Keating, Michael and Liesbet Hooghe (1996) 'By-passing the Nation State? Regions and the EU Policy Process', in Jeremy Richardson (ed.), *European Union: Power and Policy-Making* (London: Routledge).

Keohane, Robert O. and Stanley Hoffmann (eds) (1991) *The New European Community: Decisionmaking and Institutional Change* (Boulder, CO: Westview Press).

Kupchan, Charles A. (1998) 'After Pax Americana: Benign Power, Regional Integration, and the Sources of a Stable Multipolarity', *International Security*, vol. 23, no. 2, pp. 40–79.

Lasok, Dominik *et al.* (2001) *Law and Institutions of the European Communities*, 7th edn (London: LexisNexisUK).

Layne, Christopher (1993) 'The Unipolar Illusion: Why New Great Powers Will Arise', *International Security*, vol. 17, no. 4, pp. 5–51.

Lewis, David P. (1993) *The Road to Europe: History, Institutions and Prospects of European Integration 1945–1993* (New York: Peter Lang).

Lindberg, Leon N. (1963) *The Political Dynamics of European Economic Integration* (Stanford: Stanford University Press).

Lindberg, Leon N. and Stuart A. Scheingold (1970) *Europe's Would-Be Polity: Patterns of Change in the European Community* (Englewood Cliffs, NJ: Prentice Hall).

Lindberg, Leon N. and Stuart A. Scheingold (1971) *Regional Integration: Theory and Research* (Cambridge, MA: Harvard University Press).

Lindblom, Charles (1959) 'The Science of "Muddling Through"', *Public Administration Review*, vol. 19, no. 2, pp. 79–88.

Lister, Frederick K. (1996) *The European Union, the United Nations, and the Revival of Confederal Governance* (Westport, CT: Greenwood).

Lodge, Juliet (2001) *The 1999 Elections in the European Parliament* (Basingstoke and New York: Palgrave Macmillan).

Lundestad, Geir (2003) *The United States and Western Europe Since 1945: From 'Empire' by Invitation to Transatlantic Drift* (Oxford: Oxford University Press).

Magnette, Paul (2005) *What is the European Union? Nature and Prospects* (Basingstoke: Palgrave Macmillan).

Mancini, G. Federico (1991) 'The Making of a Constitution for Europe', in Robert O. Keohane and Stanley Hoffmann (eds), *The New European Community: Decisionmaking and Institutional Change* (Boulder, CO: Westview Press).

March, Steve and Hans Mackenstein (2004) *The International Relations of the EU* (New York: Longman).

Marks, Gary (1993) 'Structural Policy and Multi-level Governance in the EC', in Alan Cafruny and Glenda Rosenthal (eds), *The State of the European Community*, vol. 2 (Boulder, CO: Lynne Rienner).

Matláry, Janne Haaland (1997) *Energy Policy in the European Union* (Basingstoke and New York: Palgrave Macmillan).

Mazey, Sonia and Jeremy Richardson (1996) 'The Logic of Organisation: Interest Groups', in Jeremy Richardson (ed.), *European Union: Power and Policy-Making* (London: Routledge).

Mazey, Sonia and Jeremy Richardson (1997) 'The Commission and the Lobby', in Geoffrey Edwards and David Spence (eds), *The European Commission*, 2nd edn (London: Cartermill).

McCormick, John (1995) *The Global Environmental Movement*, 2nd edn (London: John Wiley).

McCormick, John (2001) *Environmental Policy in the European Union* (Basingstoke and New York: Palgrave Macmillan).

McCormick, John (2007) *The European Superpower* (Basingstoke: Palgrave Macmillan).

McCormick, John (2008) *The European Union: Politics and Policies*, 4th edn (Boulder, CO: Westview).

McDonald, Frank and Stephen Dearden (eds) (2005) *European Economic Integration*, 4th edn (New York and Harlow: Prentice Hall Financial Times).

Menon, Anand, Kalypso Nicolaidis and Jennifer Welsh (2004) 'In Defence of Europe – A Response to Kagan', *Journal of European Affairs*, vol. 2, no. 3, August, pp. 5–14.

Menon, Anand and Martin Schain (eds) (2006) *Comparative Federalism: The European Union and the United States in Comparative Perspective* (Oxford: Oxford University Press).

Milward, Alan S. (1984) *The Reconstruction of Western Europe, 1945–51* (Berkeley, CA: University of California Press).

Mitrany, David (1966) *A Working Peace System* (Chicago, IL: Quadrangle).

Molle, Willem (2007) *European Cohesion Policy* (London and New York: Routledge).

Monnet, Jean (1978) *Memoirs* (Garden City, NY: Doubleday).

Moravcsik, Andrew (1998) *The Choice for Europe* (Ithaca, NY: Cornell University Press).

Morris, Chris (2005) *The New Turkey: The Quiet Revolution on the Edge of Europe* (London: Granta).

Neal, Larry (2007) *The Economics of Europe and the European Union* (Cambridge and New York: Cambridge University Press).

Neal, Larry and David Barbezat (1998) *The Economics of the European Union and the Economies of Europe* (New York: Oxford University Press).

Nugent, Neill (ed.) (2000) *At the Heart of the Union: Studies of the European Commission*, 4th edn (Basingstoke and New York: Palgrave Macmillan).

Nugent, Neill (2001) *The European Commission* (Basingstoke and New York: Palgrave Macmillan).

Nugent, Neill (ed.) (2004) *European Union Enlargement* (Basingstoke and New York: Palgrave Macmillan).

Nugent, Neill (2006) *The Government and Politics of the European Union*, 6th edn (Basingstoke: Palgrave Macmillan).

Nye, Joseph S. (1971a) *Peace in Parts: Integration and Conflict in Regional Organization* (Boston, MA: Little, Brown).

Nye, Joseph S. (1971b) 'Comparing Common Markets: A Revised Neofunctionalist Model', in Leon N. Lindberg and Stuart A. Scheingold (eds), *Regional Integration: Theory and Research* (Cambridge, MA: Harvard University Press).

Nye, Joseph (2004) *Soft Power: The Means to Success in World Politics* (New York: Public Affairs).

Occhipinti, John D. (2003) *The Politics of EU Police Cooperation: Toward a European FBI?* (Boulder, CO: Lynne Rienner).

Occhipinti, John D. (2004) 'Police and Judicial Co-operation', in Maria Green Cowles and Desmond Dinan (eds), *Developments in the European Union 2* (Basingstoke: Palgrave Macmillan).

OECD website (2007) http://www.oecd.org.

Owen, Richard and Michael Dynes (1992) *The Times Guide to the Single European Market* (London: Times Books).

Padoa-Schioppa, Tommaso (2004) *The Euro and Its Central Bank* (Cambridge, MA: MIT Press).

Page, Edward C. (2003), 'Europeanization and the Persistence of Administrative Systems', in Jack Hayward and Anand Menon (eds), *Governing Europe* (Oxford: Oxford University Press).

Pagden, Anthony (ed.) (2002) *The Idea of Europe: From Antiquity to the European Union* (Cambridge: Cambridge University Press).

Palmer, Michael (1968) *European Unity: A Survey of European Organizations* (London: George Allen & Unwin).

Peters, B. Guy (1992) 'Bureaucratic Politics and the Institutions of the European Community', in Alberta Sbragia (ed.), *Euro-Politics: Institutions and Policy-making in the 'New' European Community* (Washington, DC: Brookings Institution).

Peters, B. Guy (2001) 'Agenda-Setting in the European Union', in Jeremy Richardson (ed), *European Union: Power and Policy-Making*, 2nd edn (New York: Routledge).

Peterson, John (2003) 'The US and Europe in the Balkans', in John Peterson and Mark A. Pollack (eds), *Europe, America, Bush: Transatlantic Relations in the Twenty-First Century* (London: Routledge).

Peterson, John and Mark A. Pollack (eds) (2003) *Europe, America, Bush: Transatlantic Relations in the Twenty-First Century* (London: Routledge).

Peterson, John and Michael Shackleton (eds) (2006) *The Institutions of the European Union*, 2nd edn (Oxford: Oxford University Press).

Peterson, John and Margaret Sharp (1998) *Technology Policy in the European Union* (Basingstoke and New York: Palgrave Macmillan).

Phinnemore, David and Clive H. Church (2005) *Understanding the European Union's Constitution* (London: Routledge).

Piris, Jean-Claude (2006) *The Constitution for Europe: A Legal Analysis* (Cambridge: Cambridge University Press).

Prestowitz, Clyde (2003) *Rogue Nation: American Unilateralism and the Failure of Good Intentions* (New York: Basic Books).

Pye, Lucien (1966) *Aspects of Political Development* (Boston, MA: Little, Brown).

Reiff, K. and H. Schmitt (1980) 'Nine Second-Order National Elections: A Conceptual Framework for the Analysis of European Election Results', *European Journal of Political Research*, vol. 8, no. 1, pp. 3–44.

Richardson, Jeremy (ed.) (2006) *European Union: Power and Policy-Making*, 3rd edn (London and New York: Routledge).

Rifkin, Jeremy (2004) *The European Dream: How Europe's Vision of the Future is Quietly Eclipsing the American Dream* (New York: Tarcher/Penguin).

Roberts, Ivor and Beverley Springer (2001) *Social Policy in the European Union: Between Harmonization and National Autonomy* (Boulder, CO: Lynne Rienner).

Rosamond, Ben (2000) *Theories of European Integration* (Basingstoke and New York: Palgrave Macmillan).

Ross, George (1995) *Jacques Delors and European Integration* (New York: Oxford University Press).

Salmon, Trevor and Sir William Nicoll (eds) (1997) *Building European Union: A Documentary History and Analysis* (Manchester: Manchester University Press).

Sapir, André, *et al.*, (2004) *An Agenda for a Growing Europe: Making the EU Economic System Deliver* (Oxford: Oxford University Press).

Sbragia, Alberta (1992), 'Thinking about the European Future: The Uses of Comparison', in Alberta Sbragia (ed.), *Euro-Politics: Institutions and Policymaking in the 'New' European Community* (Washington DC: Brookings Institution).

Schlesinger, Philip and François Foret (2006) 'Political Roof and Sacred Canopy?', *European Journal of Social Theory*, vol. 9, no. 1, pp. 59–81.

Schmitter, Philippe C. (1971) 'A Revised Theory of Regional Integration', in Leon N. Lindberg and Stuart A. Scheingold, *Regional Integration: Theory and Research* (Cambridge, MA: Harvard University Press).

Scruton, Roger (1996) *A Dictionary of Political Thought*, 2nd edn (London: Macmillan).

Shaw, Jo (2000) *Law of the European Union*, 3rd edn (Basingstoke and New York: Palgrave Macmillan).

Shawcross, William (2004) *Allies: The US, Britain, Europe, and the War on Iraq* (New York: Public Affairs).

Sherrington, Philippa (2000) *The Council of Ministers: Political Authority in the European Union* (London: Pinter).

Smith, Andy (ed.) (2004) *Politics and the European Commission* (London: Routledge).

Smith, Graham (1999) *The Post-Soviet States: Mapping the Politics of Transition* (London: Edward Arnold).

Smith, Michael (1997) 'The Commission and External Relations', in Geoffrey Edwards and David Spence (eds), *The European Commission*, 2nd edn (London: Cartermill).

Smith, Michael (2006) 'The Commission and External Relations', in David Spence (ed.), *The European Commission*, 3d edn (London: John Harper).

Spence, David (ed.) (2006) *The European Commission*, 3rd edn (London: John Harper Publishing).

Spinelli, Altiero (1972) 'The Growth of the European Movement Since the Second World War', in Michael Hodges (ed.), *Europe Integration: Selected Readings* (Harmondsworth: Penguin).

Springer, Beverly (1992) *The Social Dimension of 1992: Europe Faces a New EC* (Westport, CT: Praeger).

Stirk, Peter M. R. and David Weigall (eds) (1999) *The Origins and Development of European Integration: A Reader and Commentary* (London and New York: Pinter).

Strange, Susan (1996) *The Retreat of the State: The Diffusion of Power in the World Economy* (Cambridge: Cambridge University Press).

Sweet, Alec Stone (2004) *The Judicial Construction of Europe* (New York: Oxford University Press).

Taggart, Paul and Aleks Szczerbiak (2004) 'Supporting the Union? Euroscepticism and the Politics of European Integration', in Maria Green Cowles and Desmond Dinan (eds), *Developments in the European Union 2* (Basingstoke: Palgrave Macmillan).

Thatcher, Margaret (1993) *The Downing Street Years* (New York: HarperCollins).

Tsoukalis, Loukas (1997) *The New European Economy Revisited: The Politics and Economics of Integration*, 3rd edn (Oxford: Oxford University Press).

Unwin, Tim (1998) 'Ideas of Europe', in Tim Unwin (ed.), *A European Geography* (Harlow: Longman).

Urwin, Derek (1995) *The Community of Europe*, 2nd edn (London: Longman).

van Eekelen, Willem (1990) 'WEU and the Gulf Crisis', *Survival*, vol. 32, no. 6, pp. 519–32.

Van Oudenaren, John (2004) *Uniting Europe: An Introduction to the European Union*, 2nd edn (Lanham, MD: Rowman & Littlefield).

Vincent, Andrew (1987) *Theories of the State* (Oxford: Blackwell).

Wallace, Anthony (2004) 'Completing the Single Market: The Lisbon Strategy', in Maria Green Cowles and Desmond Dinan (eds), *Developments in the European Union 2* (Basingstoke: Palgrave Macmillan).

Wallace, Helen, William Wallace and Mark Pollack (eds) (2005) *Policy-Making in the European Union*, 5th edn (Oxford: Oxford University Press).

Wallace, William (1990) *The Transformation of Western Europe* (London: Royal Institute of International Affairs).

Waltz, Kenneth N. (1991) 'America as a Model for the World? A Foreign Policy Perspective', *PS*, vol. 24, no. 4 (December), p. 669.

Warleigh, Alex (2001) *Understanding European Union Institutions* (London: Routledge).

Weigall, David and Peter Stirk (eds) (1992) *The Origins and Development of the European Community* (London: Pinter).

Werts, Jan (1992) *The European Council* (Amsterdam: North-Holland).

Westlake, Martin (1994) *A Modern Guide to the European Parliament* (London: Pinter).

Westlake, Martin and David Galloway (2004) *The Council of the European Union*, 3rd edn (London: John Harper).

Wexler, Immanual (1983) *The Marshall Plan Revisited: The European Recovery Program in Economic Perspective* (Westport, CT: Greenwood).

Williams, Shirley (1991) 'Sovereignty and Accountability in the European Community', in Robert O. Keohane and Stanley Hoffmann (eds), *The New European Community: Decisionmaking and Institutional Change* (Boulder, CO: Westview Press).

Wood, David and Birol Yesilada (2006) *The Emerging European Union*, 4th edn (London: Longman).

World Bank website (2007) http://www.worldbank.org/data.

World Tourism Organization website (2007) http://www.world-tourism.org.

World Trade Organization website (2007) http://www.wto.org.

World Travel and Tourism Council website (2007) http://www.wttc.org.

Zurcher, Arnold J. (1958) *The Struggle to Unite Europe, 1940–58* (New York: New York University Press).

Index

234

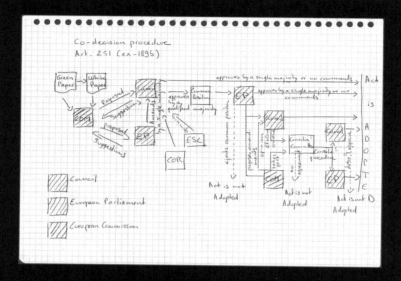